REDBIRDS REVISITED

REDBIRDS REVISITED

Great Memories and Stories from St. Louis Cardinals

David Craft and Tom Owens

Bonus Books, Inc., Chicago

94   93   92   91   90   5   4   3   2   1

International Standard Book Number: 0-929387-12-0
Library of Congress 89-81939

Bonus Books, Inc.
160 East Illinois Street
Chicago, Illinois 60611

Printed in the United States of America

This book is dedicated to our parents, Everett and Eunice Craft, and Ernie and Jeanette Owens.

CONTENTS

FOREWORD

Let's go back to the 1950s. That's when I discovered the St. Louis Cardinals. I was six years old at the time, and I haven't been the same since. Nothing has.

You must understand that at age five I was still a cowboys fan, not the yet unborn Dallas Cowboys, but the kind that rode the range in the Wild West, toting six-guns and chasing outlaws. My range was Rivermont Avenue in Lynchburg, Virginia, but that wasn't the problem. My problem was that I didn't like my cowboy hat. It wasn't shaped like a real cowboy hat but more like the hats worn by the Royal Canadian Mounted Police. You know, like Sergeant Preston of the Yukon. To me it was something a cowgirl would wear. I was ready for a change.

Then I met Wallace Hawkins, an older boy who lived across the street. Wallace was seven or eight. He was even in school. Wallace knew everything, and he shared his wisdom with me. He told me all he knew about the St. Louis Cardinals and their Class B farmclub in the Piedmont League, the Lynchburg Cardinals. I immediately put away my six-gun.

Soon after, I got a Cardinals uniform for Christmas. It was all spread out on the blue chair by the Christmas tree when I vaulted down the stairs. It was just about the best Christmas gift I ever got.

The Lynchburg Cardinals weren't a very good team, but I loved them and listened to all of their games on the big floor-model radio in the living room. It sure beat listening to Gabriel Heatter talking about some war way off in Korea.

Wallace was my baseball guru, and how many little boys

had their own guru in the '50s? He taught me how to read the box scores and the league standings, and he introduced me to baseball cards. (They didn't have bubblegum with them yet but slabs of chocolate candy.) Wallace told me about all of his favorite local Cardinals from days gone by, everyone from pitcher Floyd Melliere to outfielder Bobby Powledge who made somersaulting catches in center field.

Soon I developed my own heroes: sluggers Miff Davidson and Dick Cordell, shortstop Herb Mancini, big first baseman Nick Ananias, pitchers Paul Dewey, Dick Ban, and John Romonosky. Later there was Roland LeBlanc, who served as both the catcher and manager of the team. Boy, could LeBlanc hit.

I remember listening to one game on a Sunday afternoon when the Cardinals were playing York. York was one of two teams in the league named the Roses, but I could never remember which one. Lancaster was also in the league, and one of them was the Red Roses and one the White Roses, but that's not important. What is important is that Roland LeBlanc's batting average fell under .300 that afternoon for the first time all season. But the Lynchburg manager broke out of his slump the next day and was never under .300 again. I just knew he would be a big star for St. Louis in a very short time.

It was wonderful to listen to the games on the radio, but I wanted to go to the ballpark and see a game in person. There was a big double-header coming up, and one of the ways to get a free ticket was to save bottle caps from Nehi orange and grape drinks. It got down near the deadline and I still needed six more bottle caps. I explained this to my mother, and she gave me thirty cents from her purse and said I could go to the store. It may not have been wise to gulp down six Nehi grape and orange drinks in one sitting. But it *was* important, very important. And my mother understood.

One year I remember going to see the Lynchburg Cardinals play the Roanoke Red Sox in a July 4 afternoon game. In the first inning, Lynchburg's Nick Ananias hit a grand slam home run of Biblical proportions. I can still see it sail into the blue sky, high above the left field fence. Being fans of the Cardinals even helped Wallace and me understand a bit more easily our Sunday School lessons at church. For example, our Ananias of the Lynchburg

Cardinals helped pitcher Paul Dewey, just like the Biblical Ananias helped Paul in the New Testament (Acts 9:10).

Lynchburg never won a pennant or even came close in my day. That always went to the bad guys like the Norfolk Tars, a farm team of the wretched New York Yankees. You just had to hate a team known as the Tars, just like you had to hate a team that called itself the Yankees.

Not many Cardinals advanced from Lynchburg to St. Louis; however, one year John Romonosky won 10 games with Lynchburg and had a sip of tea with St. Louis. No, he wasn't there long enough for a cup of coffee.

In spring training one year, the St. Louis Cardinals came to town for an exhibition game against the Philadelphia Phillies. Mr. McGhee, an older man from our church, invited me to go to the game. Mr. McGhee not only loved baseball, but he was rich and was the only person in the whole world that I knew who had two cars. Right in front of his house sat two 1953 Buicks.

Mr. McGhee and I went to the ballpark, and there, at age nine, I had one of the greatest thrills of my life. Sitting on the bank in right field, I witnessed Stan Musial come to bat in the first inning and promptly line a double off the green right field wall. After the game, Mr. McGhee wanted to take me down into the dugout to meet "The Man." I was terrified, so I begged off. I wanted to meet Stan; he was my favorite player. But I just couldn't.

As happy as I was to see Stan's double that year, I was equally saddened about a year later when my father called me into his bedroom to show me something in the newspaper. He wasn't a big baseball fan, so I knew this had to be important. It was, but it was also more terrible than anything I could imagine. There on the sports page was a picture of my second favorite player, Enos Slaughter, and he was crying. Enos had just learned that he had been traded to those wretched Yankees in New York. I cried, too.

A year or two later, disaster struck again. I was in the fifth grade when I found out that my parents were moving to Georgia. Could I survive living in a town without a Cardinals baseball team or without Wallace, my baseball guru? I didn't think so, but I decided to go along anyway.

Gainesville, Georgia was a very nice town, even if it didn't have a minor league baseball team. The Atlanta Crackers of the

Southern Association were only fifty miles away, and they were a Double A team, though they were a farmclub of the Milwaukee Braves and not St. Louis.

The Crackers were the Yankees of the minor leagues. Now that sounds like a terrible thing to say about my new team, but I'm referring strictly to their history of winning pennants. I finally had a winner, even though my major league allegiance was still with St. Louis.

I listened to the Atlanta games on the radio following announcer Hank Morgan's every word. Then the next day I would cut out the game story and box score from the *Atlanta Constitution* for my file. I enjoyed listening to Hank and the Crackers on WSB, but I couldn't understand why the crowds sounded exactly the same whether the team was in Nashville or Birmingham or New Orleans or Shreveport. And half the time, it seemed, the crowd was cheering for the wrong team. The fans surely didn't sound like this when the Crackers were at home at Ponce de Leon Park. I didn't know until years later that Hank Morgan didn't actually go on the road with the team but recreated those games from a studio in Atlanta.

The Crackers didn't have Miff Davidson or Dick Cordell or Nick Ananias, but one year their outfield was Dick Stuart, Ken Guettler, and Bob Montag. They had combined for an incredible 155 home runs the year before; however, as a Cracker triumvirate, they managed to hit only 30 homers, and "Der Tag" hit 20 of those. (Stuart, who had blasted 66 homers the previous season, hit only 8 for Atlanta. Guettler's total fell from 62 to 2, and Bob Montag's Cracker totals dropped from 27 to 20.)

One night I was fiddling with the dial of my hand-me-down 1946 RCA tabletop radio when I made a great discovery. I picked up station KMOX in St. Louis and heard Harry Caray broadcasting a Cardinals game, the ST. LOUIS Cardinals. Joe Garagiola was also there, and from that night on, I would tune in KMOX every evening and listen to the Redbirds on my red-painted radio. If I couldn't get the station, I would listen to the Crackers or other teams, but every few minutes I would once again go looking for the Cardinals. I would even listen in the winter, eager to pick up any news about the Cardinals during the basketball broadcasts of the St. Louis Hawks in the NBA or the Billikens of St. Louis University.

To improve the reception, I would connect a wire to the back of my radio and then climb out my upstairs window and extend the wire onto the roof and around the side of my house, running it down a drainpipe to the ground. This made Harry Caray louder than ever. It also made the late-night crackles and pops more noticeable, but I didn't mind as long as I could hear every pitch.

During the afternoons I would often listen to the "Mutual Game of the Day." One day the Cardinals were on the game and were getting beaten soundly by, I think, the Phillies. St. Louis went to its bullpen and brought in the Cardinals' newest pitcher, a bonus baby who had just been signed out of high school. His name was Von McDaniel. He had just recently turned eighteen years old, and he was the brother of Cardinal pitcher Lindy McDaniel. As I recall, Von pitched near perfect baseball for the final three-plus innings of the game. I suddenly had a new hero. I liked Lindy, too, but he was old: twenty-one. Von was young and a phenom.

Von pitched a few more games in relief and then got his chance to start. He won his first four games, and as I remember it, he even pitched a two-hit shutout against the Brooklyn Dodgers on the "Saturday Game of the Week" on TV. The McDaniels reminded Cardinal fans of the Dean brothers, Dizzy and Paul (or "Me and Paul"), who won 49 games for the Cardinals in 1934.

I wrote my new hero, Von, and his brother and requested an autograph. I then waited on the swing of the front porch every day, waiting for the mailman to deliver my mail from St. Louis. One day toward the end of July, it finally came, a picture postcard of a Cardinal with a handwritten and personalized inscription: "Best Wishes Warner." But then the disappointment. It was signed not by Von McDaniel but by Lindy. Little could I imagine at the time that Von would never win another game after that season, while Lindy would go on to a brilliant career and become one of the game's great relief pitchers.

That same year, 1957, was also the year that the Milwaukee Braves called up Hurricane Hazle who batted over .400 and led the team to its first pennant. Hurricane Hazle was a sensation, but the second-place Redbirds had Joe Cunningham who was just as hot down the stretch. When Jersey Joe was hot, no one could get him out. It seemed like he got three hits every game that summer as the Cardinals battled the Braves for the National League pennant.

The Cardinals and Crackers were my teams, and a few years later I got my ultimate wish. Atlanta became the Cardinals' Triple A team. Now I had it all. I could even go see the young Redbirds as Crackers before they got to the major leagues.

The Crackers were great. They had players such as Tim McCarver, Ray Sadecki, Fred Whitfield, Jerry Buchek, Phil Gagliano, Johnny Joe Lewis, Mike Shannon and "Hot Foot" Harry Fanok.

One night a buddy of mine and I went to see the Crackers play at Ponce de Leon Park. After the game we saw two girls sitting in a car in the parking lot. We bravely approached and struck up a conversation. What a thrill it was to find out we were actually talking to girls who were waiting on their dates, Tim McCarver and pitcher Paul Toth. For weeks I told all of my friends that I knew the girlfrields of Tim McCarver and Paul Toth.

Two decades later in my office at Major League Baseball Productions in New York City, I would tell Tim McCarver about my great "conquest" outside the ballpark in Atlanta. Jokingly, I asked Tim if he remembered that night. He laughed and said of course he remembered that night, but what he couldn't remember was what on earth he was doing double-dating with Paul Toth.

In the 1960s my loyalty to the Cardinals grew even stronger, and in 1964 I was finally rewarded with a Cardinal pennant. It almost happened in 1963. There was a late-season spectacular surge, but Sandy Koufax, Don Drysdale, Johnny Podres, and Dick Nen proved to be too much. Dick Nen? He had only one RBI that season, but without that home run against St. Louis, the Dodgers might not have had the chance to sweep the Yankees in the World Series.

In 1964 I made my first trip to St. Louis and saw the Cardinals play the Dodgers at what Harry Caray had described to me for years as beautiful Busch Stadium. Well, on first glance it was an old ballpark, and it didn't seem to be in a very good section of town, but it was still beautiful to me. It was just different.

I can still see Bob Uecker line a shot down the left field line off Don Drysdale in a big game. The Cardinals played well but were about seven games out with a month to go when I left town. The Cardinals then got really hot. The Phillies got cold. And St. Louis, in a miracle finish, ended the year as the National League champions. They even beat the wretched Yankees in the World Series. It was the grandest moment of my life.

In 1967 while serving in the infantry of the U.S. Army some 10,000 miles away from home, I volunteered for guard duty at three o'clock in the morning, just so I could secretly listen to the Cardinals and the Boston Red Sox in the World Series.

By 1969 I was back in the "world" and could listen to the Redbirds at a more normal hour. I heard Steve Carlton strike out nineteen Mets one evening, but Ron Swoboda hit two home runs and New York won the game. Then there was the final game of the season. That game would become Harry Caray's final Cardinal broadcast. That night he discussed the rumors of his firing on KMOX and said that you would think that after putting in twenty-five years announcing Cardinal baseball you just might be presented with a gold watch. Instead, Harry got a pink slip. Harry promised his audience that he would be somewhere broadcasting baseball games for many years to come. I was crushed, but I still loved Harry and wanted to become a baseball announcer someday.

In the 1970s I got my chance to broadcast baseball in the minor leagues. Without the St. Louis Cardinals and KMOX, I might have chosen an entirely different field. Later I would even narrate baseball shows such as "This Week in Baseball" which aired on KMOX. What could be better than that?

In 1988 I became the host of ESPN's new weekly baseball show: "Major League Baseball Magazine." I guess I must have really been lucky, because I was able to work in the baseball broadcasting world without ever having been a catcher for the Cardinals. In 1965 alone, the three Redbird catchers were Tim McCarver, Bob Uecker, and Mike Shannon. Before that was Joe Garagiola. After that came Joe Torre. All became big-league announcers.

Although I was never able to catch for the Cardinals, I did catch FROM the Cardinals the baseball and broadcasting bug that has lasted to this day.

It's ironic that once I became a baseball announcer and then moved to New York, I could no longer listen to my favorite base-ball broadcasts. Not only was KMOX out of listening range, but in order to tune in the local Mets, I would have to prop my radio up-side down across the room on the window sill. At least I had many years of experience in knowing how to do that.

As baseball enters the 1990s, I can no longer hear those far-away sounds of the St. Louis Cardinals. But I still have my memo-ries, and thanks to authors David Craft and Tom Owens, those memories of my childhood are enhanced today as I can actually feel the presence of my old heroes in *Redbirds Revisited*.

Warner Fusselle
January 1990

ACKNOWLEDGMENTS

This book is the culmination of nearly a decade's worth of sharing one common obsession: the St. Louis Cardinals. When we first met in an Iowa State University journalism class in the early 1980s, our first conversation resulted after we noticed we were the only two people in class sporting Cardinals caps.

Since then, we've drawn many others into the study of our beloved Redbirds. We're grateful to the crew at Bonus Books, a bunch of creative Chicagoans who are courageous and impartial enough to publish a book about a "rival" out-of-state team. For that rebellious dedication to literature, we are deeply appreciative. We're grateful to St. Louis Browns fan Rich Hawksley of St. Louis, Missouri, for his charitable assistance in securing photographs of all the players. Rich and partner Bill Goodwin sponsor sensational sports memorabilia conventions in St. Louis on a regular basis. They make a huge effort to bring former Cardinals to the collector gatherings to meet fans and sign autographs. Many of the players interviewed in this book are regular attendees of the Hawksley-Goodwin functions, which are open to the public. Any dedicated Cardinals fan near St. Louis would savor the experience of one of these hobby spectaculars.

In St. Louis, we thank Kip Ingle, Brian Bartow, Marty Hendin and the St. Louis Cardinals public relations department. All offered encouragement and assistance which gave great aid to our efforts.

A special tip of the Cardinal cap goes to the venerable Bob Broeg for his input and support; Jack Smalling for information on

Tom Alston's minor league career; Harry and Wanda Lone for putting up D.C. on his visits to St. Louis (and Roger and Diana Killian for providing his room and board along the way); and Warner Fusselle, "The Voice of Major Leage Baseball Productions," for leading off this book with an all-star foreword.

Additional applause goes to Karen Craft and Diana Helmer, two unfailingly patient women who never knew Redbird rooting was an unspoken part of their wedding vows to us. They are All-Star editors, cheerleaders and friends. Las Vegas oddsmakers rank them as "can't miss" material for the Marriage Hall of Fame.

Most of all, we salute all of the men profiled in this book who've given freely of their time and memories. Each of these people has gladly relived his days in a Redbirds uniform to transform this book into a half-century retrospective of life with the Cardinals. Speaking with each of these men gave us joy that many fans can only imagine. Each former player shared that same joy with us. Because no matter how long each of these men played pro baseball, all of them considered their years in St. Louis unforgettable. We offer this book in tribute to the countless years of excitement these memory-makers have provided for fans like us.

—David Craft
—Tom Owens
February 1990

Sportsman's Park, home of the St. Louis Cardinals from 1920 to 1966.

Manually operated left field scoreboard at Sportsman's Park in 1957.

SPORTSMAN'S PARK AND BUSCH STADIUM

Two Regal Roosts

for the Redbirds

Robison Field, dubbed "Shoot the Chutes" due to gaps in the outfield fences that allowed balls to bounce out of the park, was host to the Cardinals from 1893 through 1920 when they moved to Sportsman's Park. Robison may have been first, but Sportsman's Park and Busch Stadium became the shrines where St. Louis fans worshipped.

Sportsman's Park had been the home of the American League St. Louis Browns since 1909 when the Cardinals arrived in 1920. The Brownies shared their residence with the Redbirds for thirty-three seasons, the longest cohabitation ever recorded in the majors. The Cardinals office was located beneath the first base grandstands (at 3623 Dodier), while the Browns were headquartered around the block on North Grand, the right field side of the stadium. Because Browns team owner Phil Ball owned Sportsman's Park, the Cardinals paid yearly rent. When the American League team saw its attendance seriously dwindle during the 1930s, the Cardinal rent money helped keep the Browns afloat.

In 1926, only six years after moving into Sportsman's, the Cardinals became World Champions for the first time. They beat the highly-favored New York Yankees in a seven-game World Series, the first of ten Fall Classics which would be hosted in the St. Louis stadium.

Night baseball arrived in St. Louis in 1940. The Redbirds played their first contest under the lights on June 4, 1940, against the Brooklyn Dodgers. A decade later, the Cardinals opened their 1950 season under the stars, beating the Pittsburgh Pirates by a 4-2 margin.

St. Louis native Nate Williams attended his first Cardinals home game in 1945. Since making his initial visit to Sportsman's Park at age eight, Williams has remained faithful to the Redbirds. Even though he now lives in Middleton, Wisconsin, this true-blue fan makes yearly treks back to St. Louis to see the team he discovered more than four decades ago. "It's like a religious experience for me and my family," Williams says. "Trips back to Busch Stadium are like pilgrimages back to Mecca."

As a youngster, Williams was one of many youths who cashed in on the team's free "Knothole Gang" program. "Team owner Sam Breadon and general manager Branch Rickey initiated the Knothole Gang," Williams says. "They let the kids in free, knowing they'd be the paying customers of the future." According to Williams, the majority of fans would be clustered in the bleachers, while most of the more expensive reserved seats would remain empty. "It became a sport for Cardinals fans to slowly drift into choice empty seats as the game progressed," Williams remembers. "I liked to sneak into seats somewhere on the third base line behind the Cardinals dugout."

Every old ballpark has its legends, and Sportsman's Park is no different. Legend has it that one pillar in Sportsman's Park may have won the 1944 World Series for the Redbirds. The town was abuzz over its first and only all-city Series. Supposedly, Browns management provided the wife of Emil "the Antelope" Verban with a poor seat behind a post. The incensed second baseman took out his frustration on the Browns by batting .412 in post-season play, helping the Cardinals to a six-game Series triumph.

During the 1930s and 1940s, Sportsman's Park saw virtually no remodeling. Cardinals fan Williams remembers that the humid

Missouri summers would bake the stadium infield into a concrete consistency. "The ground would become incredibly hard. I saw balls take some mighty strange hops there," he says. Because of the arid summers and near-continual field use by two teams, Williams says that the grass at Sportsman's usually was green only in spots.

However, Browns owner Bill Veeck sold the ballpark to Cardinals owner August A. Busch, Jr., in order to stay financially solvent. Busch, after toying with the idea of renaming the park "Budweiser Stadium," decided on Busch Stadium instead. Thanks to Busch, the park got a $1.5 million renovation which included refurbished dugouts and clubhouses and new box seats. Advertisements for Sayman's Soap, Kellogg's Corn Flakes and Buick cars, which once dotted the scoreboard and outfield walls, quickly disappeared. While most fans may have been relieved by the departure of numerous billboards, St. Louis native Williams was one fan who missed the ads plastered throughout the park. "One of the biggest thrills for fans attending doubleheaders was watching the Star of the Game sign operated by the *Globe-Democrat* newspaper," Williams says. "After the first game of a double-header, fans would consult their scorecards and try to predict what player would get his name placed on the board. There'd always be great anticipation when a groundskeeper would ride his cart into the outfield to post the name of the new star."

Those sometimes-charming signs became ballpark institutions when early broadcasters would use them as landmarks in attempts to give additional mentions of sponsors. "When Harry Caray first started announcing Cards games on radio, he'd describe every fly to right as 'all the way out to the Griesedieck Beer sign on the right field wall,'" Williams remembered. "Once TV came in, everyone could see how far the flies really went. Then we knew that Harry sometimes exaggerated for the sake of the sponsors."

With the renovations, the only memory of those gaudy advertisements were a few discreet signs for products from the new owner's brewery. The Busch Eagle, an eternal symbol of the brewery, now rested atop the left-center field scoreboard. For any Cardinal home run, the electronic eagle would flap its wings in tribute. Nearly forty years later, the bird still takes flight for any Redbird round tripper hit in present-day Busch Stadium.

Busch Memorial Stadium, present day home of the St. Louis Cardinals.

Pre-1970 Busch Memorial Stadium with natural grass and dirt basepaths.

The enormous scoreboard in left center field was scaled down when Sportsman's Park was sold. Williams says that the manually-operated scoreboard is one of his most vivid memories of the 1940s. "Watching the scoreboard was exciting. No one had a transistor radio back then to get immediate news at the park," he recalls. "People would gasp as the numeral plank was drawn up, telling how many runs other teams scored during their most recent inning. It was a dramatic way to keep track of the pennant race." An ultimate test of strength for a batter was to homer over the scoreboard. Mike Shannon highlighted the Redbirds' 1964 World Series victory over the Yankees with a 450-foot shot which topped the mammoth monument.

When he was away from the stadium, Williams listened to Cardinals games on several low-power radio stations. He jokingly calls the period up to 1945, "BHC" (Before Harry Caray). In 1943, Dizzy Dean called games with Johnnie O'Hara and J. Taylor Grant on KWK, a part of the Falstaff Beer Radio Network. He remembers O'Hara and veteran 1930s announcer France Laux teaming up to broadcast both Cards and Browns games in 1945 for WTMV and WEW. "These were low-power 5,000-watt stations with limited coverage, compared to the 50,000-watt broadcasts of KMOX," Williams says. He adds that broadcasts of road or Sunday games were unheard of. "I remember that Cardinals owner Fred Saigh wanted to play a Sunday night game in the 1940s, because of the humid summer days. The protests came out of the woodwork."

Williams often watched Cardinals games from the vantage point of the right field pavilion, where a roof sheltered the plank seating. The area was separated from the field by a screen every season except 1955, when the Cardinals hoped to boost their local home run production. At only 310 feet down the right field line, the pavilion was a tempting target. One permanent change in Sportsman's Park was the closing of the center field bleachers. Batters in the 1940s had problems spotting pitches when those bleachers were filled with white-shirted fans.

From his sixty-five-cent perch in the right field pavilion, Williams studied the uniforms of the outfielders. Like countless other fans, Williams loved the two birds perched on a baseball bat, which appeared on the fronts of Cardinals jerseys. He shared the local shock when the team scrapped the familiar shirt for one season in the 1950s in favor of a simple, modern shirt which simply read "Cardinals" in a generic script. The team took its fans' reactions to heart and restored the traditional jersey after one season.

Memorizing details of the Redbird uniforms seemed natural for young fans like Williams. "It didn't take long to recognize the players by number, because the Cardinals had the jerseys numbered in sequence," he recalls. However, Williams says that in 1945 it was necessary to use a scorecard to identify players because most Cardinals regulars were in the military. "Red Schoendienst broke in as a left fielder that year. He wore number 6 for only that year, because it belonged to Stan Musial," Williams says. "Schoendienst took his familiar number 2 the next year when Stan returned."

Following the 1966 closing of the historic baseball cathedral, Sportsman's Park's grounds became the home of a boy's club. Youngsters finally got the chance to patrol the same pasture where Redbirds once roamed.

Anheuser Busch created an ultra-modern new home for the Cardinals only thirteen years after acquiring the club. The team christened new Busch Stadium on May 12, 1966, with a twelve-inning, 4-3 win over the Atlanta Braves. Opening-night fans, all 46,048 of them, excused sweltering temperatures, a hot dog shortage and undependable elevators in exchange for a look at the glorious scoreboard made up of 35,000 lights. Prior to the new stadium's debut, a helicopter transported home plate from the team's old home to new Busch Stadium.

All of America took notice of the new baseball domicile when St. Louis hosted the 1966 All-Star game. Cardinals catcher Tim McCarver scored a tenth-inning run in front of 49,936 fans as the National Leaguers earned a 2-1 victory. Only one year later, a World Championship flag would fly over the new ballpark. What housewarming party could top a seven-game World Series win against the Boston Red Sox?

In 1968, two events marked the third season of life at Busch Stadium. A lifesize statue of Stan Musial, who concluded his career in 1963, was erected outside the park. Meanwhile, the Cardinals claimed their second straight National League crown, only to fall to the Detroit Tigers in seven games.

In the following two decades, the cavernous St. Louis

ballpark featured nearly everything but home runs. Aside from Dick Allen's 34 dingers in 1970, no Cardinal would surpass 30 round-trippers until Jack Clark posted 35 in 1987. Speed and pitching became the staples of games at Busch Stadium. An electronic Cardinal flew about the scoreboard every time Lou Brock earned one of his record 118 stolen bases in 1974. Although Busch dwellers missed out on Brock breaking Ty Cobb's career stolen base record in 1977, they saw their favorite outfielder get his 3,000th hit at home versus arch-rival Chicago on Aug. 13, 1979.

Hall of Fame hurler Bob Gibson made his last mound appearance in Busch Stadium in 1975, rounding out a career of 17 years and 251 victories. His 1968 season was highlighted by a record-setting 1.12 ERA and 22 wins, which earned him both the Cy Young and Most Valuable Player Awards. Ironically, the only no-hitters spun by a Cardinal in Busch Stadium belong to another Bob, this one named Forsch. On Sunday, April 16, 1978, he registered the first, a 5-0 victory against the Phillies.

The 1980s became the era of "Whitey-ball," the run-and-gun offense engineered by Cardinals manager Whitey Herzog. Fans flocked to Busch with the team's 1982 World Series triumph against the Brewers. Crowds kept coming and were rewarded with National League pennants in 1985 and 1987.

While the Cardinals have kept life at Busch Stadium exciting, so have their fans. The Redbirds packed Busch with a record 3,072,122 fans in 1987, and yearly attendance has approached league highs ever since. The team proved to be surprising pennant contenders throughout 1989 as they mounted their second charge at the illustrious three million mark.

Team supporter Williams remains one of the Redbirds' faithful three million. With his loyalty to the Cardinals approaching its sixth decade, Williams considers his remembrances of old Sportsman's Park especially dear. "Sportsman's Park is gone now, which is sad," Williams says with a sigh. "I'm afraid that no one will even know about the old park in another twenty years.

"Someone has to remember."

TOM ALSTON

Was "It" Lost

in Las Vegas?

At 6'5" and 210 pounds, Thomas Edison Alston was a natural for the nickname, "Tall Tom," and seemed a natural as well to anchor first base for the Cardinals in 1954.

Quick, agile — "a good glove man" said baseball pundits who'd seen him play in the minors — Alston gave his infield mates the perfect target for their assists. At the plate, he hit ropes, and showed some power, too. So, as spring training segued into opening day, the job of Cardinal first baseman was his to lose.

But with his love for the game and a desire to succeed as the team's first black player, the North Carolinian also brought with him a troubled spirit. Alston claims that for several years prior to joining the Cardinals he had been plagued by a mysterious physical ailment that left his body tired and his throwing arm weak.

Over the years, he says, a number of physicians and physical therapists examined him, yet this mysterious ailment persists even today. To what degree this strange malady actually existed, its apparent presence most definitely tormented Alston's soul nearly as much as it impaired his ability to hit big league pitching.

To this day, Alston remains puzzled, though surprisingly matter-of-fact, about what he simply calls, "that time in Las Vegas" in 1952 that he says was the beginning of the end of his baseball career.

As Alston tells it, he was for a short time hitting above .400 for the Class C minor league squad at Porterville, California, of the Southwest International League. That made him a shoo-in for the league's All-Star game in Yuma, Arizona, a game in which he recalls hitting a home run and a single.

"After the game a couple of us drove to Las Vegas all morning long to meet our teammates for a regular game against the Las Vegas club," Alston said.

"We got into town that morning about eight o'clock. Las Vegas was Jim Crow then, and we blacks couldn't stay with our white teammates in the same hotel. We had to stay in a rundown, Negro Baptist hotel."

After Alston ate his breakfast, he and a teammate decided to see what was doing in "the city that never sleeps." Never a gambling man or a carouser, Alston cut short the pair's sightseeing tour by announcing he wanted to head back to their hotel to get some sleep before the ballgame that night.

It was not a restful sleep and when he awakened he was groggy, almost disoriented. Still, he managed to eat a light meal before heading to the ballpark. It was there, Alston says, that he realized something was terribly wrong.

"I went out to take infield and my arm was gone," he said. "I couldn't throw, or, barely, anyway. I felt weak. I didn't know what was wrong. The night before I'd hit a home run and a single in the All-Star game, and here I was the next night, barely able to play."

Somehow, he played, and he says he even managed to get a hit in four times at bat. But he was tired the whole game, and didn't appear to be himself. Everybody was worried about Tom, but he told them he'd be all right once he got a good night's sleep.

But he wasn't all right the next morning, and a teammate, on the pretext that *he* needed to go see one of the local doctors, convinced Alston to accompany him to the doctor's office. Once inside the office, Tom was surprised to learn it wasn't his team-mate the doctor wanted to see. The attending physician, though troubled by the apparent weakness in Tom's right arm, could not determine what was wrong.

Alston continued to play at less than 100 percent. His batting average dropped below the magical .400 clip (though he managed a nifty .353 in 54 games). Still, his totals were good enough to interest the San Diego Padres (then an independent club in the Triple A Pacific Coast League), and Tom tried to turn it up a couple of notches as he faced a higher caliber of minor league hurlers.

"Lefty O'Doul was my manager at San Diego," Alston said. "I rode the bench a little for a time, just to observe things, but I continued to take batting practice and infield. My arm was weak. I was tired. But eventually he put me in the lineup, and I hit pretty well at first. And then the bottom dropped out.

"Oh, I felt miserable. But I was tryin' not to show it. I wasn't hittin' much, and on about the next-to-last day of the season I went to the team owner and told him I wanted to quit baseball because I wasn't helpin' my team any battin' .243 or whatever it was [.244]. So he chewed me out real nice. He told me I should be proud of myself for havin' moved all the way up to Triple A from Class C in one season.

"He told me to go home and rest after the season ended. He said, 'Tom, just start thinkin' about how well you'll do next year. Look ahead to spring training; don't worry about what's past.' So, I felt a lot better after he said all of those things to me."

Indeed, Alston must have taken to heart the pep talk. He put up some solid numbers with San Diego in 1953, including a .297 batting average, 101 RBI, 23 home runs, 25 doubles, 5 triples and 101 runs scored.

"But I wasn't proud of my record for that season," Alston said, without a hint of facetiousness in his voice. "I knew I could have done even better if I'd felt better physically, if I hadn't worried so much about what was wrong with my arm. I was looked at a few times, but nobody, including me, knew what was wrong."

The Cardinals purchased Alston from San Diego in January of 1954 for a reported $100,000. St. Louis scouts were high on the young man, emphasizing his tremendous defensive work around first base. Alston remembers having enjoyed only a "fair" spring training that year, but the Cardinals still saw enough potential in him that "they just handed me the first base job."

The team as a whole got out of the box slowly in 1954. The Cardinals lost their first three games, including a 23-13 drubbing by the Cubs at Wrigley Field. In that game, the third of the new season, the rookie from Greensboro socked a home run. It was his first hit in the major leagues.

On the following day, Alston, good Methodist that he is, observed Easter Sunday by sitting out most of the game in the dugout "pew" with the other non-starters. In the sixth inning, however, with the score tied at three runs apiece and the Cardinals rallying, manager Eddie Stanky called on Tom to pinch hit for Steve Bilko. Alston promptly drove the first pitch from Cubs' reliever Jim Davis over the right field wall for a three-run homer that proved to be the game winner. It was the Cardinals' first victory of the season.

After struggling for a couple of months to bring his average and his power numbers up, Alston was sent packing to Rochester for more seasoning. To take his place the Cardinals brought up Joe Cunningham. At season's end, Alston's totals with the Cardinals read: .246 with 34 RBI and 28 runs scored in 66 games; 3 stolen bases in 5 attempts; 14 doubles, 2 triples and 4 home runs. His fielding average was .989 with 7 errors.

Alston returned to the Cardinal lineup periodically through 1957, but spent most of his time at either Rochester or Omaha during those years. In contrast to his often anemic hitting while with St. Louis, Tom hit .297, .274 and .306, respectively, in 1954, 1955 and 1956, for those two Cardinal farm clubs. His last hurrah in the big leagues came in 1957, when he went 5-for-17 (.294) in nine games for the Cardinals.

"I got a fair shake," Alston said of his brief stint in the bigs. "It was just my physical condition that kept me from playin' ball the way I knew I could play, the way the Cardinals expected me to play. My throwin' arm, my right arm, continued to give me trouble. And because I was a left-handed hitter, I just couldn't *drive* the ball the way I should have been able to.

"My teammates treated me fairly. I don't think they thought I was that good a hitter, though, and I guess I didn't show 'em much while I was there. I heard, while I was back in the minors at Triple A, that they believed that I would come back and play regular for 'em again someday.

"It's tough enough to hit major league pitchin' when you're feeling OK, but when you're not, it's almost impossible. I believe to this day that if I'd been well, I could have hit major league pitchin' much better than I did. I *know* I could have. But when I came down sick, and my arm started givin' me trouble, that messed up my career for good. Messed up my whole life."

When the Cardinals were home, Alston lived with a local black family that he lovingly calls "my baseball mother and father." When the Cardinals were on the road, Alston roomed by himself.

"I just ate, slept and went to the ballpark," Alston said of his travel routine. "Nightclubs, bars, drinkin'—that stuff wasn't for me. I just kept to myself. No, I wasn't lonely at all. It was nice, though, when the Cardinals brought up Brooks Lawrence [the team's first black pitcher] later on. Then I had somebody to talk to back at the hotel. I had a roommate on the road then.

"I'd been readin' *The Sporting News* early in my life. Also, my mother, who worked as a maid for a white man, would bring back an armful of papers sometimes for me to read, and I'd just look at the sports pages to see who was doin' what. I'd just look at the stats and box scores and read about the games. But when I was playin' for the Cardinals, especially when things weren't goin' well for me, I didn't read the sports pages anymore. I didn't want to see where I'd gone 0-for-4 or somethin' like that."

Alston's natural mother died when Tom was serving a peacetime hitch in the Navy in Washington state. When he left the service in the late 1940s he enrolled at North Carolina Agricultural and Technical State University, where he played for the baseball team. He graduated in 1951 with a B.S. degree in physical education and social sciences.

Tom then resumed his pre-A & T career in semipro baseball, this time in western Canada. There he met and played alongside former Negro League great Chet Brewer, of whom Alston says, "even then, he could still pitch after all those years."

Brewer was later given the opportunity to manage briefly in professional baseball—he was Alston's skipper at Porterville in 1952—and served as something of a mentor to Tom.

"If you ask me," Alston argued, "Chet Brewer was the first black manager in professional baseball, but they never give him credit for it."

Of course, it wasn't long after Alston began his stint at Porterville that his troubles began. And it was at the end of the decade that his troubles came to a head.

"The Cardinals didn't release me so much as I just decided to leave," Alston said. "My father, who had remarried about a year or so before I came home, had sent one of my brothers and my sister on the bus from Greensboro to St. Louis to bring me home.

"So, I just packed up my things and came home. I just left. That's the way I ended up in baseball."

When he returned to Greensboro Alston was "broke, dejected and physically weak," with little hope of finding a good job because of his arm problem. Depression, a skirmish with the law —he says he set fire to a building—and a combined ten years spent in a pair of mental institutions followed. Alston says that he has "been on disability" for the past thirty years.

Tom had been living with his sister until about two years ago. ("She had a nervous breakdown in the 1970s, and they had to finally put her in a rest home," Tom explained.) So now he lives alone in Greensboro, where he reminisces about his playing days, and compares his batting style with the styles of more recent major leaguers.

"I had kind of a medium, open stance," Alston said. "I was, specifically, a line drive hitter. I didn't hit these towering home runs that guys like Reggie Jackson and Darryl Strawberry and these other guys nowadays hit, where they stand there and look at the ball goin' out. When I hit mine, most of the time the ball left the park early. I was mostly a pull hitter.

"Line drives. That's what I hit. Singles, doubles, triples, home runs. I almost always hit 'em on a line. When I was at Omaha I once hit a line drive home run over the fence in dead center field, 420 feet away. They told me I was the first one to ever hit a home run to that part of the ballpark.

"The fans treated me fairly when I was with St. Louis. You see, as a ballplayer, I belonged to Mr. Busch. All of the players did. The fans respected Mr. Busch so much that they had to respect me. And Brooks came along, and they treated him fine, too.

"I never married, even though I could have, I guess. I never got a promotion in pay when I was with the Cardinals, and I knew I couldn't make it on a rookie's salary with a wife and family. Seven-thousand-five-hundred dollars...that's what I made my rookie year with the Cardinals."

Alston says he is "barely making it" these days. Yet, with all the ordeals, all the disappointments he has experienced in his life, he does not talk like a bitter man. Wistful, perhaps, but not bitter. He still follows baseball. Still loves the game that he played from the time he was a youngster back in North Carolina after being inspired by watching local semipro teams.

His allegiance to one major league club has given way to just following baseball in general.

"I used to pull for the Atlanta Braves because they were nearest to me," Alston said. "They didn't amount to much until they got Joe Torre as their manager, and they haven't done nothin' since they got rid of him. They made a mistake. He was a good man.

"I get the newspaper every day and read about the games, keep up with the standin's, and read the stats.

"Sometimes I think about what might have been if I'd been well when I first came up. I might not have hit that many home runs in the major leagues, but I know I would've done respectably well, especially in battin' average and RBIs.

"When I was playin' baseball with the Cardinals, I didn't believe in swingin' at anything but strikes, no matter who that pitcher was or what he threw. Robin Roberts...all those guys...I had respect for them, but I didn't let myself be affected by their names. I just wanted to swing at strikes."

Tom Alston—Cardinal Stats

	G	AB	H	2B	3B	HR	R	RBI	BB	SO	SB	BA	SA
1954	66	244	60	14	2	4	28	34	24	41	3	.246	.369
1955	13	8	1	0	0	0	0	0	0	0	0	.125	.125
1956	3	2	0	0	0	0	0	0	0	0	0	.000	.000
1957	9	17	5	1	0	0	2	2	1	5	0	.294	.353

DON BLASINGAME

Red's Replacement

One of the most controversial trades made by the St. Louis Cardinals in the 1950s involved the departure of local hero Red Schoendienst. The transaction, completed on June 14, 1956, was made possible in part by the improvement shown by twenty-four-year-old Don Blasingame. Though the young Mississippi native did not chase incumbent second baseman Schoendienst out of town, the talented rookie infielder had the dubious chore of trying to replace one of the team's perennial All-Stars.

"I knew that Red was popular," says Blasingame. "I was a little apprehensive when he was traded. I played about six weeks at shortstop while he was at second base. When he went to the Giants, I was moved to second base. I didn't know how the fans would react to that. But they were good fans and treated me well."

After three years in the minor leagues and a five-game debut in St. Louis near the end of the 1955 season, Blasingame landed a starting job with the Cards at the beginning of 1956. A career infielder who possessed quick hands and fast feet, the transition to second base was natural for Blasingame. He wound up the season with only eight errors in 98 starts at second, good for a .986 fielding average. The only second baseman in the league with a better fielding mark was—you guessed it—Schoendienst, at .993.

Offensively, Blasingame was blossoming. Fresh from a .302 average at Triple A affiliate Omaha in 1955, the Cardinals had high hopes for their highly ranked prospect. He delivered a respectable .261 average with no homers and 27 RBI. Blasingame attributes his modest output to switching positions and "being a rookie who was trying to ping the ball around." Once new shortstop Alvin Dark arrived from the Giants as part of the Schoendienst deal, the Redbirds installed "Blazer" Blasingame as their leadoff man.

To this day, Blasingame isn't sure when his nickname was born. "It might have started in Omaha," he says. "Sportswriters hung it on me somewhere along the line. I was fairly quick, and the nickname was derived from my last name."

Surprisingly, the Cardinals didn't harness Blasingame's speed on the basepaths. In his four full seasons with St. Louis, he swiped only 64 bases (including 21 in 1957 and 20 in 1958). Yet, he led the team in steals from 1957 through 1959. He credits teammate Dark for much of his base-swiping success. "Dark batted behind me, and we had our own hit-and-run," Blasingame remembers. "He'd ask me before a game if I could get a good jump on a certain pitcher. He said, 'If I call the hit-and-run and it's a breaking ball down low which the catcher might not handle, I'll just take the pitch. Then you just steal it.' That's how I had that many stolen bases."

Aside from collaborations with Dark, Blasingame didn't get many chances to run. "I never had the green light in my life," he sighs. "They didn't give me the steal sign that much. In those days, the Cardinals just didn't run that much. I always felt that I could have stolen 40 to 50 bases easily if they'd have green-lighted me." He adds that Ken Boyer and Bill White were two of his surprisingly-fast teammates who could've had more stolen bases, "if we had had the opportunities."

Blasingame made his sophomore season in 1957 one of his best. His 650 plate appearances topped the National League, while he played in all 154 games for St. Louis. Despite hitting leadoff, Blasingame belted a career-high eight home runs and 58 RBI. His 176 hits tied Stan Musial for the team lead, while his 21 stolen bases and 108 runs scored, both personal bests, led the club.

"I never thought about the fences," Blasingame says, in an attempt to explain his homer binge. His eight dingers are even more impressive, considering that he never hit more than two homers during any other season of his twelve year career. "I think that more than half of those came in other ballparks. I was a line drive hitter who tried to keep the ball out of the air. When I hit homers, I usually had done something wrong."

The Blazer helped blaze a path for the Cardinals in 1957, sparking the team to a healthy second-place finish. "I'm proud of that year," he says. "That team went farther with less than any team I ever played on. Just look at the personnel. We didn't have a strong pitching staff or a strong bench." But the underrated Cardinals posted an 87-67 record, finishing just eight games behind the pennant-winning Milwaukee Braves. Blasingame praised Joe Cunningham (.318 in 122 games) and Walker Cooper (.269 in 48 games) for outstanding part-time work that year. Although 1957 was Cooper's final season, he later became Blasingame's father-in-law.

Two "unsung heroes" Blasingame cited from 1957 were Ken Boyer and Eddie Kasko. "Kenny played center field that year. He did it unselfishly, because we needed someone. Playing out of position, he hit just .265, but he was great in the field." In fact, Boyer paced all N.L. center fielders with a .996 fielding percentage. Rookie Kasko filled in well at the hot corner, batting .273. On the mound, Lindy McDaniel and Larry Jackson each chipped in with 15 victories. "Even though the Braves had great talent, I didn't think they could beat us. I had total confidence. Maybe I was naive in my youth, but I felt we could win against anybody that year."

Thanks to manager Fred Hutchinson, that underdog 1957 squad kept winning, Blasingame says. "He got the most out of what we had. With Hutch as manager, we really jelled. We knew he'd be behind us and let us play." Although Hutchinson didn't last three seasons as Redbirds skipper, Blasingame gave the manager high marks. "He was a man's man. I enjoyed playing for him. If you got a pat on the back, you damn well earned it. If he criticized you, you knew you deserved it."

According to Blasingame, he wasn't bothered by playing for different managers. "No manager ever had a bad year for me," he says philosophically. "I did my job, and no one ever gave me problems." When Solly Hemus was named as Hutchinson's replacement in 1959, he used Harry Walker as hitting coach. "Walker was a good line drive hitter," the left-handed hitting Blasingame says. "He wanted me to go the other way with the ball and hit to left field all the way, just to get on base. I got on base a lot like they wanted, but my RBIs went down. But a leadoff man isn't supposed to have lots of RBIs."

Eddie Stanky, Cardinals manager from 1952 to 1955, provided a springboard for Blasingame to reach the majors. "The general manager at Houston in 1954 really didn't want me there," he says. During his first year at Winston-Salem, Blasingame endured a back injury, often playing while wearing a brace. "But Eddie Stanky had seen me in spring training and liked my quickness. He told them at Houston to use me until I played myself out of the lineup. If I did, then they could send me wherever they wanted. Well, I was one of six .300 hitters on the team. That established me as a prospect." Dixie Walker at Houston and Johnny Keane at Omaha were two more supportive managers along the way, Blasingame adds.

After the 1957 season, Blasingame remained offensively steady for the Cardinals. He lifted his average to .274 in 1958, and up to .289 the next year. Despite missing 11 games in 1958, Blasingame earned a spot on the National League All-Star team. His 20 stolen bases that year ranked fourth in the league, 11 back of N.L. leader Willie Mays. In 1959, Blasingame collected a career best 178 hits, and led the Cardinals in runs and hits, while he tied White for the team lead in stolen bases with 15.

Because the Cardinals desired additional long-ball power to supplement Boyer and an aging Musial, they dealt Blasingame to the San Francisco Giants for outfielder Leon Wagner and starting second baseman Daryl Spencer on Dec. 15, 1959. Back in his hometown of Corinth, Mississippi, the news reached Blasingame in a shocking fashion. "I was back home visiting my parents, and I had gone to buy Christmas cards from a crippled friend of mine," he says. "When I got back in the car to go home, I turned on the radio and heard, 'Local Cardinals player Don Blasingame was traded...' That comes as a shock. Back at my folks' house, there was a message from general manager Bing Devine. I'm not bitter, but I never understood why he couldn't have called beforehand."

Part of Blasingame's disappointment surrounding the trade was the fact that he had come up through the Cardinals farm system. One friend he had to leave was Boyer, who was a teammate in the minors and winter league, and had been a roommate as well. "He was a good talent," Blasingame remembers. "He was a fun-lover, a good friend I enjoyed being with. I've always valued that friendship."

Before Boyer died of cancer in 1982, the old friends had a final meeting. "Before I returned to Japan [to manage a baseball team], I had lunch with him," Blasingame says. "Joe Cunningham came along. It was tough, but I knew this would be the last time. It was a sad time, but he never said anything. No one let on about what was going to happen. We laughed and joked through the whole lunch. He was that kind of guy."

Those five years with the Cardinals represent only a small portion of Blasingame's career in organized baseball. After stints with the Giants, Reds, Senators and Kansas City Athletics, Blasingame played baseball in Japan for three years. After his retirement, Blasingame worked as a Japanese League coach for eight years, and managed for four more.

Despite all the years with various organizations, Blasingame still views his time with the Cardinals as special. "I was raised in small-town Mississippi, and that was all Cardinals country," he says. "My hometown station carried Cardinals games, so we'd listen every night. For everyone there, playing with the Cardinals would have been the ultimate experience. The Yankees or anyone else would have been secondary."

Blasingame grew up without ever attending a game in St. Louis. Finally, when he entered the military, he was able to hitch a ride with an Air Force pilot headed for St. Louis. "All I remember is that they were playing Brooklyn," he says. Obviously, the ballgame experience didn't match the excitement of becoming a co-worker of boyhood idols. "I'll never forget the excitement of walking into my first major league camp and actually seeing Musial, Schoendienst and all the players. I was in some company. Being there was really special."

Don Blasingame—Cardinal Stats

	G	AB	H	2B	3B	HR	R	RBI	BB	SO	SB	BA	SA
1955	5	16	6	1	0	0	4	0	6	0	1	.375	.438
1956	150	587	153	22	7	0	94	27	72	52	8	.261	.322
1957	154	650	176	25	7	8	108	58	71	49	21	.271	.368
1958	143	547	150	19	10	2	71	36	57	47	20	.274	.356
1959	150	615	178	26	7	1	90	24	67	42	15	.289	.359

HARRY BRECHEEN

A Redbird-loving

"Cat"

In the animal kingdom, birds and cats seldom mix. But in the world of baseball, Harry "The Cat" Brecheen thrived as a bird, hurling for the St. Louis Cardinals for eleven of his twelve major league seasons.

Brecheen was dubbed "The Cat" by J. Roy Stockton, former sports editor of the St. Louis *Post-Dispatch*. Stockton affixed the nickname after seeing Brecheen's feline-like agility in fielding his position. The Oklahoma-born cat prowled mounds for the Cardinals from 1940 through 1952. Redbird fans remember Brecheen most for his three World Series wins versus the Boston Red Sox in 1946.

Looking at the regular season stats, fans would have predicted that teammate Howie Pollet would have been the clutch pitcher for St. Louis. After all, he had 21 wins, 5 saves and a 2.10 ERA that year, and topped the Cardinals in six out of ten pitching categories that season. Brecheen, meanwhile, had led the Cards with 5 shutouts and 117 strikeouts. Yet, he finished the season at only 15-15.

"In my last twelve to fifteen ballgames, I couldn't get any runs," Brecheen explains. I wasn't giving up more than one or two runs per game in the last dozen or so games, but I was losing. If you draw Warren Spahn, Johnny Sain or Schoolboy Rowe, all top pitchers to throw against, you won't get many leads to work with. Orel Hershiser had the same problem in 1989. If you give up two or three runs, you could get beat." Despite his record, Brecheen's arm was healthy, he was throwing well, and he always prospered in September. "The last month, I could pitch well and I wouldn't be tired," he says. After surviving the traditionally humid St. Louis summers, Brecheen always welcomed the declining temperatures during the final weeks of the season.

Brecheen was well prepared for his start in game two of the World Series. He had the advantage of having faced the Red Sox in spring training. "I had a good idea of how to pitch them. They had a great hitting club; if you didn't stay ahead, they could hurt you," he remembers.

After St. Louis had dropped game one, 3-2, the Cardinals needed a win to avoid going into Boston down two games. Brecheen not only notched a complete game, four-hitter; he singled in the first run in the 3-0 victory. His next starting assignment came in game six with five days rest. He again went the distance, allowing just seven hits en route to a 4-1 win that set the stage for game seven.

Thanks to an off day before the seventh game, Brecheen had a brief rest before being called on to relieve in the eighth inning. If you want to make Brecheen laugh, even today, ask him if he was tired before entering the final game. "If you're going for the Series, it doesn't make any difference if your arm is hanging," he says with a snort. "You'll warm it up and go out there." Regardless of his physical condition in that final matchup, Brecheen remained effective in those last two innings. "I only made one bad pitch. On a 3-and-2 count, I gave Dom DiMaggio a high screwball; he hit it off the right field fence. You couldn't fool him too much." Brecheen says that if his pitch had been low like he wanted, DiMaggio might have grounded it to second base or popped it up. As it was, the hit capped a two run rally that tied the score at three.

Brecheen's win was made possible by Enos Slaughter's famous "mad dash" to score the winning run in the ninth inning.

Brecheen vividly remembers third base coach Mike Gonzales trying in vain to stop Slaughter at third. "Mike thought he'd be thrown out," he says. But, when shortstop Johnny Pesky hesitated with the relay throw from center fielder Leon Culberson, Brecheen says Slaughter gained the "two or three steps" necessary to score.

When Brecheen points to his personal success, he overlooks the 1946 Series in favor of his 1948 accomplishments. In his finest season, Brecheen paced the Cardinals with a 20-7 record. In addition to his career-high win count, Brecheen led the team in five categories: ERA (2.24); starts (30); complete games (21); shutouts (seven) and strikeouts (149). "The Cat" received his second-ever N.L. All-Star roster spot. His ERA, shutouts, strikeouts and .741 winning percentage were all league bests.

What made the difference for Brecheen? "Runs, for one thing," he says. "That way, you win games even when you don't have your best stuff. With leads to work with, at least I made enough good pitches to get out of jams." Starting in 1947, after the Cardinals lost pitcher Max Lanier to the Mexican League the year before, Brecheen got more work by pitching in a four-man rotation. His success flowed into 1948, when his arm remained sound. "I had no elbow problems even though I was throwing lots of screwballs," he says. Brecheen's increased usage of his "out" pitch as his career advanced risked arm injury because of the unorthodox reverse-spin delivery needed to throw the screwball.

Additionally, Brecheen was grateful to have the milder temperatures of night games for many of his starts. "In the beginning when I came up, we only had sixteen to eighteen night games," he says. "The team always wanted a hard thrower under the lights, so my only chances to pitch when it was cooler came in relief. Of course, you might not call eighty to ninety degrees cool, but it could be for St. Louis."

During his career, Brecheen set himself apart from many left-handers by his mastery of the screwball. As a youth, he admired fellow lefty Carl Hubbell. However, Hubbell did not teach him the special pitch. "Pittsburgh pitcher Cy Blanton taught it to me when I was playing American Legion ball," Brecheen recalls. Blanton and teammates Paul and Lloyd Waner would return to their home state of Oklahoma and play exhibition games for extra money. "Blanton showed me how to put the reverse spin on the pitch." Brecheen says the pitch didn't wreak havoc on his arm like it has other pitchers, partly due to not throwing many in the minors. "It'll cause your arm to draw up and cause your hand to turn out. Because of that, it was easy to spot Hubbell walking down the street." To add to his pitch assortment, he varied the spin on his screwball to produce different breaks.

Brecheen wasn't an overnight sensation in the majors. In fact, he was twenty-five before he made his major league debut in 1940. Two more minor league seasons with Columbus followed before he played his first full major league season in 1943. Before Brecheen escaped from the minor leagues, he had won more than 100 games. "You just had to wait your turn and wait for the pitchers up there to grow old," he says. "At that time, the Cardinals had three Triple A clubs. Back then they could option a guy out three times, once to each class. There was someone wanting you all the time, but the Cardinals wouldn't sell you. There were scouts looking at you every day in the American Association, but the Cards wouldn't put a price on you." In fact, Cardinals general manager Branch Rickey wanted Brecheen so much that he paid him more money at Columbus than he would have gotten in St. Louis. "The average salary in Triple A was $400 a month," he says. "With the Cardinals, you might make $600. The pay was skimpy."

In order to stick with the Cardinals in 1943, Brecheen pitched as a reliever and a spot starter. Back then, relief pitching played a less significant role than in today's game, witnessed by Brecheen's club-leading four saves. "The pitchers in the pen would relieve long or short. The best control pitchers were in short relief because they'd be more likely to get the ball over. In those days, relieving was just a job," Brecheen says. "You took it if you couldn't break into the starting rotation, just to stay on the ballclub."

When he first made the club, Brecheen was befriended by veteran pitchers Lon Warneke and Curt Davis. (After coming from the Cubs in the Dizzy Dean deal, Davis was 22-16 for the 1939 Cardinals.) "I talked with them a lot in spring training. They had lots of good ideas," Brecheen says. "They were both low-ball pitchers." During his stay with the Cardinals, Brecheen roomed with Murry Dickson, Debs Garms and "Gas House Gang" star Pepper Martin.

Being from Oklahoma, Brecheen knew that playing for the nearby Cardinals could have been the dream of every boy in his state. "Where I lived, the Cardinals were the only close big league club," he says. "Everyone was a Cardinals fan. Weekends in St. Louis, we'd have sellout crowds. We had a tremendous weekend following. People would come to town by train or would drive up for a game."

Once he made the majors, Brecheen was the model of consistency with St. Louis. From 1944 through 1949, Brecheen posted at least 14 wins and 13 complete games. Today, he ranks among the top ten career leaders in seven of ten team categories. Brecheen is one of only six Cardinals to lead the league in strikeouts and one of just seven to lead in ERA.

After Brecheen pitched eleven years with the Cardinals, he became a free agent. He was able to sign with the St. Louis Browns in 1953, inking a two-year contract both to pitch and coach. "I wanted to go with Marty," Brecheen says of former teammate Marty Marion, who was managing the team. The Cardinals, who had hoped to retain Brecheen as a coach, unsuccessfully filed tampering charges against the Browns. "The Cat" became an original Baltimore Oriole when the Browns moved East. Brecheen stayed as pitching coach through 1967, overseeing the development of young aces like Dave McNally and Jim Palmer.

But Brecheen's heart remained in St. Louis. "Growing up, the Cardinals were the only team I knew," he says. "When I joined the team, I knew all the people. On off days, almost all the players would go on picnics or do things together. It isn't that way today, where players always go off by themselves. They were all good people, people like Musial, Marion and Schoendienst. To me, just being able to be around them was special. They played together.

"That's why I call the team *my* Cardinals. They'll always be my number one team."

Harry Brecheen—Cardinal Stats

	W	L	PCT	ERA	G	GS	CG	IP	H	BB	SO	SHO	SV
1940	0	0	—	0.00	3	0	0	3.1	2	2	4	0	0
1943	9	6	.600	2.26	29	13	8	135.1	98	39	68	1	4
1944	16	5	.762	2.85	30	22	13	189.1	174	46	88	3	0
1945	14	4	.778	2.52	24	18	13	157.1	136	44	63	3	2
1946	15	15	.500	2.49	36	30	14	231.1	212	67	117	5	3
1947	16	11	.593	3.30	29	28	18	223.1	220	66	89	1	1
1948	20	7	.741	2.24	33	30	21	233.1	193	49	149	7	1
1949	14	11	.560	3.35	32	31	14	214.2	207	65	88	2	1
1950	8	11	.421	3.80	27	23	12	163.1	151	45	80	2	1
1951	8	4	.667	3.25	24	16	5	138.2	134	54	57	0	2
1952	7	5	.583	3.32	25	13	4	100.1	82	28	54	1	2
World Series													
1943	0	1	.000	2.45	3	0	0	3.2	5	3	3	0	0
1944	1	0	1.000	1.00	1	1	1	9	9	4	4	0	0
1946	3	0	1.000	0.45	3	2	2	20	14	5	11	1	0

LOU BROCK

It's All in the

Mind's Eye

In retelling the story of how Lou Brock first became interested in baseball, it's important to highlight the "growling tummy" factor.

In the small, one-room schoolhouse in rural Louisiana, where he soon learned the third "R" (as in readin', 'ritin' and...) could also stand for "redemption," a young Lou Brock once misdirected a spitwad meant for a female classmate but which hit the teacher behind her ear. To redeem himself, the little mischief maker was required to research the lives of several big league baseball players—Stan Musial and Jackie Robinson among them—and deliver a report to the rest of the class.

"That was the punishment, to read to the rest of the class," Brock said of that childhood incident. "And it *was* a punishment, too, standing before all these people and trying to read about something I knew little about. Baseball. Wasn't anything exciting about that. Just a bunch of grown men chasing a little ball around a field. But in stumbling through what I'd read about these ballplayers, I guess there was this one paragraph that stated these guys got something like $8 to $10 a day meal money. This was an economically-poor rural community, remember, and one thing school kids identified with was lunch. Eating. A meal.

"I had trouble gettin' a quarter for meal money and these guys were gettin' maybe forty quarters a *day*. I thought, 'Wow! Can you believe that?' That stayed with me, and I wanted to learn more about baseball."

Brock chuckles when he tells the story, but he is quick to add that the experience of having to recite information to his classmates was incentive enough for him to settle down in school.

"I never wanted to be put in that situation again," Brock said.

Something else happened to Brock not long afterward that drew him into the game of baseball to stay. A city sandlot team of older youths and young men had formed, and twelve-year-old Lou would go to see them play.

"I was always fascinated by the sound of a ball off a bat," Brock said. "To this day, to me, there is no greater sound than a bat hitting a baseball in an open field or park. It's a sound that breaks you into what I call a fantasy world where you begin to—not daydream—but, rather, live through your mind's eye.

"As I sat there watching and listening, a lot of wonderful things would come racing across my mind's eye. What's beautiful about that is that you can be the fielder, the pitcher, the hitter, all the things you might be doin' if you could have a chance to be out there on the field."

One day, Brock got that chance. The right fielder didn't show up for a practice game. Another player was needed. A yell rang out, "Hey, kid! Can you play ball?"

In his mind's eye, Lou Brock had played ball a thousand times. He answered with a resounding "Yeah!" and ran onto the field.

If the ball is hit to you, the older players told him, wait till it stops rolling and then pick it up and throw it in. Instead, he charged the first ball knocked in his direction.

"And that ball hit me all over," Brock remembered, "but I picked it up, threw it in, and the ball sort of sailed. I'm not sure how I even held it. When the inning was over they asked me if I could make the ball do that again. In my mind's eye, I had done it before, so I told 'em, 'Sure.' So they had me take the mound, but the ball would never do that for me again. I tried, but I could never make it sail like a cut fastball again.

"Yet based on that time and place, I became a pitcher on that sandlot team. And I continued to pitch clear through high school. But still, it was the sound of the bat on the ball that fascinated me and got me involved."

As he matured Brock played most, if not all, nine positions on the diamond. A left-handed thrower as well as left-handed hitter, Brock even tried his hand at shortstop for one game. ("It wasn't a difficult throw, either," he insists, "despite what people say.")

Brock was primarily a pitcher until he reached college. Once enrolled at Southern University in Baton Rouge, Louisiana, he tried out for the outfield. Opposing hitters, then, must have figured out his pitching repertoire.

"Repertoire? I threw the express," Brock said, smiling. "Only the express."

Brock's development as a good, all-round amateur athlete at Southern caught the attention of some people in key places, and Brock was chosen for the baseball squad representing the United States in the 1959 Pan-American Games. He remembers getting "a couple hits" for an American team that took home a bronze medal that year.

Coincidentally, Wrigley Field in Chicago, which mathematics major Brock saw during the Pan-Am Games, became his first major league home after he signed with the Cubs in 1961. And it was no surprise that the perennial also-rans were anxious to bring the budding star to the big leagues. All he did at St. Cloud was lead the Northern League in hitting (.361); runs (117); hits (181); doubles (33) and, on defense, in putouts, with 277. For that Brock received the league's "Rookie of the Year" award.

Lou played reasonably well for the Cubs in the early 1960s, but in June of 1964 the club dealt him, along with pitchers Jack Spring and Paul Toth, to St. Louis for pitchers Ernie Broglio and Bobby Shantz, and outfielder Doug Clemens. Brock and Broglio were the key figures in the deal. The Cubs wanted to improve their mound corps, and Broglio, who went 18-8 with a 2.99 ERA for St. Louis in 1963, appeared to fit the bill.

For their part the Cardinals desperately needed a catalyst for their sputtering offense and a speed merchant to help in the outfield, and team officials felt Lou Brock was their man on both counts.

"There was one cheerful reporter who covered the story," Brock said. "I don't remember who he was working for at the time. He'd say, 'We like you' while his smile during our interview said, 'We're glad to see you go because we're getting a great pitcher [in Broglio].'

"That young reporter, maybe on his first assignment, was Brent Musburger," Brock added, breaking into a grin. "To this day, whenever I see Brent, I always rub it in."

Rather than view the trade as a message that he was no longer wanted by the Cubs, Brock took it as a sign that the Cardinals had evaluated his talents and wanted him badly enough to trade a starting pitcher who'd notched seventy wins for them in just over five seasons.

"In Chicago I wasn't too successful," Brock admitted, "and in the back of my mind I knew there was a chance that any day I'd be sent to the minor leagues. When it turned out that I was instead going to St. Louis, that gave me a new sense of purpose. It was a fresh start, a change of scenery; and I felt I was leavin' all my troubles behind.

"Remember, too, that I had grown up in the South. There was radio and Harry Caray and Stan Musial and all that when I was a kid, so I knew a little about the Cardinals, about their history. Even though I'd seen Wrigley Field in college during the Pan-Am Games, I didn't have any sense of its history. Traded to St. Louis, I had a sense of Sportsman's history. And when I walked in there as a Cardinal for the first time in 1964, I really felt that history all around me. And I wanted to fulfill the level of tradition of that place, of the men who'd come before me.

"One of the things missing in baseball, it seems, is current players' sense of what's come before them, especially of their own particular clubs. Walkin' into a ballpark—can he hear footsteps of the past? If he can, then there is a certain tradition the ballplayer is keeping alive just by his awareness.

"Players today don't really get in touch with the history of baseball or of their particular team, either through hand-me-down information from others, or from books. I think they're missing out on something. It's intriguing...fascinating...what happens to you after you do begin to appreciate what went before you. It can be a humbling experience, but it serves to give each generation of players that extra sense of purpose. You feel it, whether those ghosts exist or not. You're not only playing against the opposition that day, you're playing against history, and history has a way of living on through stats and through the events that happen year after year."

Lou played all or part of sixteen seasons in a Cardinal uniform. In that time, he reached the 3,000 hits plateau, set the career mark for stolen bases with 938, hit close to .300 lifetime and starred in three World Series. He was inducted into the National Baseball Hall of Fame—the ultimate shrine of baseball knowledge for the history-respectful Brock—in 1985. One wonders if Brock ever set such lofty goals for himself.

"You know who really sets your goals?" Brock countered. "The public. You have performed to a certain level and the public begins to hold you to it. That established level of play: you know where it is, they know where it is. The whole question is whether you can sustain that level of play and for how long. That's where the excitement comes in."

And excitement is exactly what Lou Brock provided during the course of his career. Eight times he led the National League in stolen bases; six times, he was the major league leader. Eight times he hit better than .300. In 1968 he led the majors in doubles and triples. "He was," as longtime teammate Curt Flood says of him, "the guy who made us go."

Yet with all the numbers he put up, including those in World Series play, and all the accolades he received during and after his playing career, Brock points to his final season as one of his more satisfying, if least talked about, accomplishments.

The 1978 season was a personal disaster for Brock who, at thirty-nine, hit an anemic .221 with 12 RBI in 92 games. He hit no homers, no triples and only nine doubles. He swiped seventeen bases but was caught stealing five times.

Actually, the whole Cardinal team suffered through a bad year. More than a fair share of dissension reportedly riddled the team; there were three managers; no pitcher won as many as fifteen games; and the Cardinals finished twenty-one games out of first place in the N.L. East. Not exactly a dream season.

Brock's pride and work ethic brought him into the 1979 season with more confidence than one might expect from an almost-forty-year-old star at the end of his great career. All he did was bat .304 in 120 games, steal 21 bases, hit 15 doubles, 4 triples and 5 home runs while plating 38 runners. He was named N.L. "Comeback Player of the Year" by *The Sporting News*. And with that final burst of excellence, Lou Brock could walk away from the game.

A whole decade has passed since the Arkansas-born Brock graced the green and tan fields of our National Pastime. But the memories, the images, linger—for Brock as well as his fans.

"I was a good one for using all kinds of bats," Brock said. "I used a 35-inch bat down to a 32-inch bat; 33 ounces up to 36, 38 ounces. It all depended on who the pitcher was.

"I think the pitchers who gave me the most trouble were the ones who short-armed the ball. One was George Stone, a lefty who pitched for the Mets and Atlanta. I never got a good swing against him. Twice in a month's time he ended hitting streaks I had going at the time. Everybody else on our team could get a hit off him, but he just wore me out. Couldn't hit him with an ironing board.

"Bob Apodaca was another one. He was a right-handed relief pitcher I couldn't hit. Gaylord Perry...I never got a good swing against him. [Ron] Perranoski, Jim Rooker, Dan Osinski — never a good swing against them, either. Oh, I probably got my hits off these people, but it never was to the point where I felt I took my best swing against any of 'em.

"One of the biggest aspects of baseball is the one-upmanship between batter and pitcher. It's called the big payback. A guy strikes you out one time, you go up there in your next at-bat looking to pay him back. Or, if you get a hit off the pitcher, he's not going to forget it, so the next time he faces you his idea of the big payback is to get you out. It becomes a series of these paybacks, and those who are highly motivated along these lines are flipped into another level of play.

"It's fascinating to see what happens to veteran players who perform below their self-established standard of play. Mental anguish sets in, in some cases. Guys have to be real careful here. If a guy's playing strictly for the money, or because he doesn't have a crystal clear reason for staying in the game, then he's more likely to accept the fact that he's not playing up to his previous levels. He won't care if some gunslinger comes in and mows him down. He won't care if his last at-bat is a home run or a strikeout thrown by some fresh kid barely out of high school.

"But if he's got a single purpose in mind, whether it's a record he wants to break, or if he wants to keep playing because his team has a chance to win a pennant, or some other reason that's important to him, then his quest becomes the one animal that will force him to accept play at a certain level—even when he knows that level is not where it once was."

Today, Brock wears several hats, including a baseball cap that he dons for the Equitable Old-Timers Games. He has been in business for a number of years and his Broc-World Products International Inc. is involved in retail and wholesale soft goods and gift items, including several products licensed by Major League Baseball.

Card shows are on Brock's appointments calendar, too. One annual show in which he has a vested interest is held in St. Louis every year by St. Louis Sports Collectors. Proceeds from the show go to the Lou Brock Scholarship Fund. The fund was created in 1979 to provide St. Louis-area high school students the opportunity for one four-year college scholarship to Brock's alma mater or one of several $1,000 cash grants to the college or university of their choice.

That Brock is such a strong proponent of higher education underscores his change from a spitwad-firing grade school kid to a serious college student to a former major leaguer who is giving something back to his community through a scholarship program. Perhaps that is because Brock understands as well as anyone what competition in life is all about.

For nineteen seasons he competed against the best the game of baseball had to offer. And though he wasn't always rewarded for his efforts, as his following stories about umpires point out, knowing he'd given his all on every at-bat, every leaping grab in the outfield, every stolen base attempt, still gives him the greatest satisfaction.

"Well, I spent about twenty years in baseball, and for the

first fifteen or so I never got thrown out of a ballgame. The first
umpire to throw me out was Frank Pulli. Sometimes we see each
other, and we reminisce about that. Once he did it though, the
umpires must've nailed me four or five times a year after that. But
Frank...I accuse him of opening the gate.

"We were arguing a play at first base. In fact, I had walked
away and was all the way down to second base when it happened.
I had said to him, 'The play was close. I thought I was safe. Pulli,
you realize we're in a pennant race? It's the players who're supposed to be crackin'—not you guys.' And he said, 'I'm not
crackin'.' And I said, 'Then why'd you choke?' And he said, 'I'm
not chokin'.'

"So we got into a crackin'-chokin', chokin'-crackin' thing. I
said, 'Frank, you are chokin' 'cause the veins are stickin' out of
your forehead and burstin' out of your neck!' But as I walked
away, he yelled, 'I'm not chokin'!' But I looked back at him and
put my hand around my neck and made the choke gesture, so he
ran me from the game.

"The late Dick Stello was a good umpire. A good guy. But
he ran me twice, including one time when a call he made went
against us and some of the guys in the dugout threw all these tow-
els out on the field to protest the call. Just as I was wavin' my towel
around my head to let it go, Stello sees me and yells, 'If that towel
hits the ground, Brock, you're gone!' I tried to catch it, but I
couldn't stop it from landing, so I showered early.

"The other time resulted from an ongoing game the two of
us had with each other. I used to yell to him, when I was standin'
on first base and he was umpiring second, 'Hey! I'm comin' down
there! Be ready! One time I yelled that to him and on the next
pitch I took off for second. I came slidin' in in a cloud of dust and
he yells, 'Y-e-r-r-r out!' I looked at him and said, 'Dick, I asked
you to be *ready.*' And he thumbs me outta the game.

"But I think the most memorable incident concerning an
umpire involved Bob Engel, a great umpire. But he had a tendency during those years...well, if it was an action play and he
was trailing the play, nine times out of ten he'd call you out because he'd run with his hands up so that his elbows were actually
in front of his head and his momentum would turn into the signal
for 'out.' We always wanted to tell him, 'Wait until the play ends

and then exact the sign.' Everybody had that feeling—that was the book on him. But nobody would tell him.

"One time I walked up to him and said, 'Bob, we've been friends for a long time. And as a friend, I'm going to tell you what *they* are saying about you.' And I told him about the tendency we felt he had toward calling guys out on close plays. And Bob says, 'Oh-h-h, they are saying that, huh? More you then they, I think.' And I said, 'No, Bob, I thought you should know. Really.'

"But about a year, maybe two years, had passed, and Bob still had that same habit. I don't remember the player's name but, Bob was trailing the play and everybody thought the runner was safe but Bob called him 'out.' So, I wrote on a ball right in the middle of this game in Philadelphia, something like: Bob Engel—One of the best umpires in baseball. But if the little S.O.B. would ever wait until the play stopped before he makes the call, he'd probably be the greatest umpire in the world.

"So I take the ball, roll it between the pitcher's mound and home plate over to the Philadelphia dugout. [John] Kibler was behind the plate, and he had to call time when the ball rolled across the infield. When the ball got to their dugout the Philadelphia players picked up the ball and started reading what I had written on it, and they're all nodding their heads in agreement that yes, this is true. They pass the ball from one guy to the next, but when it gets to Jose Cardenal, he reads it and then takes it and tosses it out toward Engel.

"And now this ball is rollin' out to Engel, and I'm thinking, 'Oh, no, I gotta get outta here, because I'm the only guy he's going to tie into this.' I left our dugout and ran up the chute, but then I had to come back out a few minutes later because we had to take the field. As soon as I reappeared Engel sees me and yells, 'You!'

"I said, 'What about me?' And he says 'You did this!' I said, 'Did what?' And he says, 'I'm gonna turn this into the league office, Brock!'

"Well, a few years later—it was after I had retired —I was at the 1982 World Series to watch the Cardinals and Brewers. I'm sitting in a box seat next to Chub Feeney, who was the National League president at that time. A foul ball, or a ball thrown by a reliever during his warm-ups, came rollin' up against the stands near us. Chub leans over toward me and says 'You know, Lou, that reminds me, I've got a ball that was given to me a few years ago by one of my umpires.'

"Well, I knew exactly what he was talking about, but I just made some face or something, and he says, 'And the public thinks you're such a *nice guy!*'

"I'm *still* tryin' to get that ball back!"

Lou Brock—Cardinal Stats

	G	AB	H	2B	3B	HR	R	RBI	BB	SO	SB	BA	SA
1964	103	419	146	21	9	12	81	44	27	87	33	.348	.527
1965	155	631	182	35	8	16	107	69	45	116	63	.288	.445
1966	156	643	183	24	12	15	94	46	31	134	74	.285	.429
1967	159	689	206	32	12	21	113	76	24	109	52	.299	.472
1968	159	660	184	46	14	6	92	51	46	124	62	.279	.418
1969	157	655	195	33	10	12	97	47	50	115	53	.298	.434
1970	155	664	202	29	5	13	114	57	60	99	51	.304	.422
1971	157	640	200	37	7	7	126	61	76	107	64	.313	.425
1972	153	621	193	26	8	3	81	42	47	93	63	.311	.393
1973	160	650	193	29	8	7	110	63	71	112	70	.297	.398
1974	153	635	194	25	7	3	105	48	61	88	118	.306	.381
1975	136	528	163	27	6	3	78	47	38	64	56	.309	.400
1976	133	498	150	24	5	4	73	67	35	75	56	.301	.394
1977	141	489	133	22	6	2	69	46	30	74	35	.272	.354
1978	92	298	66	9	0	0	31	12	17	29	17	.221	.252
1979	120	405	123	15	4	5	56	38	23	43	21	.304	.398
World Series													
1964	7	30	9	2	0	1	2	5	0	3	0	.300	.467
1967	7	29	12	2	1	1	8	3	2	3	7	.414	.655
1968	7	28	13	3	1	2	6	5	3	4	7	.464	.857

JACK BUCK

A Voice That's a

Winner

In his acceptance speech at the National Baseball Hall of Fame during the 1987 induction ceremonies, Cardinal announcer Jack Buck talked of wanting to be back in the radio booth that day to broadcast the Cardinals-Giants clash.

All Jack Buck ever wanted was to be in the booth, announcing the game. Just ask his close friends. Ask his brothers. Ask him.

"To tell you the truth, as a kid of fifteen or sixteen I would listen to some of those guys broadcast games on the radio and think to myself, 'Hey, I can do that,' or even, 'I can do better than that.' Some of the guys I listened to were good announcers, but some were not," Buck said.

"I used to drive my brothers crazy when we'd go to ballgames together. We'd sit out in the bleachers and I'd talk to myself out there. They all thought I was nuts. I'd call the plays as they happened out on the field."

On the playgrounds or in the tree lined streets of suburban Cleveland, where the Buck family moved when Jack was a teenager, the cocky youngster

called the play-by-play of his own moves: "Buck fades to throw long to his receiver," or, in that split second before his wiry frame met the pavement, "Buck slips and falls and lands on the street."

There was a lot of fantasizing in those days before television took some of the mystery of sports away from radio. And Jack Buck was nothing if not a radio disciple. When he saw a baseball game in person he marveled at something as simple as the pre-game ritual of fungo hitting. ("Wow! Is that Tommy Henrich? Hey, look—there's Joe DiMaggio! And that's Bob Feller!")

"Back then, you rarely saw the ballplayers outside the ballpark," Buck said. "When you went to a major league game they were like actors on a stage. Who are all these people? Well, these were people you'd only read about in the newspapers or heard about on the radio. You'd never see them up close.

"Now, Ozzie Smith walks out of Busch Stadium and all the kids yell, 'Hi, Ozzie!' like he's their next door neighbor. Back then it was like the players came alive when you saw them on the field. There wasn't nearly the familiarity then as there is now."

For millions of Cardinal fans and others who listen to Buck's play-by-play on KMOX radio, the players and their performances come alive over the airwaves, too, many miles from where the game's drama is unfolding. But as pleasing to the ear as Buck's voice remains, and as knowledgeable of the game's strategies and subtleties as he is, it is Buck's adherence to calling an "honest" game that keeps one's dial tuned in to the local KMOX affiliate.

When he talks of an "honest" game he means that if the Cardinals are behind 6-0 and one of them hits a solo shot to make the score 6-1, Buck won't call it as if the Cards have just tied the score.

"I'm not theatrical," Buck insists. "I'm not an actor or some-one who can make it sound better or more promising than it is. But if there *is* something exciting going on—good *or* bad for the Cardinals—then our listeners will know I'll be excited about call-ing it.

"I sometimes dwell on what my approach, my attitude, is going to be before a game or a series of games, but that's usually dictated by the ballclub. If we go from six games out to five games out to four games out, then our listeners' interest is going to in-crease as we zero in on first place, and so I'll get into it a little more.

"Also, who we're playing affects how listeners respond and the importance they, and I, attach to a game. It's now August of 1989, and a Cardinals-Mets game or a Cardinals-Expos game or a Cardinals-Cubs game will turn on fans, umpires, sportswriters and broadcasters much more than say, a Cardinals-Braves game. Everybody gets into the swing of a pennant race, right? That's the way it should be."

Buck isn't one to pass on a chance to liven things up when the game is out of hand, however, as a night in Los Angeles a few years ago when the Dodgers were burying the Cardinals attests.

Jonathan Winters, a former colleague of Buck's when the two worked for a Columbus, Ohio, television station in 1952, joined his friend in the KMOX booth to "help pass the time."

Winters assumed the persona of one "Whip" Willis, an "old-time ballplayer trying to make a comeback with the Dodgers." Listeners who had weathered the Cardinals' on-field debacle were rewarded for their patience with some very funny banter between the two pros.

"Jonathan and I were both staff announcers at the CBS affiliate back in Columbus," Buck said. "I had a sports show called Buck-Eye Sports, and he had a comedy show. I was never his foil; he was always a one-man show.

"But I used to give him some ideas. Once in a while he'd come to me shortly before he went on the air and say, 'I don't know what the hell I'm gonna do.' I'd give him a couple of ideas and so forth, and he'd go out and wing it. He was pretty much the wacky guy then that we all came to know later on. I saw him about a month ago out in 'Frisco and he came over to our dinner table and acted up for about half an hour. He's just a funny, funny guy."

So is Jack, albeit in a dryer, wryer manner. He and broadcasting partner Mike "Moon Man" Shannon play well in Paducah, Kentucky and any of the other 130-plus communities in an eleven state region with a KMOX affiliate. And sometimes, the two will debate the intricacies of the game.

"I'm a lot different from what I was twenty years ago or thirty years ago or forty years ago," Buck said. "I'd hate to hear what I sounded like in 1950, when I was doing play-by-play for Columbus, the Cardinals' farm club. I'd like to think that I've matured in broadcasting the game. I've also learned a few things about baseball along the way. You never know everything about this game. You're always running into people who know more than you do."

But as a student of the game, Jack Buck is well qualified to comment on some of the people and teams he's covered for KMOX since 1954. Here's a sampling of Buck's observations:

On underappreciated Cardinals: "Julian Javier, for one. People don't realize what a good, steady second baseman he was, how well he could make the pivot on a double play ball, how well he could hit left-handers. Boyer was another one. Kenny was a loping kind of guy. Even when he was trying hard, he didn't appear to be trying hard, so when he popped up it wasn't like when [Pedro] Guerrero pops up, not the same kind of animation involved. Kenny was a good ball player, and how can Cardinal fans ever forget the grand slam he hit in the '64 World Series?"

In contrasting Cardinal eras: "In the 1950s, when I first started broadcasting the Cardinal games with Harry Caray, Milo Hamilton, Joe Garagiola and others, the Cardinals never won anything. They were a perennial third-place team. The Dodgers, and to some extent the Braves and Giants, dominated the league at that time. But, that was before expansion and before divisional play, and in the eyes of some it wasn't so bad to finish third. It was actually a lot of fun to broadcast Cardinal games in the fifties, it really was. Everyone associated with the club always hoped for a pennant, but there were still some fine ballplayers on those teams who kept it interesting for the fans and the announcers. The 1960s ...well, once an announcer gets the Brock-Gibson-McCarver-Flood-Cepeda-Maris thing dumped in his lap, how could he *not* be excited about those years? The 1970s were tough, though... there were missed opportunities early on, for one thing, and for another, I didn't enjoy Cardinal baseball just before Whitey Herzog came along. Some of the people we had and the way they played on the field and the way they conducted themselves at airports and so forth with their sloppy dress and music boxes blaring ...it was embarrassing. I credit Herzog with not only infusing the proper spirit into the ballclub, but also for helping to renew my interest in doing Cardinal baseball. Most people say a manager makes the difference in six or seven games a season. Baloney. Herzog made the difference in six or seven entire seasons. He took St. Louis from a million and a half a year [in attendance] to three million a year. I can't say enough about Whitey."

On "being a Cardinal": "When I stick my hand out and meet somebody out on the field and say, 'Hi, I'm Jack Buck, one of the Cardinal broadcasters,' it means a lot to me. Not to knock the other clubs, but it's one of the grand names in baseball, the St. Louis Cardinals. There is such a rich tradition here, dating back to Rogers Hornsby and then Dizzy Dean and Pepper Martin and the Gas House Gang, through the forties with Musial and Slaughter and into the sixties with Gibson, who was at the hub of it all, and then Brock continuing through the seventies, and the pennants and World Series in the eighties. I mean, if I didn't enjoy it now, for whatever reason, I'd get out."

Buck, who was born in Holyoke, Massachusetts, about the time the Cardinals first began their switch from also-rans to contenders, attended Ohio State University following a stint in the U.S. Army during World War II. (He was wounded when his unit crossed into Germany in March of 1945.)

He parlayed his B.A. in radio speech into a professional broadcasting career that began in 1950 as the voice of the Cardinals' Columbus farm club. He also did the team's play-by-play in 1951, then switched to television in 1952. In 1953 he was the voice of the Cardinals' farm club in Rochester, and joined Harry Caray in the Cardinals' radio booth in 1954.

He left the KMOX team briefly in 1960 to call the play-by-play for ABC-TV's late Saturday afternoon baseball telecasts, but returned to the Cardinals' broadcast team in 1961. Buck left one other time—in 1975—to anchor a shortlived televised sports program, "Grandstand," but returned for good the following year. In 1990, Buck will again go national. While continuing as the voice of the Cardinals, a job he has held since 1970, Buck will team with Jim Kaat on CBS for their national baseball telecasts.

In addition to covering Cardinal games, the Hall of Fame broadcaster has announced All-Star Games, the World Series, and

NFL and AFL football. He counts among his favorite "calls" Bob Gibson's no-hitter (1971) and Lou Brock's 105th stolen base of the season in 1974, which broke Maury Wills's single-season record.

As much as Jack Buck loved sports as a youngster, he admits he was never a threat to make the big leagues.

"My father played baseball, and tried out for the New York Giants at one time," Buck recalled. "He pitched a perfect game when he was in high school back in Holyoke. I'm afraid that as interested in sports as I was when I was a kid, I still wasn't a very good player, at least in baseball. I always played right field and batted ninth. My father saw me play and he traded me for a son to be born later.

"One thing, though, I did have my voice, even when I was a little squirt. I'd say something and people would turn around and look at their eye level and find they had to look down to where I was standing. 'Oh, it's you' they'd say. Then later, I sold newspapers on the corner, and in the army I was the drill instructor. I was always developing my voice, even though I didn't know I was."

Buck, who is now sports director at KMOX, says the best piece of advice he ever received came from Rollie Hemsley, a former major league catcher who was managing at Columbus when Jack first arrived on the scene. When the rookie broadcaster asked the less-than-erudite veteran of nineteen big league campaigns how he should approach his first broadcast, Hemsley thought about it for a second and said, "If they missed it, and you couldn't have caught it either, keep your mouth shut. If they missed it and you *could* have caught it, give 'em hell."

"In other words," Buck says now, forty years after that tip, "put yourself in their shoes...be critical only when it's deserved. That's kind of been my broadcasting philosophy ever since. I also try to be fair, and use common sense when dealing with players, coaches and managers."

And, as the "Whip" Willis routine in L.A. points out, Buck also brings to the booth a sense of good-natured fun. Here's another example of that, as related by Jack himself:

"We were in Atlanta, and Silvio Martinez, one of the Cardinal players, didn't speak much English. We had a headset for the postgame show down in the dugout. During the game, he picked up the headset and began listening to me while he was watching the game. I happened to spy him down there, holding the headset to his ear.

"So I lapsed into a little Spanish, which I had studied in college, and gave him a little blurb in Spanish. You know, 'Here's the pitch, and it's a swing and a miss.' He looked at the headset as if it had a tiny translator inside it just for him. Then I saw him look up in the booth and realize it was me.

"I'm not fluent in Spanish. I need a lot of practice. Every once in a while in Los Angeles they ask me to go on and do some Spanish play-by-play, and they end up on the floor...laughing ...so I don't do that anymore."

ORLANDO CEPEDA

Sweet Music for

St. Louis

When the Cardinals obtained first baseman Orlando Cepeda from the San Francisco Giants on May 8, 1966, the fiery slugger was one of the most misunderstood players in baseball. Accused of being lazy, Cepeda was attacked by the San Francisco press regularly. Repeatedly, manager Alvin Dark had stopped Cepeda from bringing his stereo system to the Giants clubhouse.

But things were different in St. Louis. The Cardinals welcomed Cepeda's long-ball prowess and snappy defense. Teammates delighted in Cepeda's musical tastes as he filled the Redbirds clubhouse with salsa music throughout the season.

The newly-acquired first sacker meant sweet music for the needy Cardinals. St. Louis was without a cleanup hitter before Cepeda. His bat and his contagious enthusiasm earned him the nickname "Cha-Cha." Cepeda was thrilled to have his stereo in the clubhouse. "I like music. It's a big part of my life," Cepeda says. "The Cardinals had different personalities. They accepted me. In St. Louis, we had the possibility of

having fun and ribbing each other. But once the game started, it was all business."

With Cepeda on the team, the Cardinals took on an entirely different personality. The team became "El Birdos," with Cepeda leading the cheers. He credits third base coach Joe Schultz with the club nickname. The press loved the title and renamed the club temporarily.

Cepeda's problems in San Francisco had grown to epic proportions. He had bad knees throughout his career and had his first surgery at age fifteen. But manager Herman Franks accused Cepeda of faking it, which hurt the proud star's ego. The press was another adversary of Cepeda. "Unfortunately, when I came to San Francisco, they had billed me too high," he says. "When I started doing well, the people from New York told me I was doing better than Willie Mays." He realized that he had been set up to fail. When his knees plagued him and his performance slipped, writers delighted in attacking him. "I was only a baby," he explains. "I was just twenty-one and they were getting on me bad." The fans in San Francisco turned on him, too. An irate Cepeda once pursued a heckler into the stands. "The last couple years in San Francisco, I had to push myself to go to the ballpark. I would have done much better if I could have avoided conflict with those managers," he says. "In St. Louis, I had friends there. I had peace of mind. Everything started going my way."

In fact, Cepeda was in St. Louis when the trade was announced. The Giants played the last series ever scheduled for old Sportsman's Park. After getting eleven hits against the Cardinals in four games, the trade announcement was an obvious shock. Ray Sadecki, a 20-game winner for the 1964 Cardinals with a losing record the next two years, seemed like a small price for such a fabled home run hitter. At age twenty-five, Cepeda had tallied 191 homers and 650 RBI. Before his knees slowed him down, Cepeda had produced more than Hank Aaron had at the same age. Despite these past achievements, Willie McCovey had earned the starting first baseman's job in San Francisco.

The Cardinals realized how valuable Cepeda could be. Manager Red Schoendienst simply told Cepeda that he'd be a cleanup hitter and starting first baseman. "I was tired of playing different spots in San Francisco," Cepeda says. "Red let you play ball. Give him 100 percent and he was right behind you. He was a great manager who deserves to be in the Hall of Fame. He figured that we were professional ballplayers, and that we know what to do. He let us play and didn't bother anybody."

Even trainer Bob Bauman made a difference. "He told me, 'You get the hits, and I'll take care of your knee,' " Cepeda recalls. "It wasn't bad when I first got to St. Louis, but then I was hit on the knee with a pitch. Every day he worked on it for me, exercising my knee. He's the person who really helped my career."

The pleasant change of scenery made an immediate impact on Cepeda's statistics. He was named N.L. Comeback Player of the Year in 1966, when he hit .301 with 20 homers and 73 RBI. The best was yet to come both for "The Baby Bull" and for the Redbirds.

In 1967, Cepeda would become the first unanimous selection in history for the N.L. Most Valuable Player Award. His credentials included 25 homers, a league-leading 111 RBI and a career-high batting average of .325. Most impressive were his 21 game-winning hits. With Cepeda leading the way, the Cards won the pennant, a comfortable ten and a half games ahead of the Giants. While Cepeda powered St. Louis to the World Series, he had little input in the team's seven-game win against the Boston Red Sox. He wound up with just three hits, batting a paltry .103. "Yeah, it was my fault," Cepeda admits. "Because we clinched the pennant so early in 1967, I took it for granted and I became complacent. At the end of the season, I was just going through the motions. The final games didn't mean anything. When I went to the World Series, my timing was bad and I couldn't get it back."

Cepeda's fortunes were reversed in 1968. His stats dropped to .248 with 16 homers and 73 RBI. He says his proudest accomplishment that year was playing in a personal best of 157 games. However, in the World Series against the Tigers, he batted .250 with two homers and six RBI in a losing effort. Soon Cepeda and many other Cardinal fixtures would depart as part of a major restructuring program by general manager Bing Devine.

For Cepeda, his trade came only three weeks before the start of the 1969 season. He was sent to the Atlanta Braves for Joe Torre. Although he didn't suffer the shock which occurred when he was dispatched by the Giants, he was upset at the Cardinals' timing. "If you're traded during the off-season, you have time to recover mentally," he says. "But it was so close to the start of the season. Because every team is different, I had to start over. It was hard."

Before he left St. Louis, Cepeda had numerous memories of two great seasons and several great teammates. To this day, Cepeda has non-stop praise for his St. Louis contemporaries. He calls Julian Javier "the best second baseman I've ever seen. He was a great base runner, and a good hitter. It's a shame he never got more credit." Cepeda describes center fielder Curt Flood as "a complete ballplayer. He could hit, field, throw and run. He was a heck of a teammate. I believe he should be in the Hall of Fame. Not only because of his playing ability, but because he was a leader of players. He had the guts to challenge the Supreme Court for his [contractual] rights. Players today are making so much money because of Curt Flood."

He laughs as he recalls one of his surprising moments with the Cardinals. For the first and only time in his career, Cepeda was yanked for a pinch-hitter. The substitute was Lou Brock. "I was doing bad, and I was lucky to get a base hit at all," he says laughing. "One day I was going up to the plate and I hear, 'Charlie! Char-lee!' That's what they called me. Lou whispered, 'I'm hitting for you.' What a shock! It surprised me at first, but I deserved it." The story ends with Brock getting a game-winning base hit.

Despite spending only three seasons in St. Louis and playing with six different teams during his seventeen-year career, Cepeda still considers his Cardinal experiences memorable. "I enjoyed the city and my teammates," he says. "I've never seen a team that had so many different individuals hold the same approach to the game and to life. I've never seen a group work together so closely."

Orlando Cepeda—Cardinal Stats

	G	AB	H	2B	3B	HR	R	RBI	BB	SO	SB	BA	SA
1966	123	452	137	24	0	17	65	58	34	68	9	.303	.469
1967	151	563	183	37	0	25	91	111	62	75	11	.325	.524
1968	157	600	149	26	2	16	71	73	43	96	8	.248	.378
World Series													
1967	7	29	3	2	0	0	1	1	0	4	0	.103	.172
1968	7	28	7	0	0	2	2	6	2	3	0	.250	.464

JOE CUNNINGHAM

Saying "Yes" to

Their Future

Joe Cunningham pulled a letter from his office file and read it aloud to his visitor:

"Dear Mr. Cunningham," the letter began, "Thank you for visiting our school. I enjoyed Fredbird. He has skinny legs. I enjoyed your messages, and I will not try drugs even though two of my friends do."

The letter was from a third grader.

"Wow. That was enough to shake me up when I saw this," said Cunningham, a former Cardinal first baseman/ outfielder and now the director of community relations for the club.

"You talk to the FBI or your local police and they'll tell you just how bad the drug problem is in our schools nationwide, even with little kids in elementary school. Man, when I was playing for the Cardinals, the kids I saw were interested only in baseball and other kid stuff. Nowadays they've got all this other business to contend with.

"That's why we're letting the kids know—through the Cardinal organization—they should say 'No' to drugs and live their lives free of drugs."

Cunningham designed the awareness program, which includes video presentations featuring current Cardinal players delivering anti-drug, pro-school-and-sports messages. Cunningham and another former Cardinal, Ted Savage, assisted by team mascot "Fredbird," take the program into inner city schools, suburban schools and schools as far away as Jefferson City and Illinois. They even took the program to Florida for a week and did two presentations a day that reached a total of 2,000 children.

"I'm probably as proud of this program as anything I've ever done," Cunningham said. "And the Cardinal family—individual players and staffers as well as the organization as a whole—is involved in many, many charitable causes. All this is very rewarding, more rewarding than I thought it would be when I first took the job. There are so many ways we can give something back to the community. This work is so important."

When he was a player, Joe gave a lot to the community by way of his athletic talent, desire and sense of team play. Years ago, there was an article in a national, family-oriented magazine that spoke of Cunningham's popularity with the fans. Judging by the recent letter from the third grader, it seems Joe's popularity remains secure.

Cunningham began his major league career in 1954 with the Cardinals. He was one of a number of talented rookies on that team, rookies such as first baseman Tom Alston and pitcher Brooks Lawrence, the first two black players to wear the Cardinal uniform, and Wally Moon, who would go on to win National League Rookie of the Year honors that season.

Cunningham says he was surprised to be called up when he was. He notes that he was jousting with Bill Virdon and Elston Howard for the International League's batting title when he went 0-for-9 in a double-header. Instead of getting a pep talk from his manager after the game, Cunningham was told to report to the St. Louis Cardinals immediately. Goodbye Rochester, hello Cincinnati, which is where Joe introduced himself to Cardinal manager Eddie Stanky before a game with the Reds at Crosley Field.

"I was nervous, naturally, to be in the clubhouse with Musial and all those guys, but I put on my uniform and went out to loosen up before the game. I remember picking up Sal Yvars's bat, thinking, 'Boy, I better change my stance, because 0-for-9 won't cut it up here.'

"I was a great one for changing stances to suit the kind of pitcher I was facing or the game situation. Anyway, the first two times up I grounded out off Art Fowler. But the third time up I hit a three-run homer. The next time up I hit a two-run single off Joe Nuxhall. We won the game by a wide margin.

"After the game we took the midnight train to Milwaukee to play the Braves. The first two times up I hit home runs off Warren Spahn. First a solo shot, then one with two men on, and we won that game, too. But that was my introduction to the big leagues: three home runs and nine RBIs after going 0-for-9 in a double-header in Triple A a few days before."

Cunningham went on to record a .284 batting average with 50 RBI, 11 home runs, 3 triples, 11 doubles and 40 runs scored. And just for good measure, Joe even stole a base. ("I was rarely a threat to go," he quipped.) He did all that while nursing a season-long pulled hamstring.

The Cardinals moved Musial to first base for much of the 1955 season and brought up Bill Virdon from Rochester to join Moon and Rip Repulski in the starting outfield. That meant Cunningham would wear a Rochester uniform again. He did appear in four games for the parent club at the close of 1956, but went hitless in three official at-bats.

"When I joined the Cardinals for spring training in 1957," Cunningham said, "one of the coaches, Johnny Keane, told me I'd better go try it in the outfield if I wanted to go north with the team when they broke camp. By then, Musial was pretty much playing first base exclusively. Stan was still a fine ballplayer, but the club wanted to make it easier on his legs, so they kept him at first base."

Cunningham quickly took to playing the pasture, and alternated between there and first base for the next five seasons.

"I made the All-Star team one year as an outfielder," Joe said. "Can you believe that? But I remember an exhibition game ...I think it was in 1959...against the Yankees. Mel Nelson, an outfielder who later converted to pitching, let me borrow his glove. And I made two diving catches—both of them line drives— off the bat of Enos Slaughter, who'd been traded to the Yankees. I dove for the ball a lot as an outfielder. I thought if I could get to it, what the hell, I'll dive for it."

Indeed, that cunning, hammy style of play would thrill fans many times over, including once in 1988 when Joe was fifty-seven and roaming the outfield in an old-timers game in Albuquerque, New Mexico. He was there as part of a drive to raise money for a local baseball program.

"The ball was hit at me," Cunningham emphasized, "so I went back, dove for the ball, caught it, came down, and hit my head and shoulder when I landed. Knocked my back out. They had to take me to a chiropractor, and a year later I was just starting to get better. There were 6,000 people there at the ballpark who gave me a standing ovation that day, and for that I'd do the same damn thing all over again. My wife says I'm crazy, but crazy in a good way, I guess."

In the Cunningham home back in Saddle Brook, New Jersey, in the late 1940s, Joe's mother thought her son was crazy, too, when he insisted on attending Lodi High School rather than the one in Hackensack that she had in mind for him. But the teenager had played some Boys Club baseball with kids from Lodi before, and felt an allegiance to them.

The senior Mr. Cunningham had his sons playing catch in the living room before they could walk, Joe insists, and the family's chief breadwinner encouraged them to participate in various athletic endeavors, including hockey and football.

Joe's baseball coach at Lodi tipped off the local Cardinal scout that he should take a look at the seventeen-year-old. He did more than that, and Cunningham, all 5 feet, 10 inches and 160 pounds of him, was sent to Johnson City, Tennessee, on his first stop along the sometimes dusty road to the big leagues.

Even then, the left-handed hitting Cunningham stroked the ball to all fields. He hit the ball well enough at his various minor league stops to keep the Cardinal brass aware of his presence.

But in February of 1952, Cunningham was drafted by another team—the U.S. Army. Now, for some ballplayers, major leaguers or otherwise, a stint in the service can be a disruptive force in one's career. But for Joe Cunningham it turned out to be one of the biggest breaks of his life.

One evening during basic training, Cunningham talked with his captain about playing for the post team. Though not much of a baseball man, his captain was impressed when Joe mentioned that his batting statistics for the 1951 season at Winston-Salem could be found in a baseball magazine the captain possessed.

"Granted, it was only the lower minors, but he saw that I'd hit over .300, and a few days later I was on that post team," Cunningham said, "and boy, I hit real well. I led the team in home runs and RBIs. I think it was the first time I really had confidence in my abilities as a baseball player.

"Up until that time I didn't really know whether I'd have a chance to play in the big leagues. But right there, at Fort Jackson, South Carolina, Third Army, Eighth Division, there were some pretty good ballplayers. I was playing with people like Ed Bailey, Roger Craig, Haywood Sullivan, 'Hurricane' Hazle. These people went on to make the big leagues, too."

Although splitting his time between first base and the outfield during his years with the Cardinals, Cunningham preferred covering first base.

"I don't like to blow my own horn, but I was considered a pretty good defensive first baseman," Cunningham said. "And Kenny Boyer, God bless his soul, told me that with the exception of Gil Hodges, I was the best first baseman in the National League. I'll never forget that."

Cunningham used a Musial-style bat, and he choked up on its thin handle just a little. He'd swing that 34 $1/2$-inch, 32-ounce bat through the strike zone and hit to all fields, shaping a .291 lifetime batting average with quite respectable yearly walk-to-strikeout totals.

"I always had a good eye at the plate," Cunningham said, "and since I didn't try to pull the ball for home runs all the time, I could concentrate on getting on base so the other guys could drive me in. I was a contact hitter, and I worked on it, because I wasn't what you would call a natural hitter.

"As I said before, I had several stances. Plus, I was a high fastball hitter, and most of your left-handed hitters then were low fastball hitters. In fact, I heard a rumor—and it was only a rumor—that the Dodger scout who made the report on me that I was a *low* fastball hitter was fired because of that. They were pitching me those high fastballs and geez, I loved that. I hit well against the Dodgers."

There were times when Cunningham's own teammates were pitching him some fast ones—in the form of practical jokes. There had been rumors—and again, they were only rumors—that the Reds were interested in Joe, but Cincy already had "Big Klu," Ted Kluszewski, anchoring first base, so Joe gave the rumors little thought. But one day Cunningham received a telegram informing him that he had indeed been traded to the Reds. Back at his place, Cunningham packed his things and thought about saying good-bye to his Cardinal teammates when he learned one of them, utility infielder Eddie Kasko, was the culprit who sent the bogus telegram.

Mention of Kasko's name reminds Cunningham of an ongoing episode involving the two friends.

"I think I was the last single ballplayer on the team," Joe said. "Don Blasingame, another 'holdout,' had just married Walker Cooper's daughter. She was a Miss Missouri, you know. Anyway, I was receding then. Several ballplayers around the league were. We didn't want the girls in the crowd to see us with our caps off. Of course, day games were another matter, but for night games they shut the lights off for the national anthem.

"When the anthem was over and before they turned the lights back on we had our caps on our heads as quick as anybody. They say the Pirates' Dick Groat was the fastest at doing that, with Kasko second and me third. I guess they had us all timed. Once Kasko got married he didn't give a damn at all, and he was the baldest of us all."

Cunningham was traded to the White Sox in November of 1961 in exchange for Minnie Minoso. Joe put together a fine season for the Sox in 1962, hitting .295 with 70 RBI, 91 runs scored, 32 doubles, 7 triples and 8 home runs. That year he also led American League first sackers with a .994 fielding percentage. Although his power numbers were well down the following season, he still managed to hit .286 in limited action. Halfway through the 1964 season Cunningham was traded to the Washington Senators, for whom he played until they released him shortly after the start of the 1966 season.

He eventually went to work for the Herbert Hoover Boys Club, located on the former site of Sportsman's Park, for about a year and a half. Cunningham's desire to help underprivileged children formed the basis for his later work in community relations with the Cardinals.

But Joe also had a desire to get back into baseball, so he managed in the Cardinals' farm system from 1968 to 1971. He next moved to the Cardinal front office and worked in the sales department (taking over for Mike Shannon when "Moon Man" joined the KMOX broadcasting team), and eventually was named its director, a post he held until assuming his current position as director of community relations.

"You know, I really hate to admit this because I'm still in baseball with the Cardinals, but I don't see many of the guys," Joe said of his former Cardinal teammates of the 1950s and early 1960s.

"When we do get together, we don't always talk about our baseball careers, either. But we were a pretty close unit back then. We pulled together. We helped each other. I don't go on road trips with the team anymore so I don't know what it's like now...so I can't comment on it. But the gang I played with developed friendships that have lasted to this day. That means a lot to me."

Joe Cunningham—Cardinal Stats

	G	AB	H	2B	3B	HR	R	RBI	BB	SO	SB	BA	SA
1954	85	310	88	11	3	11	40	50	43	40	1	.284	.445
1956	4	3	0	0	0	0	1	0	1	1	0	.000	.000
1957	122	261	83	15	0	9	50	52	56	29	3	.318	.479
1958	131	337	105	20	3	12	61	57	82	23	4	.312	.496
1959	144	458	158	28	6	7	65	60	88	47	2	.345	.478
1960	139	492	138	28	3	6	68	39	59	59	1	.280	.386
1961	113	322	92	11	2	7	60	40	53	32	1	.286	.398

LEO DUROCHER

He Gave to

Baseball More

than Lip Service

At an auction held to raise money to send a local American Legion team to a tournament overseas, a thin, elderly, but energetic man started an impromptu bidding war.

He bid against the children; he bid against their parents; he even bid against himself, all the time razzing the audience for failing to bid higher on the posters, bats and other memorabilia being auctioned off that day.

Leo Durocher must have seemed like some elfish octogenarian carnival barker, snapping his taunts to a somewhat chagrined audience.

"Now I know exactly why they call him 'The Lip,' " said one disgruntled hobbyist, noting that Durocher had bid several hundred dollars on the items, far more than the kids (and many of the adults in the audience) could afford.

But no sooner had the crowd's low grumblings swelled to open irritation with Durocher than The Lip turned right around and gave the items he bought to the children present, who just moments before had lost in the bidding war. The

kids got their collectibles, the local team got some much-needed funding from an unexpected source, and the man once credited with saying "Nice guys finish last" was suddenly first in the hearts of the people.

Has Leo Durocher mellowed somewhat? Perhaps. He can still be gruff and demanding at times. And there's still that voice of his, which one can imagine in its prime, dueling with umpires, enemy players and teammates alike. But it probably wouldn't be straying too far off base to say he is more at peace with himself than ever before. Christianity continues to play a big role in his life, and that has contributed greatly to his present demeanor. This is a time in his life when he can bask in the warmth of fan attention without the inherent pressures of a tight pennant race.

Ballplayer, coach, manager, author, TV and radio personality; Leo Durocher has worn many caps over the years, including one signifying him as a member of baseball's Gas House Gang of the mid-1930s. Stories about that college of Cardinals, led by college man Frankie Frisch—the "Fordham Flash"— are legendary. And Durocher, a surviving member of the 1934 World Champions, has an endless supply of them.

"Tex Carleton was scheduled to be our starting pitcher one day," Durocher began one of his personal favorites, "and he was in the batting cage when the bell rang signifying it was time for the pitchers to get out of there and let the utility men and the regulars take batting practice. But Carleton wouldn't get out of there.

"Joe Medwick was my roommate then, and he told Carleton to leave. Tex said he wasn't leaving until he could swing the bat a couple more times. So Medwick walked right into the batting cage and hit him a shot that knocked him out. Blackened his eye, even. And Frisch came runnin' up all excited and said, 'What happened?'

"And I said calmly, 'Well, I think you better get another starting pitcher, Frank, because we haven't *got* one today.' "

That task probably wasn't as difficult as fans today might think, however, if Durocher's recollections are true.

"In those days our rotation was the two Deans, Dizzy and Paul; Carleton was three; and Bill Hallahan was four, although Bill Walker started for us, too, and won some games. But those guys seemed to thrive on just a few days' rest, so for the most part we went with a four-man rotation.

"We had a great pitching staff that year, too, although the rest of the league wasn't exactly handing the pennant to us. I'll tell you what the Cardinals had to face in those days back in the '30s.

"You'd walk into the Polo Grounds in New York and play the Giants, so you had to face [Roy] Parmelee, [Hal] Schumacher and [Freddie] Fitzsimmons, and if you were lucky enough to get a hit off one of them you *sure* weren't going to get anymore the next day, because Carl Hubbell would be lookin' down at you from the mound.

"Then you would walk into Brooklyn to play the Dodgers and you had to face Watty Clark and Van Mungo and Dazzy Vance. In Chicago you had to go up against guys like Pat Malone, Charlie Root, Lon Warneke, Larry French. They were all tough teams, and we didn't have any batting helmets in those days, either, you know. We got separated from our caps a few times.

"Sometimes we knew it was comin' too, but it was just part of the game. That was how we played baseball in the big leagues back then. That's how the Cardinals played it. That's how all the teams played back then. Hell, nowadays the pitcher throws on the inside part of the plate a couple of times and the hitter wants to charge the mound. It's just a different brand of baseball now, I guess.

"But the '34 club was the best of the five Cardinal squads I played for, and even though we argued and fought among ourselves, God forbid if anybody else picked a fight with us, because then they'd have to lick all twenty-five Cardinals. We stuck together, that's right, and we believed in ourselves . . . we believed in each other. We knew how to play the game."

Durocher paused for a moment, cradling in his lap a picture book of baseball stars of the past. A black and white photo of Durocher and Medwick brings a smile to Leo's face.

"There's my roomie, there's Joe!" he exclaims. "He could be mean to people sometimes, but boy, could he play. He batted fourth. Let's see, Pepper Martin was our leadoff hitter. Jack Rothrock, a good contact hitter, was our second-place hitter. Jack did all you could ask of him. With Jack you could put on the hit-and-run with Pepper, and even if he missed the ball, Pepper still had a chance to steal a base, clean as a whistle.

"Frisch hit third for us. Medwick fourth. We had some great

hitters on that ballclub. Let's see. . .Rip Collins, our first baseman, was a good hitter. . .he hit behind Joe. Then we had Bill DeLancey, a real good hitter who shared the catching duties with [Spud] Davis. Ernie Orsatti was the center fielder. He was a great defensive ballplayer—a good arm. . .smart ballplayer—he hit around .300 for us. I'd bat after him, and then whoever was pitchin' that day would follow me. We had some others on that '34 team that contributed, too, like Burgess Whitehead and Jess Haines, but those were the starters I just gave you."

Of all the starters Durocher cited, it was player-manager Frisch for whom Durocher had the kindest words:

"He was a fine manager, one of the best. He and I had a helluva relationship over the years. He and I argued all the time. We always kidded him. He just seemed suited to it. He was the target of Pepper's pranks, Diz's popping off and my mouth. 'Get over there, you dumb Dutchman!' I'd yell to him when he was playin' second base. Then, in the World Series in '34 against Detroit, I looked over at him and said, 'You oughtta give me half your World Series check, Frank. You're standing on a dime. I'm playing shortstop *and* second base. Is that fair?' "

Off the field, Durocher maintains, the Gas House Gang's behavior belied their moniker, at least to the extent that criminal activity wasn't part of the evening's entertainment. Oh, there were the usual stunts, funny incidents—both public and private—and hotel evictions resulting from pranks of "dizzying" heights, but the 1934 Cardinals were serious about baseball.

"Now, I'm not going to sit here and tell you we were angels," Durocher said, "but there wasn't a lot of drinking on that club. We'd go to movies and things like that. We'd have a few beers after the game, you know, but you couldn't be falling-down drunk or hung over and play as hard as we did, day in and day out. We did things together—play cards, go to movies and so forth, but I don't remember a great deal of socializing as such. As individuals, we generally went our own way.

"One thing I do remember us doing as a group is that we used to go over to Walsh Stadium. Pepper had built himself a midget racing car, and we'd go out there and watch this friend of his race it. The way the thing was built. . .well, Pepper would have to push the thing from behind with the driver in it to get up a head of speed before it would start. One time he showed up late for a ballgame, and when Frisch asked him where the hell he'd been, Pepper said he'd beat some guy in a race for a gallon of ice cream. That was the prize."

Durocher fashioned a playing career in the majors that lasted for seventeen seasons. He played for the Yankees, Reds, Cardinals and Dodgers. It was while at Brooklyn in the late 1930s that Leo was given an opportunity to manage by owner Larry MacPhail.

A student of the game since he was a brash rookie playing alongside Babe Ruth, Lou Gehrig and the rest of Murderers' Row in 1928, Durocher was a walking encyclopedia of hitters' tendencies and pitchers' repertoires by the time he became a full-time manager. Although noted for his run-ins with umpires over the years, Durocher was considered a smart field general who always managed at least an inning or two ahead.

He refers to himself as having been a "strict but fair" manager who only demanded of his players that they "give it their best out there," each and every game. "I didn't care if they liked me," he said.

Durocher noted that during his playing days ballplayers were fined $200 to $300 if they "dogged it." As the years passed and players earned higher salaries, the fines increased accordingly. He cited one example of when he was forced to lay down the law with a player.

"I fined him $5,000," Durocher said. "I said to him, 'Open your mouth again and say one more word to me and it'll be double.' He never moved. He was making about $98,000 at the time. That year he made about ninety-three.

"If I could manage today the fine would be $10,000 if the guy didn't hustle. Anybody making a million dollars a year and can't hustle and bear down and be ready to play every day, well, I'd fine him ten grand. And if he opened his mouth about it, it'd be twenty grand."

Leo hustled when he was a player. It was in his nature. And it didn't hurt that as a youngster he was tutored by a spunky little major league shortstop, Walter "Rabbit" Maranville, who was a neighbor of the Durocher family back in Springfield, Massachusetts. The two became good friends and Durocher, respectful of his mentor, says of him, "He's in the Hall of Fame."

Durocher played semi-pro ball in his scuffling days. By day he worked for the Boston & Albany Railroad, overseeing the crews that unloaded and cut the wood used for making railroad ties. He later worked for Wyco Electric Company, which manufactured batteries. After quitting time, the teenager played in the local twilight league featuring, as he puts it, "some pretty fair semi-pro players" from around the area, "including the Trauske brothers, Eddie and Bunny, but they never made it to the big leagues."

He was offered a two week tryout with Hartford in the Eastern League, where he performed well enough to eventually be offered a contract with the club. But within two months, the Yankee scout sent to observe the club, Paul Kritchell, bought him for the Yanks.

Durocher broke in with New York in early October of 1925. He had one official at-bat in the two games in which he appeared. He got some additional seasoning in the minors during the 1926 and 1927 campaigns before the parent club called him up in 1928. Leo capped off his partial season by playing in all four World Series contests against the Cardinals, mostly as a late-inning replacement for second baseman Tony Lazzeri.

Durocher downplays his hitting, focusing instead on his defensive contributions to the teams for which he played. Still, he breaks into a warm smile when reminded that he did have seasons when he hit as high as .270, .277 and .286, drove in as many as 78 runs and socked 8 home runs.

If ever a man had baseball history coursing through his veins, it is Leo Durocher. He barnstormed against the likes of Satchel Paige ("I couldn't hit him with this table," he muses), was befriended by the "Bambino" himself, managed such stars as Willie Mays, Billy Williams, Ron Santo and Jimmy Wynn, and helped keep the Cardinals strong up the middle during that storied season of 1934.

And then there is Leo Durocher, media star: guest shots on 1940s radio programs hosted by the likes of Jack Benny and Fred Allen; cameo appearances on numerous 1960s television programs ("The Munsters," "The Donna Reed Show," to name but two); even a brief appearance in an MGM musical in the 1950s; all are part of his resume. With so many things having the imprint of the man dubbed "Leo the Lip" by a sportswriter decades ago, just where does this man fit into baseball's overall scheme of things?

"What should people remember about me when I'm gone?" Leo reflected aloud, pondering the question for a moment. "That I loved the game. That's all. That I loved the game."

Leo Durocher—Cardinal Stats

	G	AB	H	2B	3B	HR	R	RBI	BB	SO	SB	BA	SA
1933	123	395	102	18	4	2	45	41	26	32	3	.258	.339
1934	146	500	130	26	5	3	62	70	33	40	2	.260	.350
1935	143	513	136	23	5	8	62	78	29	46	4	.265	.376
1936	136	510	146	22	3	1	57	58	29	47	3	.286	.347
1937	135	477	97	11	3	1	46	47	38	36	6	.203	.245
World Series													
1934	7	27	7	1	1	0	4	0	0	0	0	.259	.370

CURT FLOOD

Another Gem from

the East Bay

Sandlots

A few years ago, in the space of thirty-six hours and thousands of miles, former Cardinal standout Curt Flood met with hundred of fans at a Midwest hobby show, perused the script of a proposed movie of his life, and received the first-ever Jackie Robinson Sports Award from the National Association for the Advancement of Colored People (NAACP) in Los Angeles.

For a man who once found himself estranged from the game he loves, it was some weekend.

Flood starred as the Cardinals' center fielder for twelve years. From 1958 to 1969, frequently batting in the leadoff spot, he averaged .293 with 53 runs batted in, 70 runs scored, 23 doubles, 4 triples and 7 home runs. As a pinch-hitter for the Cardinals, Flood hit .326. He was a contact hitter who twice had 200 or more hits in a season (sharing the league lead with Pittsburgh's Roberto Clemente in 1964 with 211 safeties).

He was among the best glove men of his day. Flood owns the major league record for most consecutive outfield

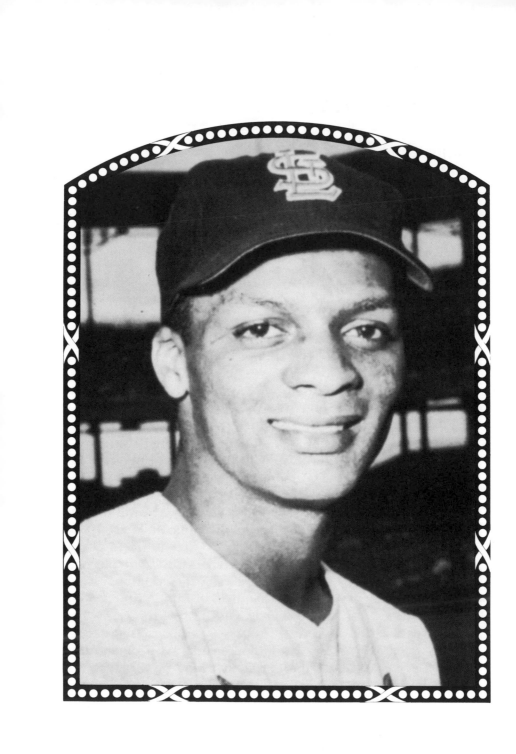

chances accepted without an error, with 568. From Sept. 3, 1965, through part of a game on June 4, 1967, Curt played the outfields of the National League—with the winds at Candlestick and the sun over Wrigley and the high bounces in the Astrodome—without a single error. He also established N.L. records for outfielders for most consecutive errorless games (226, set during that same period) and most consecutive errorless games in a season (159, set in 1966). Flood accepted close to 400 chances that year.

He played on three World Series teams, and can list among his teammates Bob Gibson, Lou Brock, Orlando Cepeda, Stan Musial and Steve Carlton.

Following the 1969 season, in which he hit .285 with 31 doubles while scoring 80 runs, Flood was traded to the Phillies—or so the Cardinal brass thought. He refused to report to Philadelphia, and in January of 1970 he filed an antitrust suit against baseball. Flood was the first baseball player with the temerity to challenge the game's reserve clause binding a player to the team holding that individual's contract. Flood wanted the right to sign with the team of his choice.

He lost his case when it was initially heard in U.S. District Court in New York City. He sat out the entire 1970 season while his lawyers prepared to appeal his case, but he eventually returned to baseball early in the 1971 season, hitting just .200 in thirteen games for the Washington Senators before hanging up his spikes for good.

Although a U.S. Circuit Court of Appeals upheld the lower court's dismissal of Flood's case that spring, Flood and his legal counsel took the matter to the U.S. Supreme Court. But the highest court in the land, by a 5-3 majority, also ruled that baseball was exempt from antitrust laws.

Later arbitration cases involving pitchers Andy Messersmith, Dave McNally and Jim "Catfish" Hunter broke the back of the reserve clause. But it was Curt Flood who, in a dedicated effort a few years before, led the charge against restricted player movement in baseball.

Of course, the irony is that Flood never reaped the benefits of the seeds he sowed. His top salary was in the neighborhood of $100,000 a year. Yet, listening to him talk about his life in and out of baseball leaves one with the impression that these days, he is not an envious man. He was crucial to the success of the Cardinals throughout the 1960s, and if his worth to the Cardinals by the end of that decade had diminished, his influence on the structure of baseball since then cannot be undervalued.

"It was just coincidental that I was born in Houston, because my family lived in East Oakland," said Flood, who was born on Jan. 18, 1938. "I guess during those years if a woman became pregnant she would always go home to her family to have the child.

"For my mother, that meant traveling from northern California to her mother's home in Quincy, Louisiana. It's just that when my mother got to Houston, it was time for me to come. My mother and I stayed there for about a year before moving back to California."

Curt and his childhood friends followed the exploits of the local minor league club, the Oakland Oaks of the Pacific Coast League. The youngsters would occasionally sneak into Emeryville Park to watch a ball game, but the diamond where they tried to emulate their Oaks heroes was on a playground just 200 yards away from the Flood family home. In time, sandlot ball gave way to organized league play.

"I think they called it the Police League at the time," Flood said. "The police officers furnished the uniforms for us and would ferry us kids around to the local diamonds. It was a good community program."

Basketball, pickup games of softball—whatever sports activities were going on at the time, Flood participated in them. But it wasn't until high school—at McClymonds and Oakland Technical —that Curt concentrated on athletics and began in earnest to develop his baseball skills.

"I had a very fine coach in high school by the name of George Powles, who was really, sincerely interested in us kids and keepin' us off the streets and out of trouble," Flood recalled. "Actually, I played for him from the time I was nine or ten years old right through my semi-pro days.

"Anyway, here was this white man who cared for us as human beings. And, I guess when you've got someone, regardless of his color, who takes time to show a genuine interest in you, who makes sure you do constructive things with your time and do your lessons, it triggers a lot of good things in young kids. I guess my interest in baseball really started with George and continued to gain momentum with his guidance."

Flood was one of many outstanding young athletes to emerge from that particular area of Oakland during the 1950s. Baseball Hall of Famer Frank Robinson, the game's first big league black manager, was one of Flood's teammates at McClymonds High. (The same Cincinnati Reds scout who signed "Robbie" to a contract later signed Flood and Vada Pinson, another McClymonds graduate and major league standout.)

"Basketball legend Bill Russell came out of that area," Flood added. "So did football great Ollie Matson. He went to school there, and he's in the NFL Hall of Fame. And I bet there were thirty or forty men who played major league baseball over the years who came out of that one little area of Oakland, which is really amazing. There were so many good players coming out of this one area that major league scouts really started to key in on it, and I was signed in 1956."

Flood's minor league career included stints in High Point, North Carolina, where, in his first year of professional baseball, he led the Carolina League with a .340 batting average while pounding out 29 home runs and knocking in 128 runs; Savannah, Georgia; and Omaha, Nebraska. In the off-seasons he played winter ball in the Dominican Republic and Venezuela.

Flood had all of four at-bats—resulting in one hit, a solo homer off the Cubs' Moe Drabowsky—as a Cincinnati Red before the club traded him, along with fellow outfielder Joe Taylor, to the Cardinals for pitchers Marty Kutyna, Willard Schmidt and Ted Wieand following the 1957 season. ("I was traded to St. Louis," he says, "because the Reds had another kid named Vada Pinson to play the outfield, and they were looking for great things from him.")

For the 1958 campaign, which saw the Cardinals fall to a fifth-place tie with the Cubs after finishing second to the Milwaukee Braves the previous season, twenty-year-old Curt Flood managed to hit just .261 with 41 RBI, although he was in double figures in doubles and home runs.

The next two years weren't much to write home about either, as far as his batting average was concerned, but again, Flood showed some occasional power at the plate.

Curt's hitting improved markedly in 1961, not in the form of runs batted in or in extra base hits, but in his overall average. He hit a healthy .322 in 335 at-bats.

"I don't think there was ever a moment when I thought I'd arrived," Flood said. "Let's just say that for any young player trying to stick with the parent club, there are moments when a lot of hard work pays off to a point where you say to yourself, 'I belong here.'

"There was a time when I was with Cincinnati, actually being tutored when I was in South America, when they were hoping to teach me to play the infield. I'd played the outfield all my life, and I had trouble making the double play, trouble throwing toward shortstop. When I got to St. Louis they decided to keep me in the outfield. I think they had about fifty different center fielders who came before me. And the outfield as a unit saw lots of changes in the late '50s and early '60s. Bill White, who became our first baseman, played the outfield for a time. Charlie James, Don Landrum, a whole bunch of guys played out there.

"Solly Hemus was the Cardinal manager then, and Solly didn't really care for either Bob Gibson or me. I'm not sure why. But both of us were trying to make the club and stay up there. I know Bob was shuffled back and forth between Omaha and Rochester and St. Louis for a couple of years before he finally stuck.

"I think it was midway through the 1961 season when Johnny Keane was named the new Cardinal manager. His first words to me, ever, were, 'Hey, you're gonna play center field for us—good, bad or indifferent—now get your ass out there.' He believed in me, and in Bob, and we finally got to show what we could do if given the opportunity."

But even with the opportunity to play full time, Flood and Gibson and other black players weren't always appreciated by the denizens of the "Gateway to the West."

"Accepted is not what we were, at least not at first," Flood said. "St. Louis was a tough town in the late '50s and early '60s. People still had a lot of the old ideas about racism bred into them. It hadn't been a very long time, I guess, since blacks and whites could sit together at the ballpark in St. Louis. At one time all of the black people had to sit together in the right field pavilion at Sportsman's Park.

"Segregation was still present, and not just in St. Louis, either, so I'm not singling out that city. You've gotta remember that I started my professional baseball career in [North] Carolina and Georgia, where it was really tough. So, coming into St. Louis, I kind of knew what to expect. Unfortunately, in many instances my apprehensions proved to be correct. By and large the people in the cities were fair to us, but there still were situations where we had to go to 'black' bars and eat in 'black' restaurants or at bus terminals. It was neither easy nor difficult back then. It was just the way things were."

Flood hit his stride with the 1962 season. His .296 batting average was complemented by 70 RBI, 99 runs scored, 30 doubles, 5 triples and 12 home runs—that last figure being the highest single season total in his fifteen-year major league career.

In 1963, the pennant-year-that-almost-was for the Cardinals and their fans, Flood hit .302 while scoring 112 runs and plating another 63. In 1964, the pennant-year-and-then-some for the Cardinals and their fans, Flood cracked a league-leading 211 hits as his average climbed to .311. He put together another solid offensive season in 1965 despite the team's collapse to seventh place, hitting .310 with 83 ribbies and 90 runs scored.

The 1966 campaign was disappointing for both Flood and the Cardinals, as his average dropped to .267 while the team could manage no better than a sixth-place finish.

But in 1967—the year of "Cha-Cha" and "El Birdos" and Roger Maris in right and a thrilling World Series against the Red Sox—Flood's bat came alive once again as Curt hit his highest season average ever, .335. A .301 season came in the pennant-winning year of 1968, followed by his .285 swan song with the Cardinals in 1969.

Flood declines to compare the three championship teams of 1964, 1967 and 1968, saying only that the 1964 season was as satisfying to him as any he ever had.

"We constantly worked on all the little things that can make a difference in the final standings," Flood said, "things like the pitcher backing up third or home on a throw, or covering first base on a ball hit to the right side, or the outfielders hitting their cutoff man. We were able to stay close to Philadelphia. It's not like both

teams lost fifteen games in a row down the stretch and we somehow backed into the pennant. We took it away from them.

"That last weekend was something else. The Phillies, the
Reds, us, we were all fighting for it those last few days. Even the
Giants had a shot at it. We knew we couldn't take the Mets lightly
because they could play the role of spoiler. We had to beat them to
stay in the thing.

"On Friday night we had to beat a very, very effective Alvin
Jackson, who shoved it up our collective ass, 1-0. The next day we
got clobbered by ten runs. But on Sunday we finally came out of
our lethargy and beat the Mets to go to the Series. Even though
we'd be facing the Yankees, I don't think fear really entered our
minds going into the Series. You have to realize we played them
for a month back in spring training that year in St. Petersburg. It
wasn't as if we'd never seen them before or anything.

"But I will say this: you talk about a thrill! To walk into Yankee Stadium to play in a World Series, it's a stunner, believe me.
All those ghosts of Babe Ruth and Lou Gehrig and the rest whisp-
ing around the place; all that Yankee mystique bullshit that makes
a visiting player's hair stand up on the back of his neck... you
better believe we felt it. But we weren't afraid. We were the National League Champions. We believed in ourselves. You kick over
Willie Mays, and stomp on Bob Clemente, and get your ass past
Jim Bunning and those guys, you have done a trick, I'm telling
you. We felt like we belonged there.

"And here I was, a twenty-six-year-old major leaguer who'd
played ball since I was about eight or nine, having a great year at
the plate, being part of a team that won the pennant on the last
day of the season, playing in my first World Series... and we *beat*
the Yankees. Will you give me a break? How fortunate can you be?
Man, I enjoyed that season."

His joy was tempered with a slight melancholy, however,
when Cardinal manager Johnny Keane announced his resignation
as soon as the season closed. Keane, unhappy with an earlier season firing of general manager Bing Devine and angered by news
that former "Gas Houser" Leo Durocher had been tabbed to succeed him as St. Louis manager for the 1965 season, told the Cardinals to "take this job and..."

Keane then took the helm of the club he'd just whipped in

the World Series. But instead of piloting a Yankee team to yet another A.L. pennant, Keane saw his crew flounder all season long. The Yankees dropped to sixth place, twenty-five games in back of the new A.L. champs, the Minnesota Twins.

Twenty games into the 1966 season, Keane was fired as Yankee manager. And within a year's time, he was dead at fifty-five, the victim of a heart attack.

"Johnny and his wife both were dear friends of mine," Flood said, "and when he passed away a little bit of me felt, very, very sad. I played for some fine managers—Fred Hutchinson, Red Schoendienst, Johnny Keane—but I was sorry to see Johnny leave the Cardinals, and even sadder when he passed away. He was a good man."

If Keane was the one who believed in Flood's abilities as a center fielder, then it was teammate Lou Brock who helped Flood realize his potential at the plate. Using a light, slender-handled Louisville Slugger about thirty-four inches long, Flood soon found he enjoyed hitting behind Brock in the Cardinal lineups of the 1960s.

"Brock made things happen for the Cardinals, just the way that Vince Coleman or Willie McGee did during the 1980s," Flood said. "He was a catalyst; the guy who made us go. Not only in terms of stealing bases, but because the pitcher was no longer that invincible presence out there on the mound when his attention was divided in half between Brock dancin' off first and me waitin' with my M114-model bat at the plate.

"Brock made me a better hitter. His ability to rattle the opposition gave me the opportunity to wait on good pitches, and gave him a chance to steal second and get into scoring position. I became a more patient hitter up there. I'd take one strike, I'd take two strikes, as I gained confidence at the plate."

All good things must come to an end, the philosophers tell us, and that exciting combo of Flood and Brock at the top of the Cardinal order was broken up when a major trade was announced a few days after the 1969 regular season. The trade, in fact, involved several big names in addition to that of Curt Flood.

Flood, along with teammates Tim McCarver, Joe Hoerner and Byron Browne were being sent to the Phillies for Richie Allen, Cookie Rojas and Jerry Johnson. But Flood refused to report to the

Phillies, setting in motion his court challenge of baseball's reserve clause. Although the trade was finally completed when the Cardinals sent Willie Montanez and Bob Browning to the Phillies the following spring, the 1970 baseball season was minus one of its most exciting players: Curt Flood.

During that time Curt traveled to Europe, spending most of his time in Copenhagen, Denmark, where he painted, wrote and, as much as anything, attempted to deal with the pain and frustration of being away from the game he loved. Did he ever feel he was standing alone in his fight against baseball's reserve clause? And what did his peers—not just on the Cardinals, but those throughout baseball—think of his efforts?

"Those are difficult questions to answer," Flood said. "Because of the insecurity all of us ballplayers felt back then about keeping our jobs and maintaining a good standard of living for our families... well, I can understand their hesitation, their unwillingness, to jump up and support me.

"The insecurity resulting from the contracts we signed back then was such that you would have to have been there to know what a stranglehold that system had on us at the time. I think there was fear, too, whether real or imagined, that by associating with me—or at least, talking openly about my challenge to the reserve clause—they would be viewed as troublemakers, or ungrateful to baseball.

"Privately, many of them *did* support me. And my family was on my side. You know, people would come up to me and say, 'Oh, Curt, you gave up so much by fighting the baseball hierarchy.' Well, my children sacrificed equally as much, because when you take away a hundred thousand dollars from the family budget, you have really done something of intense proportions.

"When I was in Europe, I guess I just tried to refresh myself and tried to overcome a lot of the hurt I felt. I tried to deal with the misunderstanding many people had of what I was attempting to do with my court case; why I was bringing all of it to light. It was a difficult year for several reasons. But as much as anything, I'm a baseball person, and to take that away from me cold turkey like that was not easy for me. I just needed to regroup."

Since his baseball career ended nearly twenty years ago, Flood has remained a busy man. He owns and runs a public relations firm in California, remains a commercial artist (having done paintings for people all over the world) when he has the time, gives as many as a dozen lectures a year on baseball, participates in the Equitable "Old Timers" games, and signs his autograph to cards, baseballs, glossies and anything else the fans proffer to him at hobby shows. He also still fights the good fight.

Flood was named the first president of The Baseball Network, an organization dedicated to helping make the hiring of minorities in baseball a little easier. It serves, in part, as a clearinghouse of information for some of the most talented black and Hispanic men in the world. TBN is one of the positive things to come out of the Al Campanis fiasco of 1987, when the then Dodger vice president of player personnel made some ill-advised remarks on national TV concerning blacks' abilities to manage in the big leagues or to serve in key front office positions.

And in 1989, Flood was named commissioner of the new Senior Professional Baseball Association, baseball's equivalent to masters tennis or seniors golf. The SPBA was created for ex-major-leaguers age thirty-five and older—catchers can be thirty-two to play in the Florida-based league—who will play their contests during the major leagues' off season.

There was talk several years ago about a made-for-TV movie about Curt Flood's life, with Flood serving as technical advisor on the film. A script was written, but to date nothing more has happened concerning the project. ("All I want," Flood quipped, "is that whoever plays me in the film must be a former athlete in some sport. I don't want somebody like William Bendix playin' me," a reference to the husky actor who was miscast for the lead role in a truly pathetic film effort, 1948's *The Babe Ruth Story*.)

Long-time St. Louis fans will remember Curt Flood for the way he played the game during his dozen years in a Cardinal uniform, for his contributions to a ballclub that went to the World Series three times and emerged victorious twice. And ballplayers—those who have benefitted, are benefitting, or will benefit from Flood's valiant court battle years ago that laid the groundwork for free agency in baseball—should thank the former Cardinal star for "taking one for the team."

At the 1987 NAACP's Image Awards ceremony at the Wiltern Theater in Los Angeles, presenter George C. Scott was right when he said Curt Flood was "respected not only for his great skill, but also for his determination to improve the lot of *all* ballplayers."

Curt Flood—Cardinal Stats

	G	AB	H	2B	3B	HR	R	RBI	BB	SO	SB	BA	SA
1958	121	422	110	17	2	10	50	41	31	56	2	.261	.382
1959	121	208	53	7	3	7	24	26	16	35	2	.255	.418
1960	140	396	94	20	1	8	37	38	35	54	0	.237	.354
1961	132	335	108	15	5	2	53	21	35	33	6	.322	.415
1962	151	635	188	30	5	12	99	70	42	57	8	.296	.416
1963	158	662	200	34	9	5	112	63	42	57	17	.302	.403
1964	162	679	211	25	3	5	97	46	43	53	8	.311	.378
1965	156	617	191	30	3	11	90	83	51	50	9	.310	.421
1966	160	626	167	21	5	10	64	78	26	50	14	.267	.364
1967	134	514	172	24	1	5	68	50	37	46	2	.335	.414
1968	150	618	186	17	4	5	71	60	33	58	11	.301	.366
1969	153	606	173	31	3	4	80	57	48	57	9	.285	.366
World Series													
1964	7	30	6	0	1	0	5	3	3	1	0	.200	.267
1967	7	28	5	1	0	0	2	3	3	3	0	.179	.214
1968	7	28	8	1	0	0	4	2	2	2	3	.286	.321

JOE GARAGIOLA

He Wasn't

THAT Bad!

Fans have taken Joe Garagiola too seriously through the years. The nine-year major league veteran spent almost five and a half seasons with the St. Louis Cardinals. Following his 1955 retirement, the St. Louis native spent the next three decades as the most famous player-turned-announcer in baseball history.

Everyone who ever listened to Garagiola as a Cardinals radio announcer on KMOX from 1955 through the 1962 season or as an NBC-TV "Game of the Week" broadcaster, "Today Show" member and quiz show host from 1963 through 1988 will remember that a great deal of his on-air charm came from home-spun tales of his mediocre days as a second-rate backstop. Long before Bob Uecker (another Cardinals catcher who turned to announcing), Garagiola had listeners thinking that he had less baseball talent than comic strip character Charlie Brown.

But don't believe it! Joe Garagiola had a respectable baseball career. In fact, he was one of the most talented rookies the Cardinals saw in the 1940s.

Just ask veteran pitcher Harry Brecheen. Garagiola was one of the receivers in the 1946 World Series who caught Brecheen's three victories. "Before he hurt his shoulder [in 1950], Joe was a super young catcher," Brecheen remembers. "He threw well and swung the bat well. He wasn't a pushover at the plate. He could hit better for average than Del Rice [who shared the catching job with Garagiola]. I don't know how great Joe would have been if it hadn't been for that accident. When he came back, he just didn't hit as well. But he was a catcher every club would want."

Garagiola may have entertained millions with his self-deprecating humor by creating a comical picture of the world's worst catcher. While he never intended to mislead fans, he says he's always wanted to shatter the god-like image athletes can create for themselves. "I've always felt that people would like hearing more about the lifestyle of baseball," he says. "People feel for a person when they realize, 'He's made mistakes just like me. He's got faults, too.' In a story, I'd rather make an out than a home run. I get tired, especially at old-timers games, when players keep talking about all their homers. I just enjoy the other side of the picture.

"But people can look up the records," he adds, noting that records can tell the best story.

Garagiola's records tell an untold story, the story of a young catcher whom the Cardinals chose over a rookie named Yogi Berra. The Redbirds plucked Garagiola off the St. Louis sandlots and had him signed to a contract by his sixteenth birthday. Neighborhood buddy Berra tried out for the Cardinals as well, but Cardinals general manager Branch Rickey thought he wasn't a disciplined hitter. Instead, the Cardinals gave Garagiola a $500 signing bonus. With the bonus, the young rookie helped his parents pay off their St. Louis home.

Actually, Garagiola says he wasn't even sixteen when the Cardinals first secured his services. "The Cardinals hired me at age fifteen as an assistant groundskeeper for their Springfield club," Garagiola says. "They actually wanted to hide me so other clubs wouldn't sign me. They paid me $60 a month to cut the grass, catch batting practice and wash the sanitary socks of the players." In 1942, Garagiola was playing for Springfield, hitting .254. After being promoted to Columbus in 1943, he hit .293 with the American Association affiliate. Following a two-year hitch in the U.S. Army (which ended on Mother's Day, 1946), Garagiola landed a spot on the Cardinals roster.

That first year, 1946, he hit a modest .237 with 3 homers and 22 RBI in 74 games. Behind the plate, he made just 3 errors for a .990 fielding percentage. The Cardinals won the pennant only after downing the rival Brooklyn Dodgers in a three-game playoff. In the opening game of the series, Garagiola tallied three hits and two RBI to give his Redbirds a 4-2 victory.

He continued excelling in post-season play. In the seven-game World Series with the Boston Red Sox, Garagiola batted a healthy .316. Appearing in five games, he earned two doubles and four singles, driving in four runs. During the fourth game, Garagiola collected four hits and three RBI.

"That was *the* highlight of my career," he says without hesitation. "I think it's a shame that there isn't some kind of system to give every player a chance to play in the World Series. There is nothing like it." He laughs as he tells how he first saw Ted Williams in person during the 1946 Series. "The first time I saw him was when I was catching. I didn't know whether to signal for a pitch or stop and get an autograph."

During his sophomore season of 1947, Garagiola boosted his production to .257 with 5 homers and 25 RBI. A horrendous start in 1948, consisting of a paltry .107 average after 24 games, got Garagiola a season-long demotion back to the American Association. He needed a .356 average with Columbus to earn a return trip to the majors. But in 1949, Garagiola was in the big leagues to stay.

The Cardinals kept Garagiola the busiest in 1949, using him in 81 games. He batted .261 and neared what could have been the pinnacle of his career. In 1950, Garagiola was hitting better than ever. His average reached a career-high .347 before disaster struck. Against the Dodgers, he tried to beat out a bunt. Second baseman Jackie Robinson covered on the play, but slipped on wet ground trying to touch first base. His legs, stretched across first base, tripped Garagiola as he tried to avoid a collision. The Cardinal catcher suffered broken ribs and a separated shoulder. Since then, he's suffered a tarnished reputation from some sportswriters. Garagiola bristles at the notion that he was trying to spike Robinson, who had fallen. "All I know is that I went to the hospital after the game; Jackie Robinson went back to the hotel," he says.

Garagiola returned to the lineup in September, but couldn't recapture his previous success. He ended the year with a .318 average for 34 games. Meanwhile, Del Rice had filled in at catcher, hitting .244 with 9 homers and 54 RBI. With Rice swinging a hot bat, Garagiola's days in St. Louis were numbered. After he hit just .194 for 27 games in 1951, the Cards sent Garagiola to the Pittsburgh Pirates with Bill Howerton, Howie Pollet, Ted Wilks and Dick Cole in exchange for Cliff Chambers and Wally Westlake. The June 15 transaction was a natural shock to the hometown talent. Although he had just 317 games to his credit, this was a man who had spent nearly a decade in the Cardinals organization.

If there was a bright side to Garagiola's 1950 injury, it caused him to look at his economic future. After being disabled, he realized he couldn't play forever. During the off-season, the popular player enjoyed success making personal appearances and giving speeches around St. Louis. Cardinals announcers Harry Caray and Gabby Street encouraged Garagiola to consider a future in broadcasting. So, Garagiola started picking up anecdotes and exploring his potential with a tape recorder at his side. Pitcher Brecheen remembers that, "He'd always keep you laughing. Even then he would sit in the bullpen and act like he was broadcasting ballgames." At age twenty-nine, Garagiola opted for retirement. After hitting .281 in September as a member of the pennant winning New York Giants, the Cubs tried to sign him for 1955.

"That's one of the things that people don't realize. My career was not over," he says. "But I felt that I had been making lateral moves and really wasn't progressing. I was ending up in the red financially." Besides keeping a home in St. Louis, Garagiola and his family tried to keep a house in Pittsburgh (and later Chicago, when he joined the Cubs in 1953). Before retiring, Garagiola approached Anheuser-Busch's ad agency for work as a goodwill ambassador and company representative. With that option, as well as broadcasting available, Garagiola seemed sure he could better the $16,000 salary he received with the Cubs. Besides, he'd have the chance to live solely in St. Louis, saving expenses.

He began his broadcasting career with KMOX Radio in 1955. Having a former player behind the microphone was common for St. Louis fans. After all, announcer Gabby Street had an eight-year career in the majors as a catcher. Garagiola points out Waite Hoyt in Cincinnati or Harry Heilmann in Detroit as pioneering the role of color commentors. "But I may have been one of the first announcers who hadn't been a big star as a player," he adds.

Memories of those first years behind the mike seem bittersweet for Garagiola today. "No question about it, I made my mistakes in the center ring," he says. "I never had training as a broadcaster. Therefore, I paid a heavy price. As I've said before, I got the job because I had been a player. But that didn't keep me there. Every day was an audition." Garagiola's broadcasting longevity is based partly on the same teamwork he practiced on the field. He compares good broadcasting teams to good double play combinations. "You've got to have faith in the guy who sits beside you," he says. "The top priority is the game itself."

While Garagiola discussed his on-field memories throughout his broadcasts, he never talked a lot about his personal reaction to playing pro ball in his native St. Louis. "Playing in your hometown is a double-edged sword," he says. "Growing up there, I've yet to find anybody in St. Louis who gave up a hit against me as a kid. Every guy I meet there says, 'Yeah, I remember you, Joe. I used to strike you out all the time.' You get used to that. People who've known you for a long time think it's OK to ask you for anything. Come to their banquet. Get them Stan Musial's autograph. Give them a baseball. If you don't do it, they're prone to say, 'He has the big head.' Every hometown boy goes through that. Everyone feels they own a piece of you."

Because the Cardinals were the southernmost National League team and the only N.L. franchise west of the Mississippi, Garagiola believes local fans viewed the team differently. "You had more people driving in for games. You got to know more people firsthand. They took a particular interest in you," he says. "Because there were no California Angels or L.A. Dodgers, geographically we had all those fans. KMOX was a powerful radio station, so it told the story. I think our fans had a different attitude, like they were part of a family."

Garagiola's real family is one of his proudest accomplishments. Wife Audrie has been a part of the team since Nov. 5, 1949. They have three children. Joe Garagiola, Jr., is an attorney and sports agent, representing players such as Detroit's Mike Heath. Steve Garagiola is a TV sports anchor in Detroit. Daughter Gina Bridgeman lives in Phoenix and collaborated with her father on *It's Anybody's Ballgame*, a 1988 best-selling book.

Looking back, the articulate baseball advocate is speechless when asked if he ever considered signing a rookie contract with another team besides St. Louis. "I never speculated on that," he admits. "Yogi wanted to play in St. Louis, but the Cardinals missed signing him. Like me, he felt there was only one team to play for: the Cardinals.

"Playing in St. Louis was the dream come true," Garagiola adds. "My hero was Joe Medwick. All of a sudden, not only am I on the same field with him, I'm his teammate for a season. This was the team I grew up with. I'll never forget that feeling."

Joe Garagiola—Cardinal Stats

	G	AB	H	2B	3B	HR	R	RBI	BB	SO	SB	BA	SA
1946	74	211	50	4	1	3	21	22	23	25	0	.237	.308
1947	77	183	47	10	2	5	20	25	40	14	0	.257	.415
1948	24	56	6	1	0	2	9	7	12	9	0	.107	.232
1949	81	241	63	14	0	3	25	26	31	19	0	.261	.357
1950	34	88	28	6	1	2	8	20	10	7	0	.318	.477
1951	27	72	14	3	2	2	9	9	9	7	0	.194	.375

World Series

	G	AB	H	2B	3B	HR	R	RBI	BB	SO	SB	BA	SA
1946	5	19	6	2	0	0	2	4	0	3	0	.316	.421

JOE HOERNER

Accidental Tourist

A wayward bus, an exploding champagne bottle and a shattered stadium club—for Joe Hoerner, they came with the territory as part of a successful St. Louis club in the 1960s.

Joe was no flake. He was, after all, the Cardinals' stopper from 1966 to 1969. And in those years he saved 60 games, fashioned an ERA that never reached the 2.90 mark, and struck out three times as many batters as he walked. He was a master out there.

It's just that when you're on a winning ballclub, "things happen." Funny things. Crazy things. And Joe Hoerner made things happen—on *and* off the field.

But to hear him tell it, one can see that things also used to happen *to* Joe Hoerner, before he became a Cardinal. Things that nearly kept him out of baseball. Things that nearly took his life. So, mixed in with the amusing tales of Joe the bus driver, Joe the celebrant, and Joe the grenadier, are stories about Joe the survivor. Hoerner's story begins, innocently enough, with his childhood in rural Iowa.

Born in Dubuque and raised in the small farming community of nearby Key West, Hoerner was drawn to baseball mostly because of his older brother, Bob, an outfielder/first baseman who notched a few seasons in the Cubs' minor league system in the late 1940s. (A younger brother, Jim, followed in his siblings' footsteps by playing briefly in the White Sox' farm system, and kid brother John also played baseball for a time.)

There was no Little League program in the area, so Joe and his childhood friends would, in his words, "Get a game going from time to time and beat the ball around out in the cow pasture."

Until he reached high school, Hoerner concentrated on playing the outfield. But his coach, James Nora, saw something in Joe that gave the successful teacher and multi-sports coach ideas about having the youth pitch for his Dubuque Rams. The idea worked. Hoerner threw hard and he threw strikes, and so, both literally and figuratively, Joe Hoerner turned his back on the outfield.

An automobile accident in his junior year nearly ended his trek through amateur sports. In the accident he sustained a shoulder separation and broken ribs. And although they could not detect anything at the time, his doctors felt Hoerner may also have suffered serious damage to muscles and tendons in his chest cavity. As it turned out, their concerns were warranted. But it would be several years before the extent of the damage to Hoerner's body was fully understood.

A year out of high school, Hoerner was entertaining thoughts of going to college, but as the fall of 1955 drew near, his thoughts turned to a career in professional baseball. The about-face was no surprise to anyone, least of all Hoerner. That spring, he had been invited to try out with the Dubuque Packers of the Midwest League, largely on the basis of his status as a local talent. Although he did not sign, Hoerner was left to savor the sweet taste of possibility.

The following summer Hoerner was pitching locally for Dyersville when the White Sox' minor league affiliate in Waterloo scheduled an exhibition game against Joe's team at Dyersville. Although he doesn't recall the outcome of the game, Hoerner says he pitched well enough that the Waterloo brass invited him to work out with their club a few days later. Though he threw only on the sidelines, Hoerner again impressed, and he signed his first professional contract with the White Sox organization and began his climb up the minor league ladder.

Joe was pitching for Davenport in 1958 when he suddenly passed out and fell to the ground. He was rushed to a local hospital where, despite immediate medical attention, he barely pulled through.

"I think I was given up for gone," Hoerner said of that scary episode. "I think they may have even given me my last rites. But the doctors there couldn't find anything wrong with me."

Yet, he continued to have problems the following year, and spent a lot of time in hospitals around the country. It was at this juncture that Joe changed his pitching motion.

"There was a chance that I would be released because of my health problems," Joe said, "but I felt I could still play. Ira Hutchinson, who pitched for the Cardinals back in the early '40s, was my manager at Davenport. He was the same man who managed the Waterloo ballclub when I pitched against 'em back in Dyersville. Anyway, he recommended I drop down and throw sidearm in hopes that that would help with whatever was wrong with me.

"It seemed to work. And along with the medication I took for a muscle condition around my heart—a medication I had to take throughout my whole career—the new pitching style helped get me to the big leagues. I owe the White Sox organization an awful lot for sticking with me and giving me that opportunity to play and have a successful major league career. If they'd said, 'Sorry, Joe, but we can't risk the chance,' then it's likely that would have been the end of the line as far as my career goes. They spent a lot of money on doctors and hospital stays to help me out."

Hoerner had some success in the minors, notably at Duluth, Minnesota, where he was named rookie pitcher of the year in 1957. He bounced around the minors for a few more seasons when, in the winter of 1961, he was selected by the Houston Colt .45s in the expansion draft.

There were stints in San Antonio and Oklahoma City before Hoerner finally got the call in September of 1963. He appeared in one game for Houston and pitched three innings of scoreless relief, allowing two hits and striking out two batters. Hoerner made the parent club in spring training in 1964, but was used sparingly by managers Harry Craft and Lum Harris: seven trips from the bullpen, no record, and a 4.91 ERA.

"I spent all of '65 back at Oklahoma City," Hoerner said, "where I had a good year. Throughout the season I was rumored to be going here or going there, or that some team was buying me because they needed pitching, and I was pitching very well at the time in short relief. But at the end of the year, I was still at Oklahoma City.

"But in the winter of '65-'66 I was drafted by the Cardinals and went to spring training with them in '66. The next four years were with St. Louis, and that's where I established myself in the big leagues."

Hoerner became the team's stopper—the Lindy McDaniel, the Al Hrabosky, the Bruce Sutter, the Todd Worrell, of his particular era. He began studying for the part when still in the Houston organization and listening to the advice of former major-leaguer Grady Hatton. Hatton felt that Joe was better suited to relief than to the starting rotation.

"At that time I was what, twenty-six years old? Hell, I'd do anything to get to the big leagues at that point," Hoerner said. "And so that's how he used me, bringing me in in the eighth, ninth inning. Grady got me to the big leagues, just as he'd promised, and I give him a lot of credit for that.

"I was mainly a fastball, slider pitcher. Mostly fastball. I might pitch an inning or more and never throw anything but a fastball. But I had excellent control and great velocity. I felt that I could throw the ball pretty much where I wanted to . . . pinpoint it in a certain location.

"And when you take a look at those walks I gave up, I think you could probably take close to half of 'em and say they were situations where I didn't really care if I walked the guy or not. If I could make a particular guy swing at a bad pitch for an out, great, but if I walked him I didn't care because in that instance I had more confidence in getting the next hitter out—an unintentional, intentional walk, I guess you could say.

"The stat that makes me as proud as anything I did out there was my earned run average. One real bad inning of giving up runs can kill you for a whole season if you're a short reliever. It just buries you for a lifetime, practically. I was able to stay away from that for the most part."

Indeed, it was only toward the latter half of his fourteen year major league journey that Hoerner posted some less than sparkling ERAs. Before they traded him to the Phillies in the deal that brought Dick Allen to St. Louis and baseball into the courts with Curt Flood's challenge to the reserve clause, the Cardinals were the beneficiaries of four exquisite seasons from Hoerner. His yearly earned run averages from 1966 to 1969 were 1.54, 2.59, 1.47 and 2.89.

"I enjoyed pitching here in Busch Stadium," he said, "because it was, and still is, pretty much of a pitcher's ballpark. There are no 'gimmes' there. If they hit one out of Busch, they've earned it. But with the clubs we had—Cepeda, Javier, McCarver, Shannon, Brock, Flood, Maxvill and Maris—if the other team put it in play, there was a pretty damn good chance of retiring the hitter. I usually made the other team hit the ball, and we usually had somebody in front of it. I challenged hitters anyway, but with the guys I had out there with me, I felt good about our defense."

The Cardinals usually had somebody in the front of the team bus, too. But when they didn't, the club's stopper became their "starter."

"It was one of the pennant years—'67 I think," Joe began. "We'd already clinched and we'd just beat up on the Braves in Atlanta. We knew we were going to the Series, and everybody was loose and feeling good. We were all showered and dressed and everything, and walking through this tunnel toward where the team bus was parked.

"But there was no driver. It turned out that the driver that had brought us to the ballpark hours before was off duty or havin' a smoke someplace. The dispatcher had sent another driver to the stadium to take us back to our hotel, but there was a mixup of some kind and he hadn't arrived yet. So a lot of the guys are sitting there on the bus, laughing and kidding among themselves, looking forward to closing out the season and playing in the World Series, when I board the bus. Somebody says something about the driver not being there and I said, 'I'll drive this damn thing!'

"The keys were there. I sat down and turned on the ignition. Some of the guys were laughing out loud, kidding me about driving the bus. They thought I was just horsing around. It didn't seem to matter to me that I knew nothing about driving a bus. Everybody was hollerin' 'Let's go!' and I put it in gear and off we went.

"The guys thought I was just going to circle around and come back . . . just go underneath the stadium without actually exiting through a tunnel to leave the park. But the closer I got to that tunnel—which was kind of a tough turn to make with a car, much less a big, long bus piloted by yours truly—a few of the guys decided they wanted off. But I thought, what the hell, I'm this far, we're goin' back to the hotel!

"So out the tunnel we go. The policeman down there was waving us through. I mean, he had no idea it wasn't the regular bus driver behind the wheel. We're out on the street and we head back to the hotel. I don't remember the trip. I don't think I clipped anybody on the way. When we got back to the hotel all the guys were hollerin' and whooping it up, just grateful to be alive and safely back at the hotel. But I had kind of forgotten how long the bus is when turning corners, and I turned a little too sharply coming into the Marriott parking lot.

"Now the guys were yelling for me to stop because I was about to cream a big neon sign with the back end of the bus. There was really no damage to the bus but, ahh, the sign . . . well, a lot of glass fell and it was kind of noisy for a few seconds. I got the bus stopped and opened the door, and everybody just sort of disappeared like ants, you know? I thought it might be a good idea if I got back to my room, too, so I just left the bus parked out there. I don't know who paid for the sign. I know I didn't."

When you're on a winning ball club and the attitude is upbeat, that kind of episode is funny. Hoerner was on a ballclub that won it all in 1967, yet a traditional victory celebration "stunt" in the clubhouse turned his elation into cause for concern in about two shakes.

In the merriment that followed the Cardinals' World Series clincher in Boston, Joe went to open a champagne bottle and the top of it exploded, shooting small shards of glass into the thumb and forefinger of his pitching hand and cutting some tendons. When told by the Red Sox' team doctor that Joe needed stitches and would likely have to catch another plane back to St. Louis, Joe told him, "No way, we just won the World Series. I'm goin' on that plane with my teammates."

So the skeptical BoSox physician, with the aid of a couple of nervous Cardinal players, got Joe stitched up. Later, after the team deplaned in St. Louis, Joe sought out Cardinal team physician Stan London and team trainer Bob Bauman for their expertise.

"From the middle of October until about Thanksgiving, I really didn't know if I'd ever be able to bend that finger again because I had tendons that were completely severed. I was very, very worried that my baseball career was over.

"Once I got it out of the cast and had all the stitches out, there was a lot of therapy. I went down to the ballpark nearly every day for therapy and ultrasound and all that. It just kept coming along and coming along, although that one knuckle at the end, out by the fingernail, still won't bend for me.

"When I went into spring training in '68 it was always on my mind. I was scared. Is this gonna hold up? Is this gonna work? But whatever we did, did work, because that year I was eight and two with a one point somethin' ERA and seventeen saves."

What was it about Joe Hoerner and broken glass? The hotel sign, the champagne bottle and... the stadium club window in L.A.

After the Cardinals had moved into their new home at Busch Stadium in 1966, some of the players would on occasion throw or hit a baseball up against the stadium club window overlooking the field. Although the glass was unbreakable, Hoerner emphasizes now, "it would scare the hell out of the people eating in there; cause 'em to spill their drinks and drop their food... there were a few messes up there."

But club officials heard the patrons' complaints about mischievous Cardinal ballplayers, and put a stop to their shenanigans.

"We were out in L.A. one day," Hoerner recalled, "and Dodger Stadium's got a stadium club out in right field, similar to what's in St. Louis, only a lot farther back. All of us pitchers were standing out there in right field during batting practice before the game, ready to run our sprints.

"There was a bunch of people sitting up there by the glass,

eating food and sipping their drinks. And Gibson picked up a ball—he had pitched the night before—and said, 'Boy if my arm weren't so sore I'd throw this thing up there an make 'em jump!'

"I said, 'Give me that thing,' and ran it up there and... it was *not* unbreakable glass. The people saw what was going to happen and they scattered in time, but about a four by eight foot pane of glass met its end. Seemed like broken glass fell for ten minutes. And since this wasn't all that long before the gates opened, and since Dodger Stadium almost always had a full house, there was quite a bit of hurried cleanup. Somebody else got blamed for it at first. There was quite a meeting out there, and it did cost about $580 to replace that window."

In 1969, which turned out to be his last year in a Cardinal uniform, Joe and teammate Dal Maxvill started a travel agency business in St. Louis: Cardinal Travel. It is still doing well, now more than twenty years later.

Hoerner says he is glad that he had the foresight to know he wouldn't pitch forever and therefore make post-career plans accordingly. He still had a pair of decent years coming to him in Philadelphia in 1970 and 1971, however, and had varying degrees of success with several other teams before retiring in 1977. In addition to his other physical ailments over the course of his professional career, Joe underwent several off-season knee operations.

"There was no consistency toward the end of my career," Hoerner said. "One day I'd go out and do a good job and the next time I couldn't. I well knew I just didn't have the velocity anymore, but what really bothered me was that I'd lost some of my control, probably due from trying to throw the ball a little harder than I was able to.

"By 1977 I was forty, and I knew it was over. It was fairly easy to accept, really, and after traveling all those years—in planes, cars and even... buses—I really didn't miss that part of the game. I went to twenty-one spring trainings in my professional career. It was time to walk away."

Joe Hoerner—Cardinal Stats

	W	L	PCT	ERA	G	GS	CG	IP	H	BB	SO	SHO	SV
1966	5	1	.833	1.54	57	0	0	76	57	21	63	0	13
1967	4	4	.500	2.59	57	0	0	66	52	20	50	0	15
1968	8	2	.800	1.47	47	0	0	49	34	12	42	0	17
1969	2	3	.400	2.89	45	0	0	53	44	9	35	0	15
World Series													
1967	0	0	—	40.50	2	0	0	.2	4	1	0	0	0
1968	0	1	.000	3.86	3	0	0	4.2	5	5	3	0	1

AL HRABOSKY

Meet "The Mad

Hungarian"

Al Hrabosky did more than become
the bullpen ace for the St. Louis Cardinals in the 1970s. He became "The Mad
Hungarian," the first superhero character
that baseball fans had ever known.

Just as Superman was Clark Kent's
alter ego, "The Mad Hungarian" was Al
Hrabosky's secret identity. Out of uniform,
he was known as a mild-mannered community resident who was an off-season
sports broadcaster and supporter of numerous local charities. However, when
summoned from the bullpen, Hrabosky
turned into "The Mad Hungarian." Re-
plete with a menacing fu manchu moustache, Hrabosky would stalk behind the
mound for a few seconds of self-hypnosis
before throwing each pitch. With his back
to the plate, he would pause to visualize
each hitter's fate. Then, the fuming left-
hander would slam the ball back into his
glove and march onto the mound.
Whether battling his foes at home or on
the road, Hrabosky's stare-down con-
frontations with batters were classic mini-
dramas. He whipped fans into a frenzy
even before a single pitch was thrown.

Even the 1975 Cardinals media guide had trouble describing Hrabosky's mystical methods. According to the official team publication, Hrabosky "used a self-psyching technique of talking to himself behind the mound to confuse batters and capture fans' fancy." Today, the forty-year-old former stopper partially agrees with the assessment. "I was doing it for myself, not just for the fans," he says of the technique first used in mid-1974. "I didn't know what it was going to do for the fans. It did get a reaction, though. On the road, I was greeted with a standing boo. That also ignited the atmosphere and sent electricity through the stadium. It motivated me both ways."

Hrabosky says this process was his "controlled hate" mood, a way of harnessing his aggression into a positive force. Contrary to popular belief, Hrabosky was never speaking aloud when he was behind the mound. "You wouldn't have heard anything," he says. TV broadcasters particularly enjoyed speculating on some of the comments Hrabosky may have been making before each pitch. "I wouldn't say anything out loud." Instead, his comments were strictly mental notes. "During the pennant stretch, I'd play scoreboard games. I'd say, 'This is a pick-up game. We can pick up a game on the leaders or we can stay ahead.' Then, after placing as much importance on the game as possible, I'd run down a scouting report on the hitter. Mentally, I'd watch myself doing everything mechanically correct. I'd imagine a positive reaction from the hitter, seeing him swing and miss."

One of the most controversial aspects of Hrabosky's pacing-and-pitching ritual was the delays it caused for batters. "If a hitter ever got into a cat-and-mouse game of stepping out, I'd say, 'Hey, he's accepted the challenge. Now bury him!'" Hrabosky says. "It psyched up some hitters and psyched some out." Of course, many managers may have worried about having infielders becoming inattentive with a slow worker on the mound. "Everyone said that, with a pitcher who takes his time, the defense gets flat-footed. My guys learned really quickly that you could play cards out there until I got on the mound. Then they should get ready. It brought out the best in my teammates. All of a sudden, they had a great deal of confidence that I could save the game. It helped my intensity and brought up the intensity of everyone around me."

While Hrabosky invented his unique pitching style, he was

given his distinctive nickname by Cardinals public relations director Jerry Lovelace. "I always had kind of an uncontrollable temper
in the minor leagues," he explains about the moniker. "I wouldn't
get in fights or break things, but I was intense. The best way to
beat me was to bunt off me. I'd charge off the mound, step on the
ball and throw it away. I'd get so mad at myself that I'd be useless
from that point on."

But why "The Mad Hungarian?" The label came partially
because the nickname of "Mad Dog" was taken by coach Lee
Thomas. "Other players had nicknames like that," Hrabosky says.
"One day, Jerry called me 'M.H.' It really fit. I was always telling
people that I wasn't Polish. I have great respect for Polish people,
but I'm Hungarian!" Noted sportswriter Jack Herman was the
first to introduce Hrabosky's title in St. Louis papers. While spelling the reliever's name wasn't that tough, a few announcers
couldn't master his name (pronounced Ra-BAH-ski). Adoring fans
learned his name early. "I Hlove Hrabosky" bumper stickers were
a favorite during the pitcher's reign in St. Louis.

Oddly enough, Hrabosky's facial hair initially got more attention from the media than his mound antics did. In the beginning, Hrabosky abandoned his clean-shaven image in preparation
for the 1973 World Series. "That was the year when owner Charlie
Finley started the moustaches in Oakland. They were winning the
A.L. West. We were fighting for the pennant, also. Someone came
up with the idea on our team that we should all grow moustaches.
We wanted to have the first all-mustachioed World Series," he remembers. But a late season swoon ended the Series dream for the
Redbirds. In 1974 in spring training, Al shaved. During the first
half of the season, Al slumped. "There were rumors that I might
be sent back down, and I was out of [contract] options," he says.
"During the All-Star break, I started growing facial hair. I knew I
wasn't pitching well clean-shaven so I decided to grow it back."

Right after the All-Star break, Hrabosky won in Philadelphia. Surprisingly, reporters weren't discussing his behind the
mound work. Instead, they wanted to know about the return of
the moustache. "It just happened that one of the reporters there
had a big fu manchu," he says. "He said, 'Why don't you grow
yours into a fu manchu?' I said, 'I might...' "

Combining facial hair and a new aggressive pitching style,

Hrabosky turned his career around quickly. After a first half re-cord of 1-1 with no saves and a high ERA, Hrabosky says his big-gest problem was a lack of concentration. "I wasn't pitching well. I didn't even know I was in the ballpark," Hrabosky jokes. With a new pitching agenda, Hrabosky went on a seven-game winning streak. He ended 1974 with an 8-1 mark and 9 saves in 65 appear-ances. In 88 innings, he whiffed 82 batters.

Hrabosky's momentum continued into 1975, when he was named the National League Fireman of the Year. The California native racked up a league-leading 22 saves and compiled a sterling 13-3 record with a 1.67 ERA. For the two seasons, he compiled one of baseball's finest winning percentages. "That was one of my trademarks," Hrabosky says. "Usually when I'd pitch, I came into the game down by one run or tied. Then the guys would get me some runs, and I'd earn the win."

Such recognition was a long time coming for Hrabosky. His professional career began in 1969 as a starter with Modesto. After an 8-1 season with Arkansas in 1970, the twenty-year-old hurler appeared in sixteen games with St. Louis in 1970. "Physically, I was probably ready. But mentally, I wasn't." An engagement with the U.S. Army limited his season to just forty-one minor league innings after missing spring training. "That really set me back. The Cardinals decided to leave me in the minors all season in 1972 to let me pitch."

Going into 1973, Hrabosky says he felt insecure about his future. "I felt there weren't that many people in my corner. I've al-ways said that sometimes you need someone that likes you more than the guys who dislike you. You have to have someone to stick his neck out and say, 'Hey, this guy can do it. Give him a shot.' " For Hrabosky, that support came from Fred Koenig, manager of the Class AAA Tulsa Oilers. "Fred got the Cardinals interested in me again. He really pushed them to bring me up at the end of 1972," Hrabosky says.

In 1973 with Tulsa, Hrabosky was 3-6 in nine starts. After four pro seasons, he began wondering what it took to get a major league job. Soon, he discovered that a new attitude could help.

"I was out in California for an Army Reserve meeting. The Cardinals were out there and I saw (PR director) Jerry Lovelace at the meetings," Hrabosky said.

"How are you?" Lovelace had asked. "I know you were disappointed in spring training."

"I think I've finally stopped feeling sorry for myself. I realize now that the Cardinals have no interest in me. So, when I go back I'm going to start pitching for the other twenty-three clubs," Hrabosky answered.

"I don't think that's true. They still have a lot of interest in you," Lovelace replied.

Still, Hrabosky remained skeptical. Nevertheless, he hurled two complete games (one a no-hitter). Bob Kennedy, chief assistant to Cardinals general manager Bing Devine, came to evaluate Hrabosky's progress. Little encouragement came from the Cardinals executive.

"Well, you're getting your fastball and curve over," Kennedy said. "Now I think you ought to start learning how to turn the ball over."

Hrabosky, who says he relied solely on those two pitches during his early years, balked at the suggestion. "I don't think so," he answered. "I'm not ready for that yet." With that, Hrabosky walked away from the conversation.

Never before had Hrabosky shown defiance toward any team brass. He liked the results. "The next day I was in the majors," he says. "It was a no-lose situation. If a guy showed defiance, one of two things happened: either they sent him to the big leagues, thinking he was finally mature and could take charge. Or, they got rid of him and traded him to the big leagues." He earned a 2-4 record with 5 saves and a 2.09 ERA in 44 appearances. Hrabosky's first major league save occurred on July 22, 1973, against the Dodgers, allowing the Cards to move into first place at the All-Star break.

Sadly, the 1973 season proved to be a heartbreaker for Hrabosky and his teammates. "That's when Bob Gibson tore up his knee in August," Hrabosky recalls. "We had a five-and-a-half-game lead at the time." He says that Rick Wise and Reggie Cleveland hit month-long slumps after getting off to great starts. "But we finished strong. Each of them threw shutouts in the last week." Ultimately, the New York Mets won the pennant title with an 82-79 mark.

More disappointment came in the 1974 season, when the Pirates took the division title away from St. Louis by the same margin of one and a half games. "That was the year Red [manager Schoendienst] was criticized for not bringing me in and relieving Gibson in the second to last day of the season," Hrabosky says. "In the bottom of the eighth, Mike Jorgensen hit a two-run homer off him in Montreal, where the wind always blows out to right field." The next day, the team spent the day in their hotel lobby in Montreal near a radio. They listened to the first place Pirates play the Cubs. "If they had beaten the Pirates, we would have played the Expos the next day. Then, if we would have won, we could have gone to Pittsburgh for a one game playoff." But Hrabosky recalls, in painful detail, how the Cubs blew a three run lead and killed the Cards' pennant hopes.

Of those glory years, Hrabosky remembers several outstanding teammates who made major contributions. "In 1975, Ron Reed pitched great as a starter," Hrabosky says. "It seemed like every single time he pitched, he came out after seven or eight innings being behind or tied. Then I'd come in and get the win. Of course, during those years, Mike Garman was an outstanding set-up guy. One reason I had such a good ERA was, when I failed and left men on base, he came in behind me and pitched well. My guys never scored." Regarding Ken Reitz, Hrabosky says, "He always played solid defense for you. He was the kind of guy who'd have a great April and May, hitting over .400. But then he'd struggle the rest of the way."

Hrabosky struggled with a leg injury in 1976, which reduced his velocity. Nevertheless, he set team relief marks (for lefties) in most appearances (68) and most games finished (45). But his biggest problems came from new manager Vern Rapp in 1977. Rapp was an accomplished manager from the Cincinnati Reds minor league system. However, in St. Louis, Rapp was in the center of constant battles with players and media. Even before arriving, Hrabosky says Rapp had a questionable reputation. "In the minors, we viewed Rapp in a very negative tone. He was part of a group of former Cardinal minor league managers and executives who defected to Cincinnati." Dick Wagner, Bob Howsam and Chief Bender were other offenders Hrabosky cited. Rapp had been a veteran Cardinal minor leaguer and manager before moving to the Reds system. "In the minors, it was instilled in us that you hated Vern Rapp and all these guys."

The biggest controversy surrounding Rapp's arrival was a new ban on facial hair. The rule meant the removal of Hrabosky's fabled fu manchu, which brought him his "Mad Hungarian" mystique.

The facial hair rule became the primary news in St. Louis that year. Newspapers delighted in showing Hrabosky's picture as proof of the typical "look" the new team rules hoped to change. The team's star reliever began to take the issue as a personal attack, pitting himself against Rapp. Hrabosky said he later found out that how "Rapp got the job was that he told Mr. Busch that he would enforce his rules. Basically, Mr. Busch didn't want the facial hair."

The disagreement plagued the team and Hrabosky all season. "I kind of liked myself," Hrabosky says. "I may have looked like a maniac on the field, but I looked as distinguished as possible with a fu manchu. I always dressed properly, I did the right things and I didn't have a criminal record. It wasn't fair that I was being used as an example." As strange as it may seem, Hrabosky does feel that the facial hair ban affected his performance that year. "The game is so mental, and they wanted to take away something I was comfortable in. It's like asking a combat soldier to go to war without a helmet or rifle."

Rapp not only had problems with his players, but with the St. Louis press. According to Hrabosky, Rapp quickly told veteran members of the St. Louis media brigade that he didn't want to be criticized or second-guessed by them. "He could not handle the media at all. The media went out and got him fired," Hrabosky claims. Hrabosky felt that Rapp's demands to the media came off as threats. "He told this to people like Jack Buck, people who had been in the business for thirty years. They said, 'Oh, yeah? We'll show you!' "

Hrabosky quickly lost faith in Rapp as the season progressed. "I decided at the All-Star break that he had lost control of the ballclub. He walked out on us in a team meeting after saying, 'We can't motivate you guys. The World Series money doesn't mean a thing to you. You're a bunch of losers.' If he couldn't stand up to players in a meeting, then that was it. I called Bing Devine and told him I wouldn't play by those rules any more. They told Rapp I'd be growing the facial hair. But, to save face for Vern, they gave him another year on his contract.

"If Vern was going to have a shot the next year without all this stuff resurfacing, I was going to have to go," he adds. "So I expected to be traded. After things had eased up between us, Devine asked me if I could get along with Vern. I said yes. But Whitey [Herzog, then with the Kansas City Royals] was convinced that he needed a left-handed reliever after getting beat by Chris Chambliss in the playoffs." The result came on Dec. 8, 1977, when the Royals swapped Mark Littell and catcher Buck Martinez to St. Louis for Hrabosky.

Because Hrabosky did not have a no-trade clause in his contract, he had no control over what team he was dealt to. He did say that contract problems weren't a factor in his trade, as they had been with Steve Carlton and Jerry Reuss in previous years. "I was in the second year of a three-year contract. I went to the Royals knowing what I'd be paid."

Al pitched for the Royals for two seasons, and then finished his career with the Atlanta Braves. Today, Hrabosky's 59 Cardinal saves and 329 appearances rank him on the team's top 10 lists in both categories.

Although he had early aspirations to have an eventual career in broadcasting, returning to work with the Cardinals seemed remote after his stormy departure from the club. "When I left St. Louis, believe me, I thought I'd never be back," Hrabosky says. "But time heals things. I was vindicated a little when Rapp was fired so early in the next season. People realized that I hadn't been such a bad guy. As time went on, people just remembered the good things." But, now, Hrabosky works as a Cardinals announcer for KPLR (channel 11). Hrabosky had prepared himself for a broadcasting career by doing sports on KPLR for two winters. "I was horrendous, by the way," he adds with a laugh. Additionally, he co-hosted a KMOX radio show with catcher Ted Simmons.

"I tried to give a lot back to the community," Hrabosky says about his feelings for St. Louis residents. "I was accessible, attending lots of charity events. Why? Because I wanted to, and because I appreciated the support fans had given me. People saw me and talked with me. They realized that I was a decent guy off the field. That has a lot to do with why I have this job today.

"Once someone's a Cardinal," he adds, "they always remain a Cardinal in their hearts."

Cardinals fans gave Hrabosky the biggest heartfelt thrill of his career on July 12, 1975. Because Dodgers manager Walt Alston overlooked Hrabosky for the N.L. All-Star squad, the Cardinals invited fans to come protest at the park during "We Hlove Hrabosky Hday." The game, versus the Dodgers, was slated for NBC-TV's "Game of the Week." Before the game, Hrabosky asked PR director Lovelace, "What if no one shows up? Does that mean they agree with Alston's All-Star selections?" But that never happened.

Instead, 50,000 banner-toting Cardinal fans appeared. Typical attendance for a Saturday game in the mid-1970s may have been 25,000 to 30,000. NBC couldn't avoid making the controversy the theme of its broadcast. Dodgers reliever Mike Marshall (an All-Star selection) wound up dueling Hrabosky in the final innings. Hrabosky, in front of Alston and an adoring mass of Cardinal fans, hurled two perfect innings to earn a 2-1 victory and avenge his All-Star exclusion. Millions of TV watchers witnessed this St. Louis-style Cinderella story unfold as Hrabosky proved Alston wrong. For an encore, he collected another 2-1 win the next day.

"I was a little queasy," Hrabosky recalls. "I didn't know what to expect. I'll always remember the day I came out on that field, and there were 50,000 fans. I don't care if you're Lou Gehrig, Stan Musial or one of the other greats of the game. None of them ever had a Hbanner Day before. When I think back, that's the moment and the day I'll always cherish with Cardinals fans.

"That was my private All-Star game."

Al Hrabosky—Cardinal Stats

	W	L	PCT	ERA	G	GS	CG	IP	H	BB	SO	SHO	SV
1970	2	1	.667	4.74	16	1	0	19	22	7	12	0	0
1971	0	0	—	0.00	1	0	0	2	2	0	2	0	0
1972	1	0	1.000	0.00	5	0	0	7	2	3	9	0	0
1973	2	4	.333	2.09	44	0	0	56	45	21	57	0	5
1974	8	1	.889	2.97	65	0	0	88	71	38	82	0	9
1975	13	3	.813	1.67	65	0	0	97	72	33	82	0	22
1976	8	6	.571	3.30	68	0	0	95.1	89	39	73	0	13
1977	6	5	.545	4.40	65	0	0	86	82	41	68	0	10

WHITEY KUROWSKI

Putting "We"

Ahead of "I"

In September of 1941, with the Rochester Red Wings eliminated from contention in the International League's pennant race, three hands from that Cardinals' farm club got the call to St. Louis: Stan Musial, Erv Dusak and George "Whitey" Kurowski.

They made their respective debuts on the seventeenth, eighteenth and twenty-third of the month which, looking back after nearly fifty years, seems so fitting. Whitey has always been happy to put his former teammates first. Is he proud of his own accomplishments? You bet. Prouder still of his *team's* accomplishments? Count on it.

Even at the mention of the decisive game of the 1942 World Series, in which he slugged a two-run homer in the top of the ninth inning off the Yankees' Red Ruffing that put the Cardinals ahead for good, 4-2, Kurowski waves it off with his hand and says:

"People always say my hit won the ballgame. No. It *helped* to win the ballgame, because I've always said that it takes nine fellas out there to win a

ballgame. In that particular one, for example, Walker Cooper, our catcher, picked off Joe Gordon at second base on a bunt play, and that was a big play right then because they had two men on base with no outs in the bottom of the ninth.

"Don't get me wrong. That home run was probably my biggest thrill in baseball. But in my mind, anyway, Walker's throw was just as important. And look at the pitching we got in the Series. Everybody contributed. Everybody."

That Kurowski even played baseball at the major league level, much less saw World Series competition, was something of a miracle. His right arm was short, the result of osteomyelitis that he endured when he was about seven years old.

There was at the time some talk of removing his arm completely, Kurowski remembers, because of the infectious nature of the inflammatory bone disease. Instead, doctors removed about four inches of bone and dead tissue from the boy's forearm, which, while saving the arm itself, resulted in a deformity that dictated a certain hitting style for the right-handed third baseman.

"I was pretty much a pull hitter early in my career," Kurowski said. "The injury to my arm made me turn my right wrist over. Much of the time I couldn't buy a base hit to right field.

"Oh, I got some hits to that side, sure, because many times the second baseman was playing me on the shortstop side of the bag, leaving a big hole on the right side of the infield.

"I stood close to the plate, practically on the line. If they pitched me inside and hit me on the fist, well, that's part of the game. Tough luck, right? But I was determined to get a piece of the ball. Sometimes, if I went into a little slump, I might try something else. But very seldom would I change my batting style. I tried to stay on top of that plate."

Kurowski stood on top of the plate, too, in softball, which he played as a boy five nights a week back in his hometown of Reading, Pennsylvania, where he still resides. On weekends he'd play baseball morning till night. If there were kids on a playground George John Kurowski was probably one of them. He later played three years of high school baseball and took his swings in the local American Legion program as well. It was in high school when Kurowski first found himself concentrating on third base.

"One of the first days out, my high school coach just said,

'Go play third base,' and I liked it once I got there. But I also played some shortstop, including way back when, when I played for a semi-pro team, and later, when I was down in Panama in winter ball in 1940, the year before I came up to the Cardinals."

His 1941 inaugural of nine at-bats produced a .333 batting average with two RBI, a run scored and two doubles. The next season, the stocky little infielder became a fixture at third base for the Cardinals when manager Billy Southworth gave him the nod over Jimmy Brown, a switch hitter whose ability to play several defensive positions made him a valuable commodity for the Cardinals.

"Jimmy Brown... now there's a guy who was hustlin' out there all the time," Kurowski said, "and if you weren't doin' the same the manger didn't have to say a word to you. Your buddies would. And you knew it, too, brother, except with the teams we had back then that didn't happen too often with guys not playing hard.

"Take Terry Moore, our captain. He was a good hitter, a great outfielder, and one of the finest guys you'd ever want to meet. He showed by example, too. Enos Slaughter, Stan Musial, the guys who pitched for us, right down the line we took pride in wearing the Cardinal uniform.

"And we'd never, *never* get out of a game when we had a hangnail or a bellyache. Unless it was something that made it impossible to play, such as a hamstring pull or a fracture, we'd go out there every day, even when we were less than 100 percent. Part of that was because there'd be six guys waitin' to take your job away from you—if not on the bench, then at Triple A. I played for the love of the game, but when I played I was also puttin' food on the table for my wife, my kids and me."

Players of Kurowski's era occasionally talk of the train travel involved in taking teams from one major league city to the next. Some liked it, some did not. Kurowski, it seems, fell into the former category.

"In this one respect we weren't any different from other teams, but when we rode the trains we used to always sit in the club compartment of our sleeper, and we'd talk about that day's game... what happened that day... whether we won or lost... what we did... who we were gonna face tomorrow, or next week.

Though we joked with each other and stayed loose, we were strictly baseball. We didn't go out and carouse around.

"Musial, I remember, used to like to try card tricks. He was like a little magician, you know. And some guys were quick wits. And there'd be the occasional practical joke played on somebody or other. When you're winning, the way we did, staying loose comes easily.

"Those were good times, and we had a lot of fun. Mostly, though, we talked baseball. We talked about the game that day, because from the time the season opened till the end of the season, we had just one thing on our minds—to get into the World Series. And I thought we did pretty good in the time I was there: four firsts and five seconds—that ain't too bad."

From time immemorial, batters have remembered the pitchers who gave them trouble during the course of their careers. Kurowski, while keeping the focus on his list narrow, is no exception to this rule. Fortunately for Whitey, one particularly breathtaking episode ended without serious consequence.

"Ewell Blackwell. A sidearmer from Cincinnati. He gave me trouble. I probably got a few hits off him, but overall, I had trouble hitting him. And with my standing so close to the plate, and him comin' sidearm at me, well, you can understand why.

"One time here in St. Louis, Blackie threw one that got away from him. My cap went up in the air, my head went down, and the ball sailed in between the cap and my head, and went all the way back to the screen.

"He was white as a sheet and so was I. We eventually knocked him out of the game, but he later came over to our dugout and apologized about that pitch. I said, 'Blackie, I know you weren't throwin' at me. You're not that kind of pitcher. Besides, I know you can hit me if you want to. It's just that you don't need to, right?' And we both laughed it off.

"Another pitcher, a left-hander by the name of Fritz Ostermueller, gave me fits. Pitched for Brooklyn and Pittsburgh when he came over here from the American League. I used to love to hit against him. But—I think in thirty times at bat against him I only got two hits.

"I could see his pitches very well. I'd pull two screaming line drives to left field that would go foul, and then I'd see him laughing to himself out there on the mound. At that point, he had any one of about four pitches he could use to get me out, which he often did. Years later, we were talkin' and I said, 'Fritzie, I used to love to face you, but you always seemed to get me out.' And he said, 'I'd *give* you them two pitches inside, and your eyes'd get big and sure enough, you'd pull 'em foul. Then I'd work on you Whitey, I'd work on you!'"

Naturally, not all of Kurowski's at-bats ended in frustration. He hit .286 lifetime for St. Louis. Twice he batted in more than a hundred runs. Three times he socked twenty or more homers, and, while not a consistent home run threat, he does hold the Cardinal club record for most home runs hit in one month, with twelve circuit clouts in August 1947.

That post-war season was, arguably, his personal best. In 146 games Kurowski hit .310 with 104 RBI, 108 runs scored, 27 home runs, 27 doubles, 6 triples, and walked 87 times while striking out 56 times.

He usually swung a 33-oz., 34 1/2-inch Hillerich & Bradsby bat, model M117. It had a medium-sized handle, Kurowski recalls, and he gripped the bat "right against the knob" because he felt that gave him better control.

One day, he lost control. Not of his bat, but of his temper. As the situation unfolded, it became evident that in the Kurowski family the old adage, "Like father, like son," was important even outside the home.

"We were in New York for a series of games, and Billy Southworth, our manager, was a good man. Once in a while when we were in New York, he'd let some of our kids sit in the dugout with us. This one time my son—he's in his late forties now, but back then we called him 'Slugger'—he was about five years old at the time, was there with me and he was sittin' in the dugout when the home plate umpire, Jocko Conlan, threw me out of the ball game for arguing a call.

"And as I was walking across the diamond past Jocko, my son came runnin' up behind me and said to Jocko, 'Well, if you throw my daddy out, I'm goin' too!' I think the next day one of the New York papers ran a picture of me going off the field, with Slugger following right behind me."

Kurowski was forced to leave the field permanently in 1949.

His arm, he says, gave him problems, and he knew he could no longer perform to the best of his ability. He stayed on the active list and pinch hit once in a while, he adds, "but it just didn't go."

To lessen the emotional pain of retiring, Kurowski entered the managerial ranks in the minor leagues and found he enjoyed it. Lynchburg. Tulsa. Winnipeg. "Name a town," he says, smiling, "and I probably managed there."

Former Cardinal star and current broadcaster Mike Shannon was one of Kurowski's proteges in the minors. So was Johnny Lewis, currently a minor league hitting instructor for the Cardinal organization. Mostly, Kurowski remembers players of that caliber, who showed class both on and off the field. But players cut from another bolt were the ones who drove Kurowski back to his Reading home.

"Toward the end of my managerial career, it got to be, I dunno. . . the ballplayers were not good listeners, many of them. A few were playing only for the money part of it. But what really got me is that some of 'em thought they could play half a season at Triple A and make it to the major leagues. Managing those kinds of guys got to be a chore, so I thought, well, better wrap it up."

When Kurowski turned seventy-one on April 19, 1989, he had been out of baseball for nine years. But he frequently listens to games on the radio and watches still others on television. And—no surprise here—he doesn't always approve of what goes on at the ol' ballpark.

"What gripes me is that I see a lot of hitters going up there and taking strikes right down the middle without ever takin' the bat off their shoulder," Kurowski lamented. "I was always under the impression that a batter should be trying to hit the ball, put it in play. When I grabbed that bat of mine out of the bat rack, I had three swings comin' to me, and brother, I'm gonna be ready.

"Another thing, I don't see that many guys standing close to the plate anymore, and they don't seem to be able to protect the plate, especially when they get two strikes on 'em. They should be trying to protect the plate, go with the pitch and make contact. Too many of these guys today are swingin' from their tails."

"You know," he said, reflecting once again on the Cardinals of the 1940s, "they were all good teams, and it was a real joy to win the pennant and hit the home run in the World Series in '42.

But I think the most exciting Series was the one in '46, when Harry Walker knocked Enos around the bases to beat the Red Sox. That was a good one, wasn't it?"

Whitey Kurowski—Cardinal Stats

	G	AB	H	2B	3B	HR	R	RBI	BB	SO	SB	BA	SA
1941	5	9	3	2	0	0	1	2	0	2	0	.333	.556
1942	115	366	93	17	3	9	51	42	33	60	7	.254	.391
1943	139	522	150	24	8	13	69	70	31	54	3	.287	.439
1944	149	555	150	25	7	20	95	87	58	40	2	.270	.449
1945	133	511	165	27	3	21	84	102	45	45	1	.323	.511
1946	142	519	156	32	5	14	76	89	72	47	2	.301	.462
1947	146	513	159	27	6	27	108	104	87	56	4	.310	.544
1948	77	220	47	8	0	2	34	33	42	28	0	.214	.277
1949	10	14	2	0	0	0	0	0	1	0	0	.143	.143
World Series													
1942	5	15	4	0	1	1	3	5	2	3	0	.267	.600
1943	5	18	4	1	0	0	2	1	0	3	0	.222	.278
1944	6	23	5	1	0	0	2	1	1	4	0	.217	.261
1946	7	27	8	3	0	0	5	2	0	3	0	.296	.407

MAX LANIER

Touring Mexico in

a '46 Chrysler

In baseball terms, Max Lanier was not well-traveled. In fourteen major league seasons—twelve of them with the Cardinals—Max Lanier pitched for only three teams. Yet in another sense, Lanier was "well-traveled" because of a trip he and several other players took that interrupted their major league careers in the late 1940s. Lanier's recollections of life in Jorge and Bernardo Pasquel's Mexican League provide a fascinating entry in baseball lore.

But before Lanier went south of the border, his was a life of small town Americana and big league games. Max begins:

"I was born and raised in Denton, North Carolina. When I was a boy, I followed the Cardinals on the radio because I liked Dizzy and Paul Dean when they were pitchin'. I was a Cardinal fan. Lou Gehrig was one of my favorites over in the American League, but really, the Cardinals were the team I followed even before I signed with 'em years later.

When Lanier was first contacted by the Cardinals, he did not behave like a typical high schooler. Anxious as he may

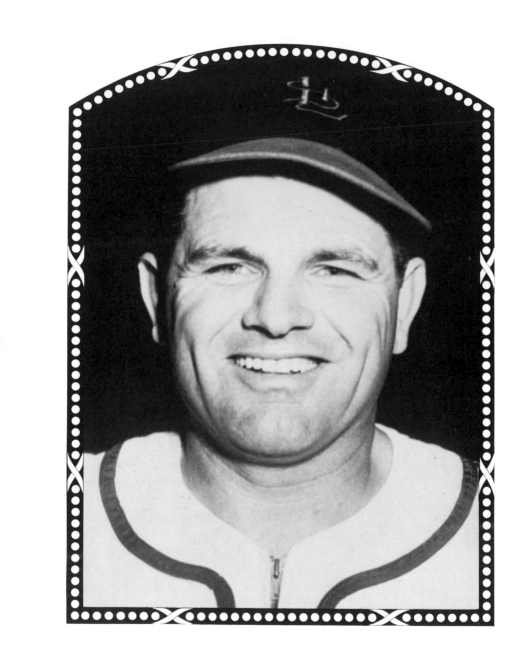

have been to sign with a big league club, the spunky teenager wasn't about to sell himself short, and he obviously wasn't overly impressed with scout Frank Rickey, brother of Cardinals' vice president and business manager Branch Rickey.

"I was pitching in a game back there in my hometown," Lanier recalled, "and it so happened I pitched a shutout. The game was over when this guy met me at the gate and said, 'Hello, Max, I'm Frank Rickey, a scout with the St. Louis Cardinals. How about if I drive you home and we can talk about your future in baseball?'

"And I said, 'Well, I dunno about that. I don't know you.' But he took out his business card and offered it to me, and again said, 'How about me takin' you back to the schoolhouse to shower, and then I'll take you home?' I just kind of looked at him funny, but after a bit I decided he was on the level, so he drove us back to my family's home out in the country.

"When we got there he seemed all anxious to get down to business, but I told him I couldn't just yet. I went out and milked a couple of cows first, and *then* we got to talkin' about my future, as he liked to put it.

"I wound up signin' a Class B contract. My dad and mother had to sign the paper, too, because I was only sixteen years old at the time. They weren't too crazy about the whole thing because I had received a scholarship to attend Duke University. But, Frank Rickey promised me that if I didn't make the club at Greensboro, North Carolina, they would release me from my contract. Well, that wasn't in writing, and after I'd stayed there a week they wanted to send me to Huntington, West Virginia, for seventy bucks a month. That's when I quit and started playing semi-pro ball."

It was in Ashbury, North Carolina, that the ubiquitous Frank Rickey later found his elusive prospect. Lanier claims he had won sixteen games in a row for his mill team, which undoubtedly put Rickey on his best behavior when next they met.

"He said to me, 'How about going to Columbus, Ohio, for spring trainin' and playing in the American Association?' I told him I'd go only if he paid me in spring training what I'd been making there at the mill, and that he promise I would be with the ball-club the whole year. And he said, 'Well, I don't know about that. How do you know you can pitch at that high a level?' I said, 'Well, we've got some pretty good ballplayers right here, and I'm doing all right against them."

Considering that the Cardinals of the 1930s had nearly cornered the market on the nation's budding talents with the organization's extensive farm system, it borders on the unbelievable that the young southpaw dickered as he did with the boss's own brother.

But when one pitches semi-pro ball while in high school, then finishes with a 10-4 record for a farm team that wins the Little World Series...perhaps there was method in Lanier's madness.

Success at the major league level, however, came slowly for Max. Noting that he was a "little wild, as most kids are when they first come up," Lanier posted an 0-3 record and 4.20 ERA in 1938, his debut year. Pitching mostly in relief, he walked 28 and struck out half as many.

As a spot starter in 1939, there was some improvement: a 2-1 record with a nifty 2.37 ERA, 13 walks and 14 strikeouts. In 1940 Lanier went 9-6 as he divided his time between starting and relieving. The 1941 season saw him post a 10-8 record with a 2.82 ERA and 93 whiffs, and from that point on, Max Lanier was on his way.

"I don't think I pitched all that differently from the way I did in semi-pro," Lanier insists, "but you learn right away, though, how to pitch to big league hitters, or you're gone.

"I sidearmed left-handers and pitched overhand, mostly, to right-handers. I had quite a high leg kick, and like most of the pitchers back then, I took a full windup. Mostly curveball, fastball and changeup, plus I threw a knuckleball later on in my career. That was somethin' I picked up on my own. There weren't too many pitchers in our league throwin' one, as I remember.

"For some reason, I was a better pitcher against the better ballclubs. I beat the Dodgers something like twenty-seven times in my career and eleven times in a row once. I never pitched much against Philadelphia, let's say, when they were on the bottom. It seemed like we were always playin' the Dodgers before or after a series with the Phillies, and Billy Southworth or Eddie Dyer would save me for the Dodgers."

Another quirk of Lanier's is that he apparently fared better in the smaller ballparks, and cites Ebbets Field, Wrigley Field,

Crosley Field and Sportsman's Park as favorite stops of his. He also preferred to face National League sluggers over their contact hitter counterparts.

"Don't get me wrong, I didn't enjoy the thought of pitching to guys like Pete Reiser and Ted Kluszewski and Ralph Kiner; it's just that I had good control and could throw hard and spot the ball. Guys who didn't strike out much *and* could punch the ball— they were the ones who always gave me trouble.

"At least with power hitters I was able to keep 'em in the ballpark. Ralph Kiner, for instance...I didn't know it till he came up to me one day years ago and told me that he never hit a home run off me the whole time we played against each other."

Lanier played for a Cardinal ballclub that by 1940 held little resemblance to the legendary Gas House Gang of the mid-1930s. But one vestige still remaining of that raucous band of ballplayers was Johnny "Pepper" Martin, whose pranks, jokes and general behavior off the field were in keeping with the moniker he earned for his hard-charging style on the field: "The Wild Hoss of the Osage."

According to a favorite story often told by Lanier, manager Frankie Frisch was among Martin's victims:

"I'm pretty sure it was in Chicago. At the hotel where we stayed there was a mezzanine floor in the hotel lobby, and you could walk up and down these stairs that led to it from the ground floor. Pepper had a sack, or maybe it was a balloon, filled with water, and he covered it with a newspaper he held in the other hand. Then he went upstairs, opened the mezzanine window, and waited patiently for Frisch to come along.

"Frisch was walkin' outside of the hotel when Pepper dropped the water balloon onto Frank's head. Pepper then dashed downstairs, ran into the lobby, and plopped down in a chair, where he opened up his newspaper. Frisch got dried off to where he could come into the lobby. He's wet, and not of particularly good humor when he looked over at Pepper and says, 'If I didn't see you sittin' over there readin' the paper, I'd swear *you* threw that damn water on me!' Pepper looked up from his paper and says, 'Hold on, Frank, what are you talkin' about?'

"Oh, that Pepper. He was a guy who'd keep a team loose. He was always pullin' tricks on people. Somehow he'd manage to nail your shoe to the floor. Or, he'd tie your clothes up in knots and you'd spend the next twenty minutes gettin' 'em untied.

"He'd use exploding cigars and exploding matches on people. One time he used both on our first base coach, Buzzy Wares, in the clubhouse. First the match exploded and then, after Buzzy yelled at the whole lot of us, the cigar. Yeah...that was Pepper. But one thing about him, though, he was the one who kind of took me under his wing when I joined the Cardinals. He was a nice guy."

Pepper Martin and the rest of the Gas House Gang had scattered as the new decade moved forward. But the Cardinal organization, under the guidance of Branch Rickey, was about to dominate the National League and Lanier was part of a juggernaut that won three consecutive pennants from 1942 to 1944.

He points to the 1942 World Championship as his most satisfying moment in the game. The Cardinals, after a valiant but unsuccessful ninth-inning rally in Game 1, came back to beat the dreaded Yankees in four straight games. Lanier was the winner in relief in Game 4 at New York.

The following year, Lanier lost the opener in the World Series, a Fall Classic that the Yankees went on to win, also four games to one. He also started the fourth game and pitched well enough to win, but the Yankees scored a run off reliever Harry Brecheen in the eighth inning to win, 2-1. For the Series, Lanier posted a splendid 1.76 ERA.

In 1944, Lanier was in top form, not only in regular season play, when he went 17-12 with a 2.65 ERA and 141 strikeouts, but in the all-St. Louis World Series, also, when he was credited with a 3-1 victory in the sixth and decisive game against the Browns.

Lanier entered the service in 1945. Because he missed most of the baseball season, he had only four decisions—two up, two down. In 1946, he was back in spring training with his mates, anxious to help the club return to the top of the National League heap after it finished a close second to the Chicago Cubs. But, he also was anxious to better his lot financially, and refused to sign a contract. At the time Lanier was making $10,000 a year.

Club officials refused to let Max work out with the rest of the team at St. Petersburg. Manager Eddie Dyer knew how crucial it was for the Cardinals' holdout to get in shape and be ready to

play when the team broke camp, so he intervened on Lanier's be-
half with club owner Sam Breadon in St. Louis.

A three-way telephone conversation resulted in an ultima-
tum from Breadon: a $500 raise, take it or go home. Under-
whelmed by Breadon's generosity, Lanier took the meager raise
and was once again wearing the Cardinal uniform.

As if to show his boss that he was worth a lot more, Lanier
burst out of the starting blocks in 1946. He started six, completed
six and won six. His earned run average was 1.93, he'd averaged
six K's in those six games, and two of the games were shutouts.
But all at a cost.

"The last couple of games I felt some pain in my pitching elbow," Lanier said. "I was pitching great, but I was worried that it
might be something serious. I didn't tell anybody, though."

After a game during an east coast swing, Lanier was approached by a couple of men who were "recruiting" major leaguers to play in a new professional league in Mexico. One of the
men, Bernardo Pasquel, was the brother of multimillionaire Jorge
Pasquel, who owned *the entire league*. He was offering the gringos
substantially more money than they were making in the States,
and a couple of big names—Sal "The Barber" Maglie and Mickey
Owen, a former Cardinal—had already taken the plunge.

Lanier made no decision until several days later. By then, he
had learned that two of his teammates, pitcher Fred Martin (2-1
with a 4.08 ERA at that juncture) and second baseman Lou Klein
(struggling at the plate with a .194 batting average) would soon be
heading south of the border. In New York Lanier talked it over
with the pair, and the pair grew to a trio.

"I wound up being offered a signing bonus of $25,000 and
$20,000 a year for five years," Lanier recalled. "You didn't need to
be a brain to see how much more that was than what the Cardinals were payin' me. After the team got back to St. Louis, the
three of us left for Mexico City.

"We drove down in a Chrysler...a 1946 Windsor. I bought it
there in St. Louis. We used that car for traveling around Mexico
when we got down there, sometimes even to the ballpark. Most of
the time of course, we traveled with our respective teams on buses
and sometimes, planes.

"I can only speak for myself. But I went down there to help

myself financially, not to hurt anybody, least of all my Cardinal teammates back home. I know a few of 'em resented it when I went, especially after I'd won all six of my starts, but they were also very good to me when I got back a few years later.

"As it turned out, of course, they did all right without me . . . won the pennant and the World Series. In the long run, I know my going helped other ballplayers. Some of our guys got a good, solid raise the day after the three of us left, just to keep 'em from going. Breadon was scared guys like Musial would take off.

"Life down there was rough. The conditions, both on and off the field, were less than ideal, as those of us who went have related many times over. It was hot, real hot. Some of the places we stayed were, well, the windows were open and no screens on 'em, so the bugs and mosquitoes ate us alive. It was terrible. For me personally, the food didn't agree with me. The water, either.

"I got sick a lot, and lost weight when I did get sick. We just had to get used to things down there, but I never really did get used to it. What made it worse for me was that my elbow problem didn't really work itself out when I was down there. I was hoping the weather would ease the situation, but it didn't. Because I got sick once in a while, they gave me some shots for this or that while I was down there, and you didn't know what you'd be getting injected with."

Not all of Lanier's Latin America stay was bad. He remembers that some of the hotels were nice—for instance, the Reforma Hotel in Mexico City, which Lanier likens to the Hotel New Yorker in New York City. And the people were kind, even generous, to their guests.

"There were a few times when fans would come to the door where I was stayin' and shake my hand and hand me hundred dollar bills for pitchin' a great game," Lanier said. "And in a game in Havana we'd have 35,000 out there for a ballgame. We played mostly in Cuba in the wintertime and Mexico in the summertime.

"The ballparks themselves could be something of a challenge, especially in some of these smaller towns we played in. Tampico was one of 'em. They had a railroad track runnin' right through center field. They'd hafta open up the fence and let the train go right through the ballpark. It never happened while I was pitchin', but boy, just that track bein' there was dangerous. Guys runnin' full speed, trippin' over that damn track, nearly killin' themselves chasin' down a fly ball.

"I can't remember all the guys who were down there when I was, but on this one team I was on at Vera Cruz, Mickey Owen was the catcher. Let's see...George Hausmann played second based for us. Danny Gardella played in the outfield, and so did Luis Olmo.

"Then you had Maglie down there, of course, and Harry Feldman and Roy Zimmerman. Maglie and I were together quite a bit away from the ballpark. We stayed at the same apartments.

"I remember Cuba was good because we played every game right there in Havana. Played four days a week, the other three we could pretty much play golf or go to the beach and swim. We could take it easy on those days. It was pretty nice down there. But in Mexico...boy, playing there could be tough. It was the high altitude and the food that got me. But I think what made me sick more than anything was that being in the high altitude, my curve wasn't breakin' the way it should. I think I aggravated my arm problems tryin' to throw that good, breakin' curveball of mine."

For Lanier, five years in Mexico and environs became less than two. He had tired of the playing conditions. Worse, the southpaw faced a substantial pay cut following the election to the presidency of a Pasquel crony.

Max Lanier was homeward bound. But he and the rest of the so-called "jumpers" found themselves barred from major league baseball by Commissioner A.B. "Happy" Chandler for their actions. The ballplayers, most of them former National Leaguers, would not be allowed back into baseball for five years, Chandler announced. The ballplayers sued to be reinstated, which they were, in 1949.

"I know I beat the Dodgers' Don Newcombe, 1-0, the first game I pitched against 'em after I'd gotten back," Lanier insisted.

Lanier was 5-4 with a 3.82 ERA during that 1949 campaign, and he went 11-9 each of the next two seasons. For Max, they formed his last hurrah as a Cardinal. In December of 1951, he was traded, along with outfielder Chuck Diering, to the New York Giants for Eddie Stanky, who was then given the Cards' managerial job in addition to his duties as part-time second baseman.

"I wound up playing out the string in St. Louis in '53, except it was with the Browns, their last year there. I pitched in about a dozen games, and lost the only decision I had," Lanier said.

In his post-playing days, Lanier owned a restaurant in St. Petersburg, Florida, for several years, managed for nearly a dozen seasons in the minor leagues ("I had Bobby Bonds his first year—great kid—and he hit 30 home runs for me"), and kept in touch with his peers.

"As for goin' down to Mexico, I've got no regrets. It wasn't all bad, but it didn't turn out the way any of us had planned. I had a good career with the Cardinals, and I played with some fine ballplayers on those clubs. We had some success. We won three straight pennants and a few World Series. I'm glad to have been part of all that.

"I think the success of our ballclub back in the '40s—other than havin' Musial in the lineup every day—was due to the fact that nobody thought of himself as a star. I bet if you talk to anybody who played on those teams, they'll tell you the same thing: we were like a big family, and I don't know if they do that anymore in baseball. We played together and we palled around together. We had a great bunch of guys. We had good people on those teams.

"I live in Dunnellon, Florida, now, but I get back to St. Louis once in a while. Back home I still follow the game. I watch games on television all the time, and turn the radio on at night. Sometimes I can get the Cardinals games on KMOX and hear Jack Buck and Mike Shannon do the games. Yeah, Cardinal games on the radio...just like when I was a kid."

Max Lanier—Cardinal Stats

	W	L	PCT	ERA	G	GS	CG	IP	H	BB	SO	SHO	SV
1938	0	3	.000	4.20	18	3	1	45	57	28	14	0	0
1939	2	1	.667	2.39	7	6	2	37.2	29	13	14	0	0
1940	9	6	.600	3.34	35	11	4	105	113	38	49	2	3
1941	10	8	.556	2.82	35	18	8	153	126	59	93	2	3
1942	13	8	.619	2.98	34	20	8	160	137	60	93	2	2
1943	15	7	.682	1.90	32	25	14	213.1	195	75	123	2	3
1944	17	12	.586	2.65	33	30	16	224.1	192	71	141	5	0
1945	2	2	.500	1.73	4	3	3	26	22	8	16	0	0
1946	6	0	1.000	1.93	6	6	6	56	45	19	36	2	0
1949	5	4	.556	3.82	15	15	4	92	92	35	37	1	0
1950	11	9	.550	3.13	27	27	10	181.1	173	68	89	2	0
1951	11	9	.550	3.26	31	23	9	160	149	50	59	2	1
World Series													
1942	1	0	1.000	0.00	2	0	0	4	3	1	1	0	0
1943	0	1	.000	1.76	3	2	0	15.1	13	3	13	0	0
1944	1	0	1.000	2.19	2	2	0	12.1	8	8	11	0	0

MARK LITTELL

An Elbow Shy of a

World Series

In Chicago the night before Cardinal manager Whitey Herzog called Mark Littell into his Wrigley Field office, the relief pitcher was using teammate Glenn Brummer as a sounding board and a support.

Littell was 0-1 with an ERA over 5.00 and no saves. Worse, he was ineffective when he did pitch, and Herzog had become reluctant to use him. Littell told Brummer that "something was up." He felt team officials would either release him or send him to the minors to recapture his skills.

It was midway through the 1982 season, and the Cardinals were contending for a division flag. It was a lousy time for Littell's pitching elbow to act up. Brummer listened as Littell pondered his own immediate future which, as Herzog informed the nine-year major league veteran the next day, would be spent in Louisville.

Well, at least Littell was still in the Cardinal organization. Given time, anything could happen, right? Even a return to the team that in a few months would star in a ticker-tape parade in downtown St. Louis.

"I went to Louisville with the idea of stretching the elbow out and getting it back close to what it had been before," Littell recalled. "I pitched in a game, and I might have gone an inning at best.

"There was a meeting at the mound, and I pulled myself out of the game. I felt some real sharp pains, and I told them I couldn't pitch, that there was just too much pain. Heck, I couldn't even bend my arm. I told the Cardinals' front office that I couldn't pitch any more. They ended up sending me to Los Angeles to see Dr. Frank Jobe, the specialist, about my elbow.

"Actually, I knew what he was going to say, that it was all over, that my arm had had it. But I wanted to hear it from him."

Littell still can't bend his right arm as much as he would like. He can throw batting practice, he says, "but that's about it."

The players now taking their hacks at Littell's "BP" offerings are minor leaguers. Littel moves to the Charleston Rainbows, a Class A affiliate of the San Diego Padres, in 1990 after spending the 1989 season as a coach for the Midwest League's Waterloo Diamonds, a Class A ballclub in Waterloo, Iowa.

"It's fun because I get to see some of the crazy things that these kids do out there, things that remind me of my own minor league days.

"I kind of look back at all the adversity that I went through at that age and wonder how I managed to stick to it and make the big leagues. The travel, the buses, the pay, the small crowds at some of the ballparks, being away from home cooking and friends. Let's face it—the minor leagues can be tough for some kids.

"There are a lot of similarities between the kids playing in the low minors today and those of us who played fifteen, twenty years ago. But I think the aluminum bat they use in college programs is really screwing some kids up, not only from a hitting standpoint, but the people who sign them aren't getting an accurate reading of the talent before them.

"Also, college pitchers don't seem to want to come inside with a pitch because they know that hitters can fist the ball over the infield when they use an aluminum bat. Pitchers aren't going inside as much as they might if the batters were using wooden bats. Sometimes that mentality carries over into the minors."

After a few years away from it, Littell is glad to be back in baseball. On the field. Helping the up-and-comers. When he was forced to retire in 1982, the native Missourian took a job with the Cardinals in group sales. Still mentally wrestling, perhaps, with the realization that his playing days were over, Littell lasted about two months before he stepped away from his suit-and-tie job.

"I really wanted to be on a baseball field," Littell said. "Only trouble was, I didn't realize how hard it was to get back *on* the field. Throughout baseball, all the positions were filled. I contacted a lot of ballclubs, a lot of organizations, but nothing ever came of it.

"I began to think maybe I'd made the wrong decision, that I should have stayed in the Cardinals' front office. At least I would have been around the game. The Cardinal organization was always good to me, but I yearned to coach. I wanted to be outside, working with young players."

When the phone call he longed for didn't come, Littell renewed his own baseball camps to help St. Louis-area youngsters with the game's fundamentals. He had always worked with kids during the off-season anyway, and he felt his know-how and personal experiences in the bigs would still mean something to wide-eyed charges. To make ends meet, though, Littell worked in advertising for a time in St. Louis.

Littell's singleminded desire to teach was underscored in recent years when he traveled to Australia and did several weeks of baseball clinics as part of a program sponsored by the International Baseball Association.

Few people consider Australia a hotbed of baseball activity, but in Littell's hometown area of Gideon, Missouri, the game was almost a religion.

"It's a farming area about seventy miles south of Cape Girardeau, which is where I was born," Littell said. "Even though Gideon had only about 800 people when I was a kid growing up there, baseball was a very large factor in our lives. And a lot of people followed the Cardinals at that time.

"I played Little League, high school, American Legion. That's really where I was looked at by scouts, in Legion ball. We played sixty- or seventy-game schedules. But I was scouted in my last high school game, too, because we went to districts in Sikeston. A number of us were being scouted then. Must've been any-where from twenty to twenty-five scouts in the stands."

Littell was eventually signed by the Kansas City Royals, for whom he pitched from 1973 through 1977. He came to St. Louis by way of the trade that sent relief ace Al Hrabosky to K.C.

As a Royal, Littell put up decent numbers in 1976 and 1977, going 8-4 each year with 16 and 12 saves, respectively. Those indi-vidual successes, however, were tempered by the fact that in both years the Royals lost to the Yankees in the American League Championship Series, three games to two.

The 1976 season was especially bittersweet for Mark, who had played a major role in getting the Royals to the playoffs. With the score tied at six apiece in the bottom of the ninth, Chris Chambliss homered off him to win the decisive fifth game of the A.L.C.S. It would be the closest Littell ever got to a World Series appearance.

When Littell joined the Cardinals for the 1978 campaign, it was almost like coming home. As a kid of about eight, Littell saw his first big league game at Sportsman's Park. Sitting in the upper deck, he watched Stan Musial & Co. take on the Giants.

"I don't remember what Stan did that day, or even who won the game," Littell said. "Unfortunately, I do recall that Willie Mays hit two out that day—one to left and one over the big screen in right."

Left and right is a subject Littell knows something about: he throws right-handed and bats left-handed. How he developed that individual habit is explained by Mark thusly:

"I was not registered to play in the Little League program where we lived, but my dad knew one of the coaches and asked of the man if he would allow me to get in and participate a little bit. The man said, 'OK' and I soon found myself playing in a Little League game.

"I'd never really hit before, so in my first at-bat I went up to the left side of the plate and took a swing at a pitch and missed it. I said to the umpire, 'Could you hold it for just a minute? I think I'd like to try it from the other side.' He said it was OK, so I stepped over to the right side of the plate and swung and missed at a sec-ond pitch, too.

"I looked up at the umpire and said, 'You care if I get back to the other side?' He started laughin' and said, 'No, I don't mind.' So, I went *back* to the left side of the plate. By this time, everybody was laughin' at me. But this time—and I'll never forget it—I got a hit. My first time up and I got a hit. I know traditional wisdom says it's better for a pitcher to bat the same as he throws so his pitching arm is away from his opponent's pitches, but at age six my aspirations were not really major league at the time."

Life for Mark Littell after that first glorious hit included games of catch with his dad and his younger brother, Eric, who would later play baseball at Mississippi State. Laughing, Littell recalls how he and his brother would sometimes simply throw rocks at stationary targets "to hone all that raw talent we had."

Because he could throw hard, even as a youngster, Littell was good enough to be chosen to pitch and play shortstop for a traveling Little League squad that went from one area town to another. It was a big thing for a youngster to make that team of budding All-Stars, and Mark enjoyed his status to the hilt.

In 1971, Littell was signed out of high school by former major leaguer pitcher Gary Blaylock. Blaylock, who was 4-5 for the Cardinals in 1959, was also Littell's first manager in the minor leagues.

It was while in the minors, at Billings, when Littell was nicknamed "Country" by traveling hitting instructor Joe Gordon, himself the possessor of the moniker, "Flash."

"Of the two dozen or so guys on that team, maybe eighteen to twenty of 'em were from California," Littell said. "And a lot of guys in the Pioneer League at that time were older, more college-type guys. When they met me, with my Missouri drawl and firm handshake, and the fact that I'd grown up on a farm and everything, it was, you know, the country boy type of thing. One day around the batting cage Joe just kept saying, 'Where's that country boy? Where's he at?' The guys picked up on that and the name stuck."

George Brett was on that Billings team. Littell insists that the career Royal remains to this day "the loosest guy on the field—ever."

"I was involved in a game one time when the batter bunted the ball between George and me," Littell related. "George called me off, fielded the ball, pulled my cap down over my eyes and completed the play. That's loose."

Littell was a hard throwing, challenge them kind of hurler. Even after two surgeries—one in 1974 to work on the ulnar nerve and remove a spur; a major, second one in 1980 to remove bone chips and spurs, plus repair a deteriorating elbow joint—Mark Littell wanted the ball. Until he pulled himself from the mound in his Louisville "rehab" game in 1982, Littell never told his managers or coaches that he couldn't pitch, even on those occasions when he was in pain.

"I pitched in pain a lot of times in my career, which I probably shouldn't have done," Littell said. "But I was headstrong. I could have made it a lot easier on myself sometimes, but I was stubborn. But I'm human, and I did feel pain, especially after I came out of surgery in Los Angeles. That was probably the most pain I've ever felt in my life.

"Funny, I was the kind of pitcher who reared back and fired to home plate … just let it ride, you know? But now I've got to impress upon these young pitchers that rather than blast it by 'em every pitch, they've got to gain a sense of what they're doing out there. The batters will get themselves out if the pitcher knows what he's doing out there on the mound."

Actually, Littell did develop a forkball late in his career, and Cardinal pitching coach Hub Kittle helped him fine-tune it. Kittle was the last in a long line of pitching pros who helped Littell along the way; Blaylock, Galen Cisco, Claude Osteen and Bill Fischer were some of the others. Littell's best pitch was his slider, which had a good, sharp break to it. But he could get people out with his fastball, too.

Littell started nineteen games in his major league career (three as a Cardinal), but it was as a reliever where he had his greatest success. Interestingly, it was a former Cardinal relief ace who roomed with Littell in his rookie season in 1973: Lindy McDaniel.

"I was twenty years old and he was in his late thirties. I guess they wanted to pair the veteran with the rookie to keep me out of trouble. Some of the best words of advice I ever got were from him. He told me not to try anything weird or different with my pitching, just stay within myself and work with what got me to the big leagues in the first place.

"I enjoyed my time in St. Louis," Littell said. "I think I was treated fairly by the fans and the press, which in my case there was no guarantee of that. People probably think it must be wonderful to pitch in your home state, to be a homegrown product and play in the big leagues, but that can make it tougher on a player, too. It's almost like an extended family of hundreds or even thousands. They want you to do well. They share in your good outings and bad. But they *do* expect more of you sometimes.

"At the professional level a guy has to say, 'To heck with it. I can't let any additional pressures affect my performances. This is baseball. This is a game. This is what I like to do. Just give me the ball.' "

Mark Littell—Cardinal Stats

	W	L	PCT	ERA	G	GS	CG	IP	H	BB	SO	SHO	SV
1978	4	8	.333	2.80	72	2	0	106	80	59	130	0	11
1979	9	4	.692	2.20	63	0	0	82	60	39	67	0	13
1980	0	2	.000	9.00	14	0	0	11	14	7	7	0	2
1981	1	3	.250	4.39	28	1	0	41	36	31	22	0	2
1982	0	1	.000	5.23	16	0	0	20.2	22	15	7	0	0

MARTY MARION

A Pre-Ozzie

Shortstop Star

Long before the birth of Cardinals star Ozzie Smith, another shortstop was the toast of St. Louis. Like Smith, he gained his early fame from spectacular defense instead of superb hitting. Like Smith, this 1940s spark plug was a surprisingly clutch hitter when games were on the line. The name of this "wizard" was Marty Marion.

"The Octopus" was a fitting title for a man who writers once said was "all arms and legs, but he can reach across the whole infield." Even the U.S. Postal Service knew of Marion's fabled reputation in St. Louis. "Once, I got a large envelope sent from a fan," he remembers. "It arrived at the ballpark, and had a large octopus painted on the front. There was no name or address on it, but I got it anyway."

From 1940 through 1950, Marion patrolled the St. Louis infield. After his retirement, while he refrained from comparing himself to Smith, he talked about the different challenges facing shortstops of his day. Playing in Sportsman's Park was one of the first obstacles. "Being an infielder, I used to call it 'The Brickyard,' " he says with a laugh. "It was the worst infield in baseball. You really had to guard yourself. I didn't want a bad hop to knock my teeth out. We had two teams playing in the ballpark and the field never got any rest. And, with the hot summers, even the infield grass had trouble surviving."

However, the biggest obstacle Marion encountered was staying healthy. Numerous injuries, some before his career began, made full-time work difficult for the ailing infielder. "I used to room with Dr. Weaver [the team physician] because they had a hard time keeping me in the lineup," Marion says, recounting how a minor league back injury plagued him for more than a decade. "I wore a corset all the time, and could hardly bend over. Late in my career, starting about 1946, I could hardly make it. I'd sit in the dugout and get chills." Painful spasms made Marion's back muscles as hard as the stadium concrete. Whenever the team played road games, the beleaguered Cardinal would spend nights sleeping on hotel floors. Normal beds weren't firm enough to support his temperamental back.

Long before his back gave him problems, Marion's athletic future was in doubt. At age nine, a near-tragic accident left him on crutches for more than a year. During his childhood in Atlanta, Georgia, Marion and his friends enjoyed playing in the woods. One day during a game of "Cowboys and Indians," young Marty tried jumping off a high embankment. He wound up with a broken leg. Worst of all, his frightened friends left him alone after he was injured.

"My father was coming home to pick me up for a dentist appointment," Marion recalls. "When Daddy got home, he found out the kids had run off and left me. When he asked them where I was, they said I was in the woods. I was by myself and couldn't move. I had a compound fracture; the bone was sticking through the skin between the knee and the hip." After a stint in traction, another shock came. "A couple of months later, they X-rayed. My leg had regrown an inch-and-a-half shorter than the other leg. The doctors went in and broke the leg again. I had forty-eight stitches, and they wired me back together. I still have wire in that leg."

Naturally, Marion's parents were worried that their son was

vulnerable to future injuries. "I drove my mother crazy. She was always screaming at the boys, 'Don't touch Marty, you may hurt his leg.' I was kind of the pet of the family because I was so frail. Mother was always trying to protect me from sports." Marion did sneak in a few informal games of football with other youngsters. The only organized sport he tackled, though, was baseball.

"I played at Tech High School in Atlanta. We won the state championship every year I was there," he says. "When I was out of school, there was a tryout camp north of Atlanta in Rome, Georgia. I tried out and the scouts liked me. I only played two innings, then they pulled me aside and asked, 'How would you like to go to St. Louis to let them look at you?' " Obviously, Marion jumped at the chance, and got a late-season workout in Sportsman's Park in 1935.

Unlike many of the Midwestern youngsters the Cardinals signed in the 1930s, Marion didn't have the same reverence for a team halfway across the country. "I had no love for the Cardinals. I didn't even know who the Cardinals were," he admits. "The Tigers were my favorite team, because I had an uncle who lived in Detroit. Living in Atlanta, you didn't know much about major league baseball. The Atlanta Crackers, a minor league club, were the closest thing we had."

But how did the Cardinals feel about Marion? The answer was found in the unusual four-year contract he received from the team. Four-year deals for any players were unusual. For a minor leaguer, such an agreement was even more stunning. "I was a good player and a pretty fair businessman," Marion says. After his career was over, Marion would back up his claim by owning a minor league team in Houston in 1960. During his career, Marion was a vocal supporter of a pension plan for former players. He handled tight-fisted team officials as well as hard hit grounders.

Marion began his career making $150 a month for the Cardinals' affiliate in Huntington, West Virginia. He was promoted to Rochester of the International League in 1937, where he spent the next three seasons. "When I made the Cardinals, I had been paid $5,000 a year for the last two seasons," he says proudly. "That's pretty good money for a rookie in those days." Even more than the amount itself, however, Marion seems most satisfied that he could get *any* money from frugal general manager Branch Rickey.

"Mr. Rickey was quite a man," Marion says. "He was a negotiator, no matter who you were. Even after you became a star, Mr. Rickey always wanted to cut you. Even if you just finished the best year in the world, he never thought about giving you a raise. That was his starting point. By the time negotiations were through, you'd think that a $1,000 raise was a big thing!"

Don't think that Rickey's overzealous guarding of the team's pursestrings made players disloyal, Marion interjects. "Back then, if I hadn't played for the Cardinals, I couldn't play for anybody," he says. "You were signed to a team forever, until they decided to get rid of you. You couldn't negotiate for yourself anywhere else. They had a lock on you. Plus, you knew that they had so many players in the minors who were as good as you were, waiting to take your job. When Mr. Rickey said, 'We're giving you a chance to play,' he was about right! At least he was giving you a chance."

Besides a long-term contract, the Cardinals quickly gave Marion a lasting nickname. Burt Shotton, best known for managing the Brooklyn Dodgers while wearing streetclothes, dubbed Marion "Slats" while managing the Cardinals' affiliate in Columbus. "In spring training before I was sent to Huntington, Shotton gave me the nickname," Marion remembers. "There was a comic strip about a tall, skinny kid named Slats. Also, people call a long, thin board a slat."

When the Cardinals lost Leo Durocher after 1937, no dominant personality claimed the shortstop's job. Although Marion was an offensive question mark, St. Louis made him a starter in 1940. He responded with a tidy .278 batting mark in 125 games. In his sophomore season, Marion was active in a career-high 155 games. While his average dropped to .252, he pounded 3 homers and 58 RBI. Today's eighth-place hitters would kill for such offensive success.

In 1941, Marion teamed with Frank "Creepy" Crespi, "the best second baseman I ever played with, at least for a single season." Marion describes Crespi as "a real lazy kid, but one with great talent. He could handle shortstop as well as second base." Sadly, after excelling in 146 games in 1941, Crespi's career was extinguished by a broken leg in World War II. But in discussing annual consistency, Marion points to double play partner Red

Schoendienst. "Overall, Red was the best. He did the job at second every year."

The baseball world fully recognized Marion in 1942, when his club whipped the Yankees in a five-game World Series. Marion led the National League with 38 doubles, and he batted .276. Although he hit just .111 in the Series, Marion gained the most attention for combining with catcher Walker Cooper to pick Joe Gordon off second base in the fifth game of the Series. Ironically, Marion remembers the incident today as a routine play. "That's the kind of play that just happens with men on first and second, when the bunt is in order," he says. "The runner tries to get a good break off second during the bunt so he won't get thrown out. The batter missed, and I broke in back of Gordon. He just got caught off. It wasn't so much that we were so great. It was Joe being a pretty bad baserunner. I was in the right spot at the right time. But it came in a timely spot."

Being a member of a World Championship squad elevated Marion's performance in 1943. He tallied 1 homer, 52 RBI and a .280 average. "When you play with better players, you become better yourself," Marion explains. "Play with jerks, and you'll be a jerk." According to Marion, he felt more confident than ever at the plate in 1943. "I was pretty good, especially with men on base. The players used to laugh and say, 'We'd rather see Marty up there with a man on third than Musial.' " Musial once told Marion, "To have a good average, you have to bear down every time you're up to bat." But for the lanky shortstop, bearing down was easier in dramatic moments. "If we were winning by a lopsided score, I wasn't nearly as intent on hitting. I didn't take it as serious. I'd hardly get any hits if we beat someone 12-0. But I hit the most during a tough game, when the outcome meant something." Marion knew the importance of the 1943 World Series, a rematch against the Yankees. Although New York avenged its five-game loss from the previous season, Marion batted .357. Among his five hits were two doubles and a home run, which provided the winning margin in the team's 4-3 win in game two.

In 1944, Marion was named the National League Most Valuable Player and baseball's Player of the Year. He was the first shortstop in baseball history to win the MVP. Previously, only leading hitters and noted pitchers won the honor. Although his stats (.267

with a career high of 6 homers) were respectable, it was clear that other contributions gained Marion distinction. Why was he selected? He credits his unseen accomplishments, the achievements not always present in box scores. "I was a leader. Everyone looked up to me. Everything I did was for the team," he says. "I had several game-winning hits, and I took away a lot of hits at shortstop." All of these elements helped the Cardinals regain their World Championship with a six-game triumph over the St. Louis Browns.

While a natural "city series" type rivalry flared in 1944 post-season play, Marion says that the Cardinals hadn't looked down on their American League relatives. "The guys who wore the Browns uniform were just as good as the guys in the Cardinals jerseys. We were lucky to beat them. The Browns outdrew us that year. The town went crazy over the Browns, because everyone loves an underdog."

As evidenced by his 1944 awards, Marion commanded a lot of respect with sportswriters. "They appreciate talent, that's all," he explained. "The press has always been good to me. You've got to be a really no-good guy for the press to dislike you." Marion still seems baffled by current stars who won't talk to the media. "I never saw anything like that in my career. I never remembered anyone who wouldn't talk to the press. The more publicity you got, the more money you could make."

Broadcaster Harry Caray started broadcasting Cardinals games in 1945. "I knew that Harry was a damn good announcer," Marion says. "He'd always come down to the bench, and we became good friends. Harry got a lot of criticism then, because he wanted to manage the team while behind the microphone. He kind of ran the ballpark from the booth. But a lot of guys with a pen or mike like to second-guess you. Harry was very opinionated, and he had the gift of gab like crazy. I don't think there was anyone better."

Marion remembers his health starting to decline in 1946, the year the Cardinals beat Boston in the World Series. The Georgia native continued as the team's full-time shortstop through 1950. In 1951, he retired and became the Cardinals manager. "I could have played, but I was in such misery. It just didn't seem worth it." As pilot of the Cards, Marion posted an 81-73 record, good for third place. He played seventy games for the Browns while managing the club in 1952 and 1953. Marion joined the White Sox coaching staff in 1954, and skippered the team for the next two campaigns.

Looking back, Marion says little about his individual career statistics, which included a .263 lifetime average in 1,572 games. "I'm not much for records," he says. "I never cared about how many hits I got, as long as we won. Today's players are more protective and play for themselves. That's why lots of good players never get in the World Series. If you're selfish and just care about your own stats, you won't be on championship teams. We sacrificed ourselves to win."

Marion talks proudly of living in St. Louis even today, and "becoming one of the community" after retirement. His memories of the Cardinals are just as glowing. "I think most about the players I played with. They made the organization. Mr. Rickey and [team owner] Sam Breadon tried to get players as cheap as they could. But when I walked out on the field with the Cardinals uniform on, I didn't think of them. I thought of Joe Medwick, Musial and Schoendienst.

"That's who the Cardinals are. That's where the memories come from."

Marty Marion—Cardinal Stats

	G	AB	H	2B	3B	HR	R	RBI	BB	SO	SB	BA	SA
1940	125	435	121	18	1	3	44	46	21	34	9	.278	.345
1941	155	547	138	22	3	3	50	58	42	48	8	.252	.320
1942	147	485	134	38	5	0	66	54	48	50	8	.276	.375
1943	129	418	117	15	3	1	38	52	32	37	1	.280	.337
1944	144	506	135	26	2	6	50	63	43	50	1	.267	.362
1945	123	430	119	27	5	1	63	59	39	39	2	.277	.370
1946	146	498	116	29	4	3	51	46	59	53	1	.233	.325
1947	149	540	147	19	6	4	57	74	49	58	3	.272	.352
1948	144	567	143	26	4	4	70	43	37	54	1	.252	.333
1949	134	515	140	31	2	5	61	70	37	42	0	.272	.369
1950	106	372	92	10	2	4	36	40	44	55	1	.247	.317
World Series													
1942	5	18	2	0	1	0	2	3	1	2	0	.111	.222
1943	5	14	5	2	0	1	1	2	3	1	1	.357	.714
1944	6	22	5	3	0	0	1	2	2	3	0	.227	.364
1946	7	24	6	2	0	0	1	4	1	1	0	.250	.333

DAL MAXVILL

Broken Windows,

but No Shattered

Dreams

It was the summer of '42. Or was it in 1943? Dal Maxvill can't recall. Besides, the important thing for him was that Stan Musial was roaming the outfield that warm day in Sportsman's Park. And sitting in the stands were Maxvill and his parents, eager to see the Cardinals nail down another victory on their way to a National League pennant.

There is something cyclical about Maxvill's story as it relates to the Cardinal legend. Dal was a pitcher at one time (as was Musial), who played on back-to-back Cardinal pennant winners (as did Musial), became a successful businessman in St. Louis (as did Musial), and eventually was named the club's general manager (as was Musial). And of course, "The Man" and his fan were teammates in the early 1960s.

But during the war years of the 1940s, when Musial was hitting his stride, Dal Maxvill was growing up in a middle class section of Granite City, Illinois, just next door to St. Louis.

"There weren't any baseball fields as such where I lived," Maxvill said, "but there were a couple of empty yards scat-

tered around the neighborhood where we played ball. We always had enough kids to get up a game.

"I remember that we sometimes ended up breaking a few windows, which was the normal thing to happen when kids play baseball in yards near people's homes. Sometimes we moved faster when we broke a window than we did running the bases."

When they weren't hightailing it off of their makeshift diamonds, Maxvill and Co. could be seen playing organized baseball on the area's Little League diamonds.

A truism of baseball—at least in one's formative years—is the kid with the strongest arm is usually chosen by his coach to pitch. Maxvill was chosen to pitch. And when he wasn't on the mound, he was playing shortstop. By the time he was playing American Legion and high school ball, however, Maxvill had completely abandoned pitching for his duties at shortstop.

The Cardinals were one of several major league clubs scouting the slick-fielding Maxvill. But tempting as it may have been to give pro ball a try, he decided instead to attend Washington University in St. Louis, and wound up playing for his collegiate team.

He attended tryout camps with the Washington Senators and the Pittsburgh Pirates, and talked to scouts from various other teams. But Maxvill, Cardinal fan that he was, signed with St. Louis after his senior year at Washington "U" in 1960.

"Kenny Boyer was the biggest help to me when I first came up to the Cardinals," Maxvill said. "Kenny was a veteran player when I joined the club. Red Schoendienst, another veteran who later became a coach and manager for us, was another one. Those two fellas, more than anyone I can think of, helped me make the adjustment to the big leagues.

"I think when I was first called up in 1962, the club looked at me as a possible backup-type guy. At the time I don't think they ever projected me as being a starting player, because they had signed other people who they felt would be everyday players. But after several years of mostly sitting around and doing the job whenever I was called on, they gave me an opportunity to play every day and I made the most of it."

The Cardinals in 1962 had Julian Javier at second and Julio Gotay at short, leaving little playing time for Maxvill. Maxvill appeared in 79 games, and finished with only 189 at-bats. About a month after the season ended, the Cardinals swapped Gotay and pitcher Don Cardwell to the Pirates for shortstop Dick Groat and pitcher Diomedes Olivo.

So, as the 1963 campaign opened, Maxvill was once again fitted for the robe of the Cardinals' bench jockey choir—this time to sing the praises of the veteran Groat, who went on to have one of his best years at the plate. Maxvill appeared in just fifty-three games that year, and only thirty-seven in 1964, when the Cardinals mounted their furious pennant drive in the final two weeks of the season and won the National League flag by a game over the Phillies and Reds.

In the World Series, Maxvill played second base in all seven games, and fielded flawlessly. He also singled in a run in the seventh game against the New York Yankees. For the Cardinals and their fans, the Series ended, happily, when "Maxie" caught a pop-up off the bat of his opposite number on defense, Bobby Richardson, to seal the victory, 7-5.

"It was a great feeling to be part of that World Championship team," Maxvill said, "especially the way we won the pennant on the last day of the season and then took the Series from New York in seven games. But in '64 I was an extra guy who didn't really have an opportunity to help a whole lot *until* the World Series, because Javier had gotten hurt and I filled in at second.

"So for that reason, I think '67 was the most exciting year for me personally because I contributed more. I was one of the regulars. I was in nearly 155 games, out there doing something to help the team almost every game that season. To me, that year stands out more than the others."

Something else that stands out in Maxvill's memory: the National League infields. And, like many of his generation, Maxvill's career spanned the period when dirt and grass diamonds gave way to artificial surfaces.

"I don't think anybody really enjoyed playing on the Dodger infield in Los Angeles," Maxvill recalled. "I understand they've improved on it considerably, but back then, with its hard, red clay, it was a tough infield. Shea Stadium was a tough place to field the ball. I liked Cincinnati. I liked the infields at Philadelphia and San Diego, too. Sportsman's was OK, and Busch.

"When Astroturf was first introduced in the mid-1960s, we

used to go out and take a lot of ground balls to get ready for it. It was such a new experience for all the ballplayers, both defensively and offensively, and we had to work at it. Originally, the 'dome featured an all-natural playing surface. You know, grass and dirt, just like any outdoor ballpark. But when club officials learned that grass would not grow under the 'dome, they installed Astroturf but left the basepaths dirt clear around the infield. That was really bad because the ball would really skip off the Astroturf and get to us in a hurry, but on that next hop—off the dirt—you didn't know how it was gonna react.

"When the Cardinals organization first installed an artificial surface at Busch Stadium in the early '70s, we also had a dirt and Astroturf infield, and it was bad here, too. Now, of course, the ballparks that feature artificial surfaces just have the dirt sliding pits around the bags. But playing on Astroturf back then was a challenge for the ballplayers."

Maxvill met those challenges throughout his career. In 1968 he was selected as the shortstop on *The Sporting News* N.L. Gold Glove All-Star Fielding Team, an honor bestowed on him by club managers and coaches.

As a member of three Cardinal squads that saw post-season action in the 1960s, Maxvill is qualified to speak on the makeup of each. They were, he acknowledges, quite different from one another.

"On the first club, 1964, there were many veteran players, with Kenny Boyer, Bill White, Dick Groat, Curt Simmons, Barney Schultz, people like that, who starred for us. There was a confidence, a maturity, on that team that contributed a lot, I think, to our winning that wild pennant race down the stretch.

"Later on, with the '67 and '68 clubs, we had more young guys it seemed: myself, Shannon, Brock, Flood, McCarver, and a somewhat younger pitching staff, with Carlton and Briles and Jaster and Washburn and Hoerner. And I guess because I was an everyday player by then, I really saw how winning breeds an awful lot of confidence in young players.

"The people we had on those two clubs—'67 and '68—just had a real professional spirit about them, the way they approached their jobs. After a game they liked to relax and have a good time, but when it was time to play baseball, you had a group of real professionals out there.

"I'm not much on recalling anecdotes. I can't tell you stories about the guys, or crazy plays or strange incidents that happened on the field. But what I do remember about those years is how fortunate I was to be part of three teams that went to the World Series and won two of them. The sense of unity, the feeling I got from being part of something very special—that's what I feel inside me when I look back on my years in a Cardinal uniform."

But baseball is a business, and Maxvill had to exchange his Cardinal uniform for that of the Oakland Athletics in late August of 1972. The Cardinals got two minor leaguers in the trade, neither of whom would make the majors. Less than a year later, Maxvill went to the Pittsburgh Pirates in a cash deal. But in 1974 he was back at Oakland. He was a pinch runner and late inning replacement at second base for the A's in the World Series against the Dodgers. With the A's in 1975 he closed out his fourteen-year major league career.

"I knew when I finished playing I wanted to stay in the game, but I didn't know for sure if I wanted to stay in the game *on the field,* á la coaching or managing," Maxvill said.

"I had several chances to manage in the minor leagues for a couple different organizations, but I turned them down because I wasn't sure I wanted to go in that direction. I thought about the front office, player development, scouting ... I thought about a lot of things. Fortunately, when the Cardinals were looking for a general manager a few years ago they interviewed me along with several other people and I was offered the job."

Maxvill left baseball for a time once he hung up his spikes after the 1975 season. (He and former Cardinal teammate Joe Hoerner have for many years owned and operated a successful travel agency in the St. Louis area called Cardinal Travel.)

He joined the New York Mets coaching staff in 1978, but returned to the Cardinal organization the following year as a coach. In 1982 the Atlanta Braves tabbed him as their new third base coach, where Maxvill flashed signs to a Braves team that won the National League Western Division that year but lost the N.L. Championship Series to the Cardinals in three straight games.

Maxvill served with the Braves until he was named Cardinals general manager in February 1985. He maintains that his experiences as a player and coach help him in his current role as team vice president/general manager.

"I understand the atmosphere, the mentality, the difficulties that go on in a clubhouse—both at home and on the road— during the course of a season," Maxvill said. "I have the perspective of having been out there on the field and experiencing the boos as well as the cheers. I know it's not that easy to perform at the major league level. I appreciate the pressures these guys have to face game after game.

"When things go well for the team the credit goes to the players on the field, and to some extent the manager and his coaches, which is the way it should be. When things don't go well the fans look to the front office to place blame. That's natural. I knew that when I accepted this position. And regardless of how the team is doing on the field, in the front office there aren't too many cheers or much applause. But I *am* back with the Cardinals, back in St. Louis, where it all started for me."

Dal Maxvill—Cardinal Stats

	G	AB	H	2B	3B	HR	R	RBI	BB	SO	SB	BA	SA
1962	79	189	42	3	1	1	20	18	17	39	1	.222	.265
1963	53	51	12	2	0	0	12	3	6	11	0	.235	.275
1964	37	26	6	0	0	0	4	4	0	7	1	.231	.231
1965	68	89	12	2	2	0	10	10	7	15	0	.135	.202
1966	134	394	96	14	3	0	25	24	37	61	3	.244	.294
1967	152	476	108	14	4	1	37	41	48	66	0	.227	.279
1968	151	459	116	8	5	1	51	24	52	71	0	.253	.298
1969	132	372	65	10	2	2	27	32	44	52	1	.175	.228
1970	152	399	80	5	2	0	35	28	51	56	0	.201	.223
1971	142	356	80	10	1	0	31	24	43	45	1	.225	.258
1972	105	276	61	6	1	1	22	23	31	47	0	.221	.261
World Series													
1964	7	20	4	1	0	0	0	1	1	4	0	.200	.250
1967	7	19	3	0	1	0	1	1	4	1	0	.158	.263
1968	7	22	0	0	0	0	1	0	3	5	0	.000	.000

LINDY McDANIEL

A Belief System

That Worked

Lindy McDaniel has given thought to someday writing a book about his life in and out of baseball. As far as Cardinal relief aces go, he "wrote the book" in 1960: 65 appearances, 26 saves, a 2.09 ERA, and a 12-4 record.

In his heyday the righty fired a good sinking fastball, broke a nasty curve and hurled a forkball that sent enemy batters muttering back to the dugout. He threw both sidearm and straight overhand, and his control was superb. Playing for five different major league teams over a twenty-one year span, McDaniel cultivated a winning record and notched 172 saves.

Lyndall Dale McDaniel grew up on the family farm in Hollis, Oklahoma. He and his brothers, Von and Kerry Don, helped their father with the chores around the farm, but there were brief respites from chores for a game of "scrub" or "workup" with kids from neighboring farms or softball with classmates on the school playground.

"At home we'd play catch more often than not," Lindy remembered, "because there wasn't a lot of time we could take off. When we were kids we made our gloves out of burlap sacks. Every once in a while we'd get a store-bought ball, and we'd play with it until the leather would fall off. Then we'd tape it up and keep playing with it till we lost it.

"We might have a piece of wood or an old broom handle or something to hit the ball, but mostly, we didn't bat a lot. I know our dad brought a bat home one time, and one whack and it was broken.

"I started playing organized baseball in high school. We had just barely enough players to make a team. There were only about forty kids in the whole school, so we might have had one, maybe two, substitutes. I played shortstop and pitched, which is normal for young players. But I progressed so fast as a freshman that our coach, Rooster Jones, wanted me to try out for the American Legion team in Altus, forty miles away.

"My dad had to drive me to Altus just so I could try out with the team. But I made it, and I was only fifteen. That team consisted basically of country players from around Altus. They played a lot of baseball throughout that area. In fact, in high school they would play some forty games in the spring, and that year in American Legion we'd play something like seventy-two games. Then in the fall they have a season, also, so we'd play about thirty games then. You're talking about a lot of baseball for young kids."

It's not surprising, then, that McDaniel quickly developed into a talented young pitcher who played for a pair of state championship teams in the early 1950s. Also not surprising is that the Cardinals at this point began to scout his progress. A few years later, when McDaniel was pitching semi-pro ball in Texas, he also caught the eye of the Phillies organization. But, it was the Cardinal organization that had McDaniel's loyalty.

"Our American Legion team made a trip to St. Louis in '52," McDaniel said. "We played the top American Legion team from that area right in Sportsman's Park. I got to meet Stan Musial and some of the others, and it's something I'll never forget. Having read about the Cardinals in the newspapers or listening to games on the radio, it was a thrill for me to be there. What kid wouldn't be thrilled?

"So, about mid-season in '55, when I was in Sinton [Texas], I took another trip to St. Louis and tried out for the team. My dad went with me. We rode in a Thunderbird with the Cardinal scout. I figured the team needed pitching, and with my strong amateur background I felt I could make the Cardinals' pitching staff. Everything worked out right for me while I was there for the tryout.

"The first day they gave me an old uniform and I just threw to a batting practice catcher along the sidelines. Harry Walker was managing the Cardinals then, and he came up to me at one point and told me, 'We'd like to see you again tomorrow.' And I turned to Harry and said, 'Don't you want to see me cut loose?' He said, 'Aren't you cutting loose now?' I said, 'No, I'm just warming up,' and I buzzed a few in there and the next day Harry had me throw batting practice.

"I wasn't throwing to any of the starters. Still, these guys were major leaguers, and even though they knew the fastball was coming, for the most part, they were not hitting it solid. So Harry —who was a good hitter in his day—took some cuts, and he was doing the same thing with my pitches: hitting them into the ground or popping them up. I had good control.

"He told me to come back the next day, which I did, and when I showed 'em my curveball, that was it. He took me into the main office. They wanted to sign me right there."

But the Cardinal officials present at that meeting wanted Lindy to tell them what he wanted as his salary. Thinking back to what an old family friend once told Lindy's father after seeing Lindy pitch, the brash young guest of general manager Bing Devine said, "$50,000."

Even Devine intervention couldn't make that wish come true. But "Der Bingle's" phone call to owner Gussie Busch, with Walker espousing Lindy's talents, did. The Cardinals' latest "bonus baby" joined the parent club about a week later. Making two starts and two relief appearances, McDaniel had no decisions to show for his 4.74 ERA. In 19 innings he gave up 22 hits, 4 of them home runs.

"When I took the mound in Chicago the plate looked like it was a mile away and the batters looked like they were ten feet tall," McDaniel remembers. "I felt lucky just to get the ball over the plate. The second hitter was Walker Cooper, a former Cardinal who was playing for the Cubs by then, and he hit a ball over the wall. That was the only damage, I think.

"Then I started a game in St. Louis. It was against the Cubs, and I shut 'em out for about the first four innings or so. Then in the fifth Ernie Banks came up with the bases loaded. No one told me *not* to throw the fastball to him on the inside part of the plate, so I did and he hit it out for his fifth grand slam of the year. The game was tied when I left, and even though I didn't win or lose any games that September, I did gain some experience."

McDaniel was used as a reliever and spot starter in 1956 by manager Fred Hutchinson. Going 7-6 with a 3.41 ERA was an improvement over his inaugural season, but McDaniel made a greater impression the following year, when he went 12-9 as a starter and 3-0 as a reliever.

McDaniel says the best thing about the 1957 campaign—and perhaps the biggest thrill of his career—was that his eighteen-year-old brother, Von, was brought up by the Cardinals to join their starting rotation. Von posted a respectable 7-5 record that year, but then, mysteriously, he "lost it" in 1958 and spent the next few years trying to make it back to the big leagues as an infielder.

"Von had a smooth delivery," Lindy said, "and tremendous poise for a young player. Nobody knows for sure what happened. He just developed arm trouble and that was it. And Kerry Don, we thought he'd be the best because he had an outstanding record in high school and American Legion ball, but he never developed in pro ball after he started having back trouble."

Lindy slipped to 5-7 with a 5.78 ERA in 1958, but fared better in 1959 when he was moved to the bullpen. Although it was fourteen up and twelve down in decisions for him, McDaniel did save fifteen games. Part way through the season, pitching coach Howie Pollet suggested a change in McDaniel's delivery, and the sidearmer started pitching overhand. It worked like a charm. For the next three months McDaniel came over the top with his fastball and curve. The bonus baby was growing up.

"The forkball was something I picked up with the help of my brother," McDaniel said, "and 1960 was when I put it all together. Once I understood the grip and the release and everything, it didn't really take me all that long to perfect it. I think I gave up two hits on the forkball all year, and got most of my strike-outs with it.

"Most people remember me for the forkball, because I used it to finish off a lot of hitters. But my control was good, and my fastball was always what set everything up."

McDaniel remembers well the ballparks in which he pitched. Sportsman's was one of his favorites because of the hometown fans. Dodger Stadium in Los Angeles was another because of the mound clay ("You could just stop dead when your foot came down—great leverage because your foot didn't slide any," he says.), and Yankee Stadium because "center and left center field were Death Valley for hitters." Old Ebbets Field, however, was not one of his choice "vacation spots," even though he recalls pitching well on the Dodgers' home turf.

"It seemed like something would always go wrong there," McDaniel said. "I lost one game 2-1, when Jim Gilliam stole home, and I lost another game by a run when Charlie Neal hit a home run to straightaway center field. I may have been 0-4 at Ebbets Field, so I was very happy when they moved out of Brooklyn and relocated in L.A."

McDaniel has not forgotten the National League hitters who consistently hurt him, either. Names such as Willie Mays, Red Schoendienst, Richie Ashburn and Jerry Lynch. If Lynch doesn't ring a bell with today's younger fans, let them know the former Pirate and Red outfielder ranks fifth all-time among the game's leading pinch hitters with 116 safeties. He led the league in pinch-hits in 1960 and 1961, and finished his career as a .277 hitter.

"He hit three home runs off me," McDaniel said. "What he'd do is go up there and look for a pitcher's best pitch on that given day, and wait for it. Over the course of several meetings, Jerry hit a home run off my fastball, one off my curveball and one off my forkball. He wasn't too particular with me."

"Mays also gave me a lot of trouble, mainly because of dumb pitching against him. Most of the home runs he hit off me were off my fastball. The first time I pitched against him the players told me that you could start Mays inside and go up the ladder with him—just keep going higher with each pitch, so I did.

"I threw the first pitch high and inside to him and he swung and missed. I went up a little higher with him on the next pitch and he swung and fouled it off. I went up higher still on the third pitch and he sent it over the fence."

Episodes such as that one aside, once McDaniel got a taste of success in relief, that is what he wanted to do. He relished being called in to snuff out an opponent's rally. He wanted to be the guy who rewarded his manager's faith in him. McDaniel wanted the ball. That could be a double-edged sword, however, and McDaniel says there were times when he *was* the bullpen. If he was having a bad outing or a series of bad outings, the ballclub probably didn't have anyone else to protect a lead.

"I might be called on to pitch as early as the sixth inning," McDaniel said, "and I would be expected to go the rest of the way. That was kind of hard, carrying that much load.

"Today, relieving is more specialized, with guys being brought in to pitch to one hitter before being removed for another reliever to get the next hitter out. Relief pitching has gone through a lot of transitions over the years. It's also thought of more highly than it once was."

The Cardinals always thought highly of McDaniel. At least, until October 17, 1962, when they traded him, along with Larry Jackson and Jimmie Schaffer, to the Cubs in exchange for George Altman, Don Cardwell and Moe Thacker. McDaniel had gone 10-6 with 9 saves and 3-10 with 14 saves in the two years following his 1960 masterwork. Also, the earned run averages those two seasons—4.88 and 4.12—were helping fan the flames of his opponents' big innings.

"I don't really blame the Cardinals for the trade," McDaniel said. "They gave up on me. They'd lost confidence in my ability to close off an inning the way I could before. Sometimes I think I was the only one who still believed I could do it, that I could put it together again. I've always said that if I'd had the same year with the Cardinals that I had with the Cubs in '63, I would probably have stayed in a Cardinal uniform for several years more."

And what a year he had with Chicago: a league-leading 22 saves, a 2.86 ERA, and a 13-7 won-lost record, all in relief. Shades of 1960.

He would pitch for the Cubs for two more years before going to San Francisco in the trade that brought catcher Randy Hundley and pitcher Bill Hands to Chicago. McDaniel stayed with the Giants for just over two years, then was traded to the Yankees, with whom he made a magnificent comeback in 1970 when he posted 29 saves, a 2.01 ERA and a 9-5 record. The veteran closer closed out his career with the Royals in 1974 and 1975. While with Kansas City, the former Cardinal pitcher roomed with a future one, Mark Littell.

McDaniel's career totals include 141 wins, 119 losses, 172 saves, a 3.45 ERA, and more than twice as many strikeouts as walks of opposing batters.

He made what he calls "a clean break" from baseball after he announced his retirement. For McDaniel, leaving the game wasn't tough; making adjustments in his personal life was. A failed marriage left him devastated, and plans for farming and preaching fell through. Yet despite all that, McDaniel was able to make another comeback—not in baseball, but in life.

"My religious beliefs really helped me face different crises over the years," said McDaniel, who put out a Christian paper for twelve years while in the big leagues. The tract was sent to major league players and fans, and McDaniel had a mailing list at one time of nearly 10,000.

Today, his home life once again on an even keel thanks to a very supportive wife, McDaniel preaches a non-denominational message in Las Vegas, New Mexico. It's a natural follow-up to his nine years of preaching the New Testament at a church in Kansas City.

"Baseball was always very good to me in that respect," McDaniel pointed out. "They knew I was going to worship on the first day of the week and that I'd be late to the ballpark on Sundays. I brought my strong religious upbringing into baseball, and baseball accepted that. That's one of the things that I want to deal with if I ever get around to writing a book: how to deal with the fact that a player is a Christian in baseball, and the problems and real-world conflicts that can cause."

McDaniel, now fifty-four, doesn't always scan the box scores in the newspaper or tune in to radio and TV to catch baseball's current events. He says he thinks of himself as the kind of fan whose senses are heightened at playoff and World Series time.

But he is proud of his accomplishments in baseball, and maintains a sense of loyalty to St. Louis and to the Cardinals. In

August of 1989, Lindy participated in his first-ever baseball card show, held in the city where he got his start as a nineteen-year-old rookie thirty-five years ago. Seated with him at the signing table was his brother, Von.

"The first team you play with, at least for me, was like having my boyhood dreams come true," Lindy said. "Wearing the Cardinal uniform, the uniform of my heroes, the guys I read about or heard about as a kid, players I looked up to...there's a lot of sentimentality connected with that.

"And there were some fine *people* on those clubs: Musial, Schoendienst, Bill Sarni, Vinegar Bend Mizell, Julian Javier and Hal Smith. Hal was perhaps the most underrated ballplayer of all, the only catcher I played with who I never had to worry about throwing one in the dirt, because he could block it. He played great defense and called a good game.

"But after you're traded you kind of lose some of that innocence, I guess. You quickly learn that professional baseball is, after all, a business. It has always been that way. But it was always more than just a business for me when I was with the Cardinals, and I don't think I had that feeling with any other ballclub I played with."

Lindy McDaniel—Cardinal Stats

	W	L	PCT	ERA	G	GS	CG	IP	H	BB	SO	SHO	SV
1955	0	0	—	4.74	4	2	0	19	22	7	7	0	0
1956	7	6	.538	3.40	39	7	1	116.1	121	42	59	0	0
1957	15	9	.625	3.49	30	26	10	191	196	53	75	1	0
1958	5	7	.417	5.78	26	17	2	108.2	139	31	47	1	0
1959	14	12	.538	3.82	62	7	1	132	144	41	86	0	15
1960	12	4	.750	2.09	65	2	1	116.1	85	24	105	0	26
1961	10	6	.625	4.88	55	0	0	94.1	117	31	65	0	9
1962	3	10	.231	4.12	55	2	0	107	96	29	79	0	14

JERRY McNERTNEY

No "Simba"? Just

Call "The

Weekend Warrior"

Can a tonsillectomy lead to a career in the big leagues? In the case of former Cardinal "supersub" Jerry McNertney, who served as Ted Simmons's backup during the 1971 season as part of a nine-year big league career, that's one way of looking at it.

McNertney's parents gave him a ball and bat when he was a little boy as a reward for having his tonsils removed. The central Iowa lad practiced swinging the bat until one day, he accidentally shattered it against a tree; symbolic, perhaps, of the nickname of one of his boyhood heroes—"The Splendid Splinter." Of course Ted Williams was known more for smashing his bat into fat pitches than into large trees.

Jerry improved his swing as he grew older. He played high school, semi-pro and college ball (at Iowa State University) before a local businessman, serving as a "bird dog" scout for the White Sox, told club officials about the young infielder.

McNertney signed with the White Sox organization in 1958 and worked dili-

gently to master the art of catching after he learned the Sox had a wealth of first basemen ahead of him. He toiled in their farm system for six years before getting the call in 1964 to share catching duties with J.C. Martin. "Mac," as Jerry was often called, played for Chicago at a time when the team twice—in 1964 and 1967—came agonizingly close to winning the American League pennant.

In 1969, McNertney played for the "legendary" now-you-see-them, now-you-don't Seattle Pilots, who acquired him in the expansion draft. For part of that season, at least, one of Jerry's batterymates was Jim Bouton, who would go on to author *Ball Four*. (Bouton, by the way, has some kind words to say in the book about his former Pilots receiver.)

When the franchise moved to Milwaukee in time for the 1970 season, McNertney moved with it. He shared the starting catcher's job with Phil Roof, batting .243 in 111 games. In October, McNertney was traded, along with pitchers George Lauzerique and Jesse Higgins, to the Cardinals for utility player Carl Taylor and pitcher Jim Ellis. McNertney's value to the Cardinals would soon become evident, when starting catcher Ted Simmons—nicknamed "Simba" for his long locks that resembled a lion's mane—was, as Jerry recalls, "called up on weekends to serve in the National Guard, or something like that."

McNertney enjoyed his best year in the majors with the 1971 Cardinals, a team that would go on to boast the season's National League Most Valuable Player in Joe Torre, the continued excellence of speedster Lou Brock (major league-leading totals in stolen bases and runs scored), 20 wins from Steve Carlton in his final season as a Cardinal, and the only no-hitter of Bob Gibson's marvelous career. The team even made a late-season run at the N.L. East title before the Pirates claimed it as their own.

And though Mac found himself on yet another big-league bridesmaid, as a ballplayer he had his most satisfying year personally. In fact, McNertney's teammates dubbed him "The Weekend Warrior." The righty hit .289 in 128 at-bats and showed occasional pop in his bat with ten extra base hits. As a pinch hitter he batted .313, with several of his hits either tying or winning ballgames for the Cardinals. He credits third baseman Joe Torre with giving him sound advice when the Cards were at bat.

"Joe was my biggest influence over there," McNertney said.

"That was my first year in the National League and I didn't know the pitchers or what they'd throw me. Before I'd go up there I'd ask Joe what kind of stuff the pitcher had. Joe knew what he was talkin' about because he wound up as the MVP that year and I had the best season of my career—even though I was a part-time player."

As for the stocky Torre—who a few years later hit into four consecutive double plays—McNertney deadpanned, "Joe didn't get too many leg hits, as I recall." Still, as McNertney quickly added, "It was great just to watch him hit, and he hit the ball often and he hit it *hard*."

Torre was indeed torrid that season of 1971. His .363 batting average produced 137 RBI, 34 doubles, 8 triples and 24 home runs. His batting average and RBI totals led the majors, as did his 230 hits.

McNertney also remembers the intensity of his battery-mates, notably Steve Carlton and Bob Gibson, when it was either man's turn to pitch.

"We were playing the Mets in New York, and before the game Steve told me he really wanted to beat those guys because they'd given him a lot of trouble in the past," McNertney recalled. "He told me he was gonna pitch everyone inside. When I called for the fastball he wanted it *in*—in to the left-handers, in to the right-handers. No finesse stuff at all.

"So, the Mets got a steady diet of fastballs and sliders in, all right, one batter after another. And we beat them. But in the process Steve beat *me* up, 'cause my hand was swollen and purple for a week after that. In that game you could hear my mitt pop on every pitch."

And though Gibson may have lost a little something off his fastball at that point in his career, McNertney insists the Cardinal ace had lost none of his concentration or desire to win once he took the mound.

"He pitched a no-hitter that summer, of course, [an 11-0 blowout] against the Pirates in August. I didn't catch him in that game. I wish I had. But on the few occasions when I did catch Bob, I remember a couple of times when I went out to the mound to ask him how he wanted to pitch certain batters. He would look at me and say, 'Just get back there and catch.'

"The outside part of the plate was his, boy, and if you were a hitter who leaned over too far he wasn't afraid to turn your cap."

Throughout the 1971 season, McNertney himself turned a few heads as he came through in the clutch. His two-run homer following a walk to Ted Sizemore powered the Cardinals to a 5-0 victory over the Phillies in a game in late April. It was his first N.L. dinger.

A month later, with the score tied, McNertney's sacrifice fly plated the go-ahead run in a wild, 15-8 come-from-behind win over the Padres.

His second N.L. home run iced a game in late May. It came off Phil Regan who served up Mac's first major league home run in 1964 when Regan pitched for the Tigers and Mac was a rookie with the White Sox.

In a game in Atlanta in June, with two outs and two on in the ninth, "The Weekend Warrior" delivered a pinch-hit double to tie the score at 6-6. The Cardinals went on to win the game in the tenth inning.

A bouncer up the middle to win a game at Wrigley Field two weeks later, a memorable four-for-five day in a losing cause against the Giants at Candlestick Park, pinch-hitting heroics and solid efforts as an occasional starter—Jerry McNertney epitomized the reliable role player throughout the 1971 season.

"Every time we pulled to within four or five games of Pittsburgh we seemed to stall out," McNertney said of his 1971 team. "But even though we fell short of winning our division, what I remember most about playing for the Cardinals that year was this: even though I was a platoon player, those guys made me feel welcome, and it was the first time in my life I felt like I was playin' alongside superstars.

"Sometimes I'd look around me and see Lou Brock and Jose Cruz and Torre and Gibson and Carlton and Teddy and Jerry Reuss...I was in awe. I couldn't believe the guys we had on that team. But '71 was the year of that Pirate team that had Clemente, Stargell and Sanguillen. Those guys could hit a little bit, too. It was no fluke they wound up winnin' the World Series that year."

When McNertney arrived in St. Petersburg, Florida, for spring training in 1972, he was looking forward to repeating his personal success while helping the Cardinals go all the way to the top. But a freakish accident—horseplay, to be precise—hampered his talents all season long, and both Mac and the team suffered through a sub-par crusade despite some decent numbers put up by Gibson, Simmons, Brock and Torre.

"One of Jose Cruz's brothers—I'm not sure if it was Tommy or Heity—gave me a bear hug and something popped in my back," McNertney remembered. "I could hardly move sometimes because of the pain. I had hoped for another good season like the one I had the year before, but it didn't work out. The pain affected me on offense and defense, and I only caught about ten games or so. I just never could get on track, and that was a great disappointment to me after '71."

The Cardinals released McNertney in October of 1972. He was hoping to stick with the Oakland A's the following spring, but Ray Fosse and Gene Tenace had a lock on the team's catching duties. The A's sold McNertney to the Pittsburgh Pirates, for whom he played in just nine games before deciding to pack it in.

In the mid 1970s McNertney, a lifelong bachelor, married and began raising a family. He re-enrolled at Iowa State University, where he soon graduated with a degree in physical education. He went back to baseball around 1977, when he joined the Yankees' minor league system as a coach. He eventually was moved up to the parent club to serve as bullpen coach.

Unfortunately for Jerry, however, he was a man in the right place at the wrong time—at least during one particular game. Dave Righetti, then a starter but using one of his off days to regale his teammates in the bullpen with stories and jokes, injured his pitching hand, apparently on a metal or concrete structure, while gesturing with his hands to make a point.

Yankee owner George Steinbrenner was so incensed that one of his aces was injured in such a screwball manner that he vented his frustration on Jerry, who was near Righetti when the mishap occurred. It was "hit the road, Mac, and don'tcha come back no more, no more" for the innocent bystander from Iowa.

McNertney returned to the coaching ranks in the Yanks' farm system, serving with clubs at Albany, Columbus and Ft. Lauderdale. During those years Mac formed a number of new friendships, including one with Bucky Dent, who managed in the organization's farm system for several years before succeeding

Dallas Green as skipper of the Yankees in August of 1989. Jerry himself left the Yankee organization a few years before that, however, wanting to devote more quality time to his wife and children.

For the past several years, Mac has served as an assistant coach to Bobby Randall at Iowa State. (Randall, as Twins fans may recall, was Minnesota's second baseman in the latter half of the 1970s.) Although a part-time job, McNertney loves it because he can stay close to baseball while staying close to home.

And to bring in a little extra income to the family budget, McNertney accepted an offer from the Red Sox to be their bullpen coach in 1988, one of the positions that opened when third base coach Joe Morgan replaced ousted manager John McNamara.

"My wife and I decided that, yes, maybe this one time I'll finally be part of a team that goes to the World Series," Jerry said. "We thought, 'What the heck, let's give it a whirl for a couple of months.' And it was fun, being part of a pennant race, even though Oakland beat us in the playoffs. But I didn't like being away from the troops over the summer, so when Boston wanted me to come back for the '89 season, I had to say no—even though they were kind enough to ask me. I just wanted to be with my wife and kids.

"Working as a part-time assistant at Iowa State is good for me. I'm on the payroll. The check isn't much, but it helps make the car payments. Bobby sent me off on a few recruiting deals last summer, but otherwise I have the summer off with my family. In the fall things start picking up, and Bobby and I hold some instructional sessions for our players who we feel need to refine certain skills.

"The team works out, of course, during the winter, and each spring Bobby's got a ten-game trip south scheduled. Here in 1990 we're goin' to play, I think, Texas A&M and Texas. For a bunch of Iowa Staters we're playin' some pretty heavy stuff for comin' out of a snowbank. But you gotta play the top teams if you're ever gonna improve."

Jerry McNertney may never completely sever his ties with professional baseball. But for now, at least, "The Weekend Warrior" spends his weekends at home. And though Jerry himself owns caps and other keepsakes of every team for which he ever played, his father has for years been wearing a Cardinals cap about town.

"I'll always remember playin' on that '71 Cardinal team," Mac said. "It was too bad we didn't win the thing that year, but we gave it a good shot. And even if it was for only a couple of seasons, I'm glad I was part of that organization."

Jerry McNertney—Cardinal Stats

	G	AB	H	2B	3B	HR	R	RBI	BB	SO	SB	BA	SA
1971	56	128	37	4	2	4	15	22	12	14	0	.289	.445
1972	39	48	10	3	1	0	3	9	6	16	0	.208	.313

JOHNNY MIZE

Big Cat with a

Big Bat

They went by Dizzy, Ducky, Daffy, Pepper, The Lip, Ripper and Spud.

John Robert "Johnny" Mize, a twenty-three-year-old rookie in the spring of 1936, found himself next to the nucleus of the legendary "Gas House Gang" of the St. Louis Cardinals. With those guys as teammates, it was a sure thing that "Johnny" would soon give way to something more colorful.

The strapping 6'2", 215-pound native of Demorest, Ga., was rechristened "The Big Cat" for the way he pounced on hard hit grounders and scooped up low throws in the dirt like a feline first baseman.

He played six seasons with the Cardinals and just over four full seasons each with the New York Giants and the New York Yankees before calling it a career. He batted .312 lifetime, knocked in 1,337 runs, and socked 359 home runs. His career slugging percentage of .562 puts him eighth on the all-time list; his run production per game ranks him tenth—just behind another Cardinal luminary, Stan Musial.

Mize spent all but eight games of a fifteen-year big league career prowling the first base area, and fielded at a .992 clip.

His love of baseball was nurtured as a youngster growing up in Demorest where, as he puts it, "I played baseball every chance I got—in the mornings before grammar school, during recess, after school and during the summer."

There was a small college, Piedmont Academy, where Mize and his childhood pals retrieved baseballs hit over the fence during the collegians' practice sessions and games. A few years later, when he was in high school, Mize was approached by a few of the Piedmont players and asked if he would like to play for their team. The exchange, Mize said, went something like this:

"How can I play? I'm in high school."

"Well, we'll talk to the coach or something. Maybe we can work it out so you can take one subject in college. We'd really like you to play for us."

"Well, OK, if you think it's all right."

But they never again mentioned the word "subject," Mize said, "And neither did I. I just went out and played. I wasn't about to bring up the topic of what subject I could take...I was havin' enough trouble in high school without worrying about another class. The next year, come baseball season, I just went over there the first day they were issuing uniforms and got mine, and nobody ever did say anything. But the yearbook came out this one year and I had my picture in it."

In fact, Mize was a "college student" for several years at Piedmont Academy. But it was while playing baseball for a lumber mill team in Helen, not far from Demorest, that Mize was spotted by people who would soon change his fortunes.

The mill was owned by a company in Rochester, New York, site of one of the Cardinals' top farm teams. Someone at the mill told officials with the Rochester club about this young slugger at the lumber camp who could "hit a ball a long ways."

It was at that point that Frank Rickey, brother of the Cardinals' general manager, was dispatched to scout Mize. Big John was making a decent wage in those days by playing for several area semi-pro teams that needed his services. Reluctant at first to sign, Mize did eventually cast his lot with the Cardinal organization, and began his professional career in 1930 at Greensboro in the Piedmont League. His opposite number at first base with the Raleigh team that year was another future Hall of Famer, Hank Greenberg.

Mize never hit below .317 in his five full seasons in the minors, and his production with the bat ensured a move to the parent club was not far off. But when Mize did finally crack the Cardinals' roster it was with a team that would fail to deliver the goods when post-season play was within its grasp.

"We always seemed to be just one more good starting pitcher short of winning the pennant," Mize said of those Cardinal teams of 1936 to 1941. "And if Diz hadn't gotten hurt when [Earl] Averill's liner hit him on the foot in the '37 All-Star Game, well, who knows?

"In three or four of those six years I played for St. Louis, we came up short because we lacked another pitcher who could win 15 or 20 games for us. But we could always hit."

Solid starting pitching is only one of several keys to locking up a pennant, but Mize's reasoning is well-taken.

In his rookie season, the Cardinals led the National League in runs batted in, slugging percentage, doubles and stolen bases. Dizzy Dean went 24-13, but fellow righty Jim Winford, at 11-10, had the staff's next best record among starters. The Cardinals' pitchers had the league's second-highest team ERA—only the last place Phillies' staff was worse—and St. Louis finished in a second-place tie with the Cubs.

In 1939, Cardinal hitters led the league in hits, runs, RBI, doubles, batting average and slugging percentage, and tied for the lead in triples. Curt Davis won 22 games, but Bob Bowman, used mostly in relief, and starter Lon Warneke, tied for second on the staff with 13 wins apiece.

That year, Cardinal pitchers notched 45 complete games, the lowest total in the majors in 1939. N.L. Champion Cincinnati got 86 complete games out of its pitching staff, and finished four and a half games ahead of St. Louis.

By the end of the 1941 regular season, the Cardinals boasted two 17-game winners in Warneke and Ernie White, but the Dodgers boasted two 22-game winners in Kirby Higbe and Whitlow Wyatt, and won the pennant by two and a half games over St. Louis.

Yet if his team's fortunes were a frustration to him, his personal accomplishments were not. In his six years with the Cardinals, Mize *averaged* .336 with 109 runs batted in and 91 runs scored, 36 doubles, 11 triples and 26 home runs. He and Joe Medwick—the last National League hitter to win the triple crown—became one of the league's most feared one-two punches at the plate.

Mize debuted in mid-April of 1936 against the Cubs. It was memorable only for its brevity.

"I struck out on three pitches from Larry French, a left-hander," Mize recalled, somewhat bemusedly. "I was pinch hitting for one of our pitchers—Paul Dean, I think—in a game we were losing in the ninth inning. Now, that was no time for a guy to go up and pinch hit when there's two out in the ninth, nobody on and you're three or four runs behind."

But that humbling debut soon turned into an assault on National League pitching that left little doubt Mize was in "the bigs" to stay. Of his first 28 hits, 17 were for extra bases: 8 doubles, 4 triples and 5 home runs.

When the dust settled at the end of his rookie season, the left-handed hitting "phenom" had a .329 batting average and 93 RBI fueled by 30 doubles, 8 triples, 19 home runs (fifth in the league) and a .577 slugging percentage, good for a second place tie with Medwick and the Phillies' Dolph Camilli. The Big Cat's fielding percentage—he played the lion's share of his games at first that year—was .994. All that, in only 126 games.

It was a portent of things to come. In his six years as a Cardinal, Mize led the league in triples once, doubles once (a tie), batting average once, runs batted in once, home runs twice and slugging percentage three times. For a power hitter he had a terrific eye at the plate, walking nearly 200 times more often than he struck out during his tenure with St. Louis.

Even after he left the Cardinals, Mize continued to put up solid numbers. As a member of the New York Giants from 1942 to 1948, he held or tied for the league lead in various offensive and defensive categories. His finest season with the Giants was in 1947, when he led the majors with 51 home runs (tied with Ralph Kiner), 137 runs scored and 138 RBI. He was a key factor in the New York Yankees' World Championship dynasty of 1949 to 1953.

In the 1952 Yankees-Dodgers Fall Classic for example, Mize, then thirty-nine, led all participants with a .400 batting average and displayed some of that old Mize magic with the long ball by pasting three Brooklyn offerings into the stands and knocking in six of his teammates.

As many triumphs as Mize had in his rookie year in 1936 and beyond, he remembers the at-bats when he didn't come through. One instance involved Giant screwballer Carl Hubbell (against whom, according to Mize, he had a fair amount of success over the years) and slugging right fielder Mel Ott:

"One day in the Polo Grounds we were losing to Hubbell by a couple of runs or something," Mize began, "but we were rallyin' with two out and a man or two on base late in the game when it was my turn to bat.

"Frankie Frisch, who was our player-manager then, told me to 'go for the outer walls,' even though the wind was blowin' in that day. Hubbell pitched and I swung up on the ball. Well, the moment I hit it, he threw his glove straight up in the air. He knew he'd thrown me a home run ball, and so did I.

"I wasn't so much of a pull hitter in those days, so Ott was playin' me over near center. As I round first, I see him runnin' the 100-yard dash toward the foul line. The ball, which was fair by twenty feet when I hit it, just seemed suspended up there in the air...floating...like a kite or something, higher than the stands, and it drifted into foul territory. Ott caught it on the run. End of rally."

Every Cardinal who ever played with Dizzy Dean has a story about him, it seems, and Mize is no exception. In 1936, Mize's first season, Dean was not only the ace of the starting rotation, he was also the team's stopper out of the bullpen. Complementing Dean's 24-13 record with 28 complete games were his major league-leading 11 saves.

"I can remember games where our starting pitcher got knocked out and we'd send in a reliever or two and every one of 'em would get hit pretty hard," Mize said. "Diz's wife, Pat, would be sittin' in the stands at Sportsman's and we'd hear her yell, 'Put Jay in there! Put Jay in there! He'll get 'em out!' She always called him Jay, never Dizzy. But we could hear her."

Mize did much of his damage against opposing pitchers'

ERAs by using a 36-ounce, 36-inch bat from Hillerich & Bradsby. (In spring training Mize often used a 40-ounce club because to him the others felt too lightweight that time of year.)

"I had big calluses on my hands when I played," Mize said, noting that many of his bats featured a tapered handle with little or no knob on the end. "And I just rested the tip of my bat in my right hand. When we were teammates on the Yankees, Phil Rizzuto used one of my bats during the 1950 season. He used to joke that the bat was nearly as big as he is. But he stuck with it. He just put the bat on the ball, hit .300-somethin' that year and was voted MVP."

But the man who had the greatest success with this particular model was Mize himself. The fact that he loved to hit—and hit to all fields—was evident early on, but crystallized in a game against right-hander Si Johnson, a hunting and fishing buddy of Mize's during the off-season.

"I hit baseballs all over Sportsman's," Mize said. "I hit a number of home runs into the bleachers in left. I hit two in a row off Si one time. He threw me two low, outside change of pace balls. Later he told me during one of our huntin' trips that after I hit the first one he knew darn well I couldn't hit another one like that, so the next time up he threw me another change an' I hit it out of there. He told me that made a believer out of him.

"I enjoyed hittin' in Brooklyn at Ebbets Field, and at old Braves Field in Boston. I even hit one out in the Polo Grounds to left field, a line drive that went up in under that upper deck section that used to stick out. I hit an awful lot of loud outs in the Polo Grounds when I tried to pull the ball and it'd be caught out in deep center field. When I got over to the American League I guess I hit pretty good in Detroit. Yankee Stadium was all right for me if I pulled the ball. If I didn't get around on it, though, it was kind of tough for me."

Get Mize in a roundtable discussion about the pitchers of his era and he'll mention Johnny Vander Meer, who, while never winning twenty games in a season, managed to top the National League in strikeouts three consecutive years, 1941 to 1943. "The Dutch Master," of course, is best known for firing back-to-back no-hitters in 1938. The hard throwing southpaw's Achilles' heel was his control.

"Vander Meer was the toughest, you know, to go up and face in the batter's box," Mize said, "especially if you were a left-hander like me. He was so wild. You never knew where the ball was going, and neither did he, at times. He was fast. And he threw a good curveball an' all. But, he might throw behind you on 3-and-2 and the bases loaded or somethin'—and you *know* he's not tryin' to hit you in that situation.

"I heard him say one time that with the rules the way they are now, he wouldn't last an inning. He'd probably rear back and throw and the ball would go behind some guy, and the next time he went back there with a pitch they'd throw him out of the ballgame.

"Same way with Tommy Byrne when I was with the Yankees, except he was my teammate. You just never knew where that ball was goin' when he threw it. One time, Tommy was pitchin' battin' practice to us. I walked up to the plate and I call to him that I'm gonna practice bunting the ball a few times. And I make a motion like I'm gonna bunt, right?

"So, I make my pivot and slowly square around to bunt the ball, and here it comes—ssfft!—right behind my head and then it ricochets off the batting cage. I just got up and walked right out of there and never went back in against him again. It's tough enough in a real game without havin' to duck a pitch from one of your own guys in battin' practice."

When it comes to hitting, Johnny Mize does not mince words regarding today's players and their approach to each at-bat.

"Some of 'em will go up there and dig a hole and put their foot in it and the next time it's the same thing," Mize said. "Doesn't matter if they face five different pitchers during the game, or whether they face left-handers and right-handers both, they're still gonna stand in those same spots. By gosh, move around with the pitcher! Learn to adjust to the situation the way you'd adjust to the different ballparks or whether the wind is blowin' in or out that day.

"And another thing I can't understand is why these hitters are so busy up there. Every time the pitcher makes a pitch that the batter doesn't hit, the batter's gotta get out of the box and walk over to pick up the resin bag, or adjust his helmet, or his batting gloves. When I went into the batter's box I never got out of it till I got a base hit or made an out. If there's a runner on first when you're at the plate, let the pitcher throw over there five or six times. Just stand there in the box and wait for that guy to pitch to you. Sooner or later he's gotta throw it home and you can be waitin' for it. I might drop my bat down in that situation when the pitcher's goin' to first, or I might rest it on my shoulder, but that's about it.

"And another thing I can't figure out is why everybody has gone to a lighter bat. Or at least a lot of hitters have. These thirty or thirty-one ounce bats, look at what happens when some of these big guys swing those little bats. The guy swings hard and half the bat's in his hand and the other half's somewhere up in the stands or out on the field. I never had a bat break in my hands. Split, yes, but I always had the bat when I went back to the dugout to get a new one."

Mize's career with the Cardinals ended on a somewhat sour note four days after the Japanese attacked Pearl Harbor. That's when he was traded to the Giants for three players and $50,000.

"I had asked them once before to trade me," Mize said. "In 1940 I hit about .315 with 43 home runs, and I drove in a 137 runs, but they wanted me to take a cut in salary. I said, 'Trade me off the ballclub,' but they wouldn't do it. They said, 'We can't. The fans won't like it.' But they did trade me after the 1941 season. I had some good years with the Giants, but we never won a pennant. I think we finished third one year.

"Then later, with the Yankees, things were turned around a little. I tailed off some, but we had some great clubs over there, and we won five straight World Series in New York. It was a lot of fun walkin' into a restaurant or something and people would come up to you or call out, 'Hey, when you gonna lose a game?'—instead of when I was with the Giants and they'd ask, 'When you guys gonna win one?'"

Like many ballplayers of his time, Johnny Mize served his country in World War II, and in the process missed several key seasons in his baseball career. His three-year stint in the U.S. Navy included a stay on the tiny Pacific island of Tinian, near Guam, in 1945 during the closing weeks of the war.

On those precious occasions when Mize and some of his Navy buddies had a day off, they would prepare a feast consisting of a large canned ham, two or three loaves of bread, a jar of mayonnaise, a jar of pickles, and a case of beer. They'd borrow a truck from the base's athletic department and drive to a hilltop overlooking the runways, ammo dumps, Quonset huts and supply depots below.

On one of these occasions, Mize and his buddies took note of an influx of Marine guards who immediately took lookout positions along a bank. Then more Marines arrived. And still more after *those* platoons.

"They watched everything like hawks," Mize recalled. "Heck, we'd just be sittin' there relaxin', eatin' sandwiches and drinkin' beer and havin' a good time, never really askin' ourselves what all those Marines were guarding."

Part of what those Marines were guarding on Tinian arrived on July 26 aboard the U.S. cruiser *Indianapolis*—the basic components of the atomic bomb that would be dropped on Hiroshima, Japan, within two weeks. On the night of July 28, transport planes landed at Tinian with the last of the uranium isotope, U-235, needed to assemble the bomb.

"We found out later that's why they were sittin' up there," Mize said of the Marine sentries. "We were told later it wasn't really armed until they got it on the plane and took off from Tinian, but my gosh, if I'd a'known we were picnicking a few hundred yards from where that thing was stored I would've asked for a transfer."

Johnny Mize still moves at a fairly brisk pace for a man in his late seventies who has undergone several knee operations and cataract surgery. He remains a solid draw at baseball card and memorabilia shows around the country, especially in New York and St. Louis, the two cities where he played major league baseball for fifteen years.

Not surprisingly, this proud but good-natured man has his generational prejudices. Talking to a group of youthful autograph seekers, some clutching baseball cards of today's top hitters, Mize winked and said, "I'd like to see some of these guys face Diz or Hubbell in their prime. Some of the numbers on the backs of those cards might not be so good."

Johnny Mize—Cardinal Stats

	G	AB	H	2B	3B	HR	R	RBI	BB	SO	SB	BA	SA
1936	126	414	136	30	8	19	76	93	50	32	1	.329	.577
1937	145	560	204	40	7	25	103	113	56	57	2	.364	.595
1938	149	531	179	34	16	27	85	102	74	47	0	.337	.614
1939	153	564	197	44	14	28	104	108	92	49	0	.349	.626
1940	155	579	182	31	13	43	111	137	82	49	7	.314	.636
1941	126	473	150	39	8	16	67	100	70	45	4	.317	.535

TERRY MOORE

Captain of the

Cardinal

Center Field

Terry Moore isn't enshrined in "The Hall," but Johnny Mize and Enos Slaughter, who are, will tell you the former Cardinal team captain was as fine a defensive center fielder as they ever saw. And both men are quick to add that Moore "could hit some, too."

Another former Cardinal, Harry Walker, who knows a little about hitting as well, talks of Moore's all-round abilities on the field and the leadership qualities he brought to the Cardinals.

"Everybody respected Terry," Walker says. "He was a leader, and a friend. I named my son after him."

Moore, born in Vernon, Alabama, spent most of his formative years growing up in the Memphis, Tennessee area, where he was playing youth baseball for a local church by the time he was seven. The family moved to St. Louis when Terry was twelve, at which point he played in the city's municipal leagues, pitching (occasionally) and playing the outfield (usually).

As a baseball-hungry teenager, Moore eventually wound up playing across the state border for an Illinois semi-pro team. It was there that the Cardinals signed Terry and he began his journey through their farm system.

When he joined the parent club in 1935, Moore was enlisting with the defending world champions of baseball. Bumping center fielder Ernie Orsatti from the starting lineup, Moore forged a solid rookie season, batting .287 with 53 RBI, 34 doubles, 3 triples and 6 home runs. He also swiped 13 bases.

"I was a low-ball hitter," said Moore, who hit right-handed. "At first I was hittin' a lot to left field, pullin' the ball. But I learned to go to right field a lot and that made a big difference in my success at the plate.

"They had a fella over there at Pittsburgh named Bill Swift, and I had a heck of a time hittin' him until I started hittin' the ball to right field on those high, outside pitches.

"And when the Cardinals had the best luck, I think, was when I was hittin' and runnin' when we had a man on first base. We had better luck winnin' ballgames when I did that. I know I helped my battin' average by twenty points a season by goin' the opposite way."

Moore's hit-to-all-fields mentality also helped avoid a potentially embarrassing outcome in Game 1 of the 1942 World Series pitting St. Louis against the New York Yankees.

With two out in the bottom of the eighth inning, Moore singled to right to break up a no-hit bid by Yankee hurler Red Ruffing, who was credited with a 7-4 win over the Cardinals.

Moore went on to hit .294 in the Series, second highest among the eight Cardinal regulars, and played flawless center field.

And although he didn't hit well against Red Sox pitching in the 1946 Fall Classic, Moore did bat .500 and score twice to help his club win the best-of-three N.L. playoffs against the Dodgers, two games to none, a few days earlier.

But it was another game against Brooklyn, in Terry's rookie season, that still brings a smile to his face, though not because of anything he did personally. The story involves several Cardinal teammates—notably, pitching legend Dizzy Dean and player-manager Frank Frisch—and the Dodgers' first baseman, Sam Leslie. As teams have always done before a game, the Cardinals scanned their opponents' lineup and discussed with Frisch how each batter should be pitched.

"We had the lead in this ballgame," Moore recalled, "and Dean had pitched Leslie the way *he* wanted to, not the way Frisch wanted him to when they discussed it before the game. I think Dean may have even struck Sam out three straight times. Late in the game, Dean went back to Frisch and said, 'Now I'll pitch him the way *you* want me to, Frank.'

"So Dean threw Leslie a high fastball with not too much on it and Leslie hit it nine miles over that outfield fence in Brooklyn, and Dean is out there doubled over with laughter as Leslie's runnin' around the bases. Dean looks at Frisch and yells, 'I told you so!' That was the kind of showman Dean was.

"There was another time...let's see, it had to be the same year I guess, '35, because that's when Babe Ruth had come over to our league to play out the string with Boston. We were playin' 'em in Boston, and Ruth was the hitter when Dean started challengin' him.

"Well, we had a lead by then, and Dean walked off the mound and walked up to Bill DeLancey, our catcher. Ruth was standin' there at the plate, of course, and Dean looks at the two of 'em and says, 'Babe, I'm gonna throw you my fastball. I'm not gonna throw you anything *but* the fastball, but I'm gonna throw it with everything I got on it. I wanna see if you can hit it.'

"And that's what Dean did. Threw every one of 'em right down the gut, and Ruth swung and missed all three. I was a rookie outfielder then, standin' out there wonderin' what the heck was goin' on. I found out about it when I got back to the bench and heard DeLancey tellin' Frisch all about it. I thought that was one of the funniest things I'd ever run into. Heck, I wish he would've hit the ball. Might've been fun to see how far it went."

Dizzy was not the only character Moore observed during his years with St. Louis. There was "Eno," of course, who played beside him in the outfield for eight seasons, and Mize, who was all business out there on the diamond but who wasn't immune from the ballclub's playful nature, either.

"I roomed with each of those fellas at one time or another," Moore said. "I saw both of 'em come up to the Cardinals after I'd been there a year. John was quiet when he came up, just like Eno.

You couldn't get a word out of 'em. But boy, once they started gaining confidence in themselves, you couldn't keep 'em quiet. Always talkin', they were.

"We had guys on the Cardinals who were pranksters, too. Walker Cooper was a good one for that. If you were readin' the paper in the hotel lobby or train station—I don't care who it was— he'd set it on fire. If you wore one of those straw hats, he'd pull it down over your head. And if he'd been drinkin' a little bit, he'd grab your necktie and either cut it in two or tie it into knots."

Cooper, Mize, Slaughter and even Moore himself received knots of a different kind in 1941. Each of them, and a few other Cardinals as well, suffered various injuries during the course of the year. Those injuries, painful as they were, may have put more hurt on the team's pennant drive against the Dodgers than they did on the individuals.

Slaughter's broken collarbone resulted from a dance floor maneuver gone awry in the outfield at Sportsman's Park. Stu Martin, once a teammate of the dynamic duo's but at that point a Pirate utility infielder, hit a liner to deep right-center that Slaughter and Moore converged on at the same time. As Moore skidded along the hard outfield surface to make the catch, Slaughter leaped over him to avoid a collision, but Eno's momentum carried him crashing into the wall.

Moore escaped that one, but not the one that got away from Boston's young lefty, Art Johnson, a few days later. When Moore crumpled to the ground after taking it in the skull, the Cardinals relied on part-time outfielders Estel Crabtree and Coaker Triplett, who wound up hitting .341 and .286, respectively, to keep them in the race. Alas, even those handsome averages were not enough to catch Brooklyn, and St. Louis finished the 1941 campaign a heart-breaking two and a half games behind the N.L. champs.

Still, Terry's cap must have had a silver lining, because the Cardinals also decided to bring up a converted pitcher from their Rochester club that September, and he wasted no time in announcing his arrival. Stan Musial hit .426 in a dozen games.

"Let me tell you one about Stan," Moore said. "As you know, he started out as a pitcher in the minor leagues before he hurt his arm. But we played against him in a game once down in

Georgia, I think it was, before we went north to start the season. And Mize and I hit home runs off him. I mean, we creamed 'em.

"So then in the fall of '41, I'm back out of the hospital and I'm sittin' on the bench 'cause I'm not able to play just yet. And Stan comes over and sits down next to me and says, 'Gosh, Terry, you oughtta remember me.' And I says, 'No, kid, I don't remember you.' And Stan looks at me for a second and says, 'You ought to, you and Mize hit home runs offa me.' 'Oh,' I says, 'No wonder you're a hitter now.'

"But Stan was a good kid. He was quiet and shy when he first came up, too, and if you'd seen him back then with that unorthodox stance of his, you'd say to yourself, 'This kid's *never* gonna hit. We soon learned otherwise, didn't we?"

Moore, although not as devastating with the bat as "The Man," had his moments. In his rookie season he once went 6-for-6 in a game. Five years later, in 1940, Moore was one-third of a .300-hitting outfield (along with Slaughter and Ernie Koy). And in 1947, his next-to-last year in the big leagues, Captain Terry fashioned a streak of nine consecutive hits on his way to a .283 batting average.

His best years on offense were from 1939 to 1941. He averaged close to .300 for those three crusades, while having back-to-back, 17-homer years in 1939 and 1940. He also spanked an average of 28 doubles, scored an average of 81 runs and plated an average of 70 runners during that period. And while stealing bases was not a big part of this game ("My speed came in to play when I was going from first to third or second to home, or when I played the outfield," he points out.), Moore stole as many as 18 bases in one season (1940) and was in double figures in that category four times.

To many long-time Cardinal observers, Moore had few peers in center field. He attributes his success on defense to a combination of natural speed and a willingness to work hard to learn the nuances of the outfields around the majors, especially the outfield at Sportsman's Park. With its often rock-hard surface, across which ground balls "could really scoot," Moore's home turf was a challenge even for someone who roamed it half the season.

"See, we played there when St. Louis had two teams—the Browns in the American League and us in the National—and the

groundskeepers rarely had the time to get the playing surface soft-
ened up just right. It wasn't that they didn't try, it's just that as
soon as one team left town, the other one would come into play a
series. It was kind of like a cow pasture out there.

"If you tried to field a ground ball and took your eye off it
for just a second, you were dead. You *had* to follow the ball all the
way into your glove. A lot of times I'd be comin' in ready to catch a
one- or two-hopper and I'd have to grab it barehanded because
it'd bounce that far over. We still charged the ball, though. Ground
balls were really tough out there."

After eleven seasons with the Cardinals, Moore called it
quits as a player. He later served as a coach with the Cards, and he
also managed the Phillies in 1954.

"I owned two bowling alleys for a time," he said, "but I sold
'em. I'm retired now. Just takin' it easy, workin' around the house.
Once in a while I'll go to one of these card shows and sign for the
kids and everything. I had two knee operations not long ago, so
maybe I'll be able to play golf now.

"Everybody says, 'Gosh, you're gettin' old, Terry.' And I tell
'em, 'Yeah, and there's one way you can get that way, too: just
keep breathing.'"

Terry Moore—Cardinal Stats

	G	AB	H	2B	3B	HR	R	RBI	BB	SO	SB	BA	SA
1935	119	456	131	34	3	6	63	53	15	40	13	.287	.414
1936	143	590	156	39	4	5	85	47	37	52	9	.264	.369
1937	115	461	123	17	3	5	76	43	32	41	13	.267	.349
1938	94	312	85	21	3	4	49	21	46	19	9	.272	.397
1939	130	417	123	25	2	17	65	77	43	38	6	.295	.487
1940	136	537	163	33	4	17	92	64	42	44	18	.304	.475
1941	122	493	145	26	4	6	86	68	52	31	3	.294	.400
1942	130	489	141	26	3	6	80	49	56	26	10	.288	.391
1946	91	278	73	14	1	3	32	28	18	26	0	.263	.353
1947	127	460	130	17	1	7	61	45	38	39	1	.283	.370
1948	91	207	48	11	0	4	30	18	27	12	0	.232	.343

	G	AB	H	2B	3B	HR	R	RBI	BB	SO	SB	BA	SA
World Series													
1942	5	17	5	1	0	0	2	2	2	3	0	.294	.353
1946	7	27	4	0	0	0	1	2	2	6	0	.148	.148

RED SCHOENDIENST

Returned by an

Unbroken Promise

Cardinal fans of different ages think of Albert "Red" Schoendienst in different terms. The over-forty set remembers Red the Player, a feisty starting second baseman in St. Louis from 1946 to 1955. Today's fans think of the 1989 Hall of Famer as an unflappable coach and manager, quietly guiding Redbirds of a different era.

Few fans realize, however, that Red the Manager almost never happened. Without a promise unbroken, Schoendienst might have spent three decades shaping the California Angels.

Following the 1960 season, the Milwaukee Braves released the savvy veteran. Before St. Louis' spring training began, Schoendienst contacted Bing Devine, then the team's general manager. Away from the Cardinals for nearly five seasons, Schoendienst decided that he'd like to end his career in the city where his big league life began fifteen years earlier.

Because of major league expansion, with new franchises in Los Angeles and Minneapolis, new teams needed personnel. Cowboy movie star Gene Autry owned the new L.A. team, and he recruited former Milwaukee Braves skipper Fred Haney to help select talent for the first-year club. Haney knew that Schoendienst, cut loose by the Braves after fighting tuberculosis for nearly two campaigns, could still play. During the 1959 season on the disabled list battling the disease, doctors removed Schoendienst's right lung. But Haney had seen before how Schoendienst's knowledge and determination could help overcome his physical shortcomings.

In the winter before the 1961 season, major league baseball held the expansion meetings at the old Chase Hotel in St. Louis. During the meetings, Haney and Autry made a valiant try at luring Schoendienst westward. "Mr. Autry got ahold of me and said, 'I'd like you to join our club as a player and help out as much as possible.'" Schoendienst remembers. "'You'd be great with an expansion ballclub. You'd be great with any baseball team,' he told me. 'But I think you'd be outstanding with us.'"

Schoendienst's reply to the Angels was typically modest but straightforward. "I told them that the only thing was that I promised Bing Devine and the Cardinals that I'd go to spring training if they'd give me a shot to make the club," he adds. "I made the promise. I didn't sign anything. There wasn't any contract. But I promised them, and I thought I should keep my promise." After the polite refusal, Haney and Autry still asked Schoendienst to keep them in mind if he needed a team.

As the saying goes, the rest is history. Schoendienst hooked on with the 1961 Cards as a utilityman. The next year, he became a player-coach under manager Johnny Keane.

But Albert Frederick Schoendienst began making Cardinals history all the way back in 1942.

Despite growing up across the Mississippi River from St. Louis in the coal mining community of Germantown, Illinois, Schoendienst wasn't pursued by baseball scouts seeking his services. Because he had quit school at age fourteen, he didn't have the exposure from playing with organized teams. At age nineteen, Schoendienst and two friends thumbed their way to St. Louis, about forty miles away. "Forty-seven years ago, Joe Lindemann, Joe Hockey and myself hitchhiked a ride on a milk truck from Germantown to St. Louis. We were going for a tryout with the Cardinals," Schoendienst said at his 1989 acceptance speech at the

Baseball Hall of Fame. "I never thought that milk truck ride would eventually lead to Cooperstown and baseball's highest honor."

Schoendienst's journey to baseball fame took many paths. His family, one sister and five brothers, all played baseball in their spare time. Joseph Schoendienst inspired his son by playing semi-pro ball when he wasn't mining or farming. "Growing up in Germantown, I could find a ballgame and play every day," he says. Prior to his tryout camp discovery, which pitted him against nearly 500 other hopeful youths, Schoendienst had been a member of the Civilian Conservation Corps. When he signed his first pro contract, the soft-spoken redhead was working as a civilian clerk at Scott Air Force Base. Before his career began, Schoendienst faced his first challenge. Vision in his left eye was spotty and weakened, due to an injury inflicted by a wayward nail from his CCC days. His solution was simple: until the eye was strengthened, Schoendienst would bat from the left side to compensate.

"Yeah, I was worried about it," Schoendienst admits. "I couldn't see very well out of my left eye at first." He says the team doctor didn't believe in having people wear glasses. Instead, a set of exercises was designed to strengthen Schoendienst's eyesight. Life as a switch hitter suited the Illinois native. After 68 games in the Florida-Georgia League, Schoendienst batted .269 with 1 homer and 28 RBI. After just nine games with Lynchburg of the Piedmont League in 1943, Schoendienst was advanced to Rochester of the International League.

His Rochester manager was former "Gas House Gang" member Pepper Martin. The one-time Cardinals outfielder was flabbergasted when the twenty-year-old first reported to his new clubhouse. Martin shut the door on Schoendienst, saying, "I don't need a batboy." Little did he know that the freckle-faced newcomer would be the team's new shortstop. By season's end, Schoendienst was the International League's Most Valuable Player, posting a .337 average in 136 games.

After just 25 games in 1944, Schoendienst's average was up to .373. But military duty caused a brief interruption to the young infielder's climb to the majors. His stint in the Army lasted less than a year. He was released early because of traces of tuberculosis found during an early physical. The first confrontation with TB, combined with a dislocated shoulder during a military baseball game, made Schoendienst's arm questionable for his entire career.

Just as he adopted switch hitting out of necessity, Schoendienst says he could have become a left-handed thrower if needed. "I was always ambidextrous as a kid," he says. "I could have thrown left-handed if I had to. It would have taken me about a year, and I don't know how strong my throws would have been. But I could have done it."

Fortunately, Schoendienst and his right arm were ready for 1945. World War II had drained the ranks of the Cardinals and all the other teams. Defensive wizard Marty Marion still held down the starting shortstop job, a fact which kept Schoendienst in the minors previously. But enthusiasm gave the talented rookie an unscheduled audition at another post. When Schoendienst asked coach Mike Gonzales if he could field some flies in left field, the impromptu workout impressed both the coach and manager Billy Southworth. He wound up patrolling left field in 118 of his 137 games during his rookie season.

Temporarily wearing Musial's jersey number 6, Schoendienst batted .278, and led the league with 26 stolen bases that year. It would be 1985, exactly forty years later, before another rookie outfielder named Vince Coleman could duplicate the feat for the Cardinals. More shoulder problems arose from the head-first slides Schoendienst used. As a result, he curbed his base thievery. Besides, stolen bases just weren't a high priority in the 1940s for the Redbirds. "We didn't steal a lot of bases back then," Schoendienst remembers. "We only went when we got the sign, and the sign started with the manager. One day I stole second on my own, and after the game I got called to [manager] Eddie Dyer's office. He told me, 'Don't do that again, kid.' And that was the end of that." Schoendienst says that his managers often wanted him to stay at first base "to keep the hole open" for RBI men like Musial, who could lace pitches to right field. Proof of Schoendienst's claim that the Cardinals seldom stole is found in the 1947 record books. Fleet-footed Red swiped six bases, leading the team!

What stopped the base stealers from stealing back then? "Pitchers used to get by with a lot more balk movements than they do now," Schoendienst says. "This lasted up to the time of the great base stealers like Lou Brock and Maury Wills. Now pitchers get called for looking crooked to first base." But don't think that the Cardinals of the 1940s were incompetent on the basepaths, warns Schoendienst. "Even guys who weren't that fast could steal a base or take the extra base on a hit to the outfield, because in that era, guys were in the minors for five or six years getting grilled on the fundamentals. Ballplayers had to be smart out on the bases."

In 1946, Schoendienst's sophomore season, the Cardinals won their fourth National League pennant in five years. When asked about that glorious season, Schoendienst's first memories aren't of the team's 98 wins (including a two-game playoff victory against Brooklyn) or the seven-game World Series win against the Boston Red Sox. Instead, he speaks of being thrilled to simply have a job. "Because everyone came back from the War in 1946, I didn't know if I was going to make the club or not," Schoendienst says. In his efforts to stay with the Cardinals, the former left fielder played second base, shortstop, and third as well.

The Cardinals tested Schoendienst's versatility early. He began the season subbing for injured third baseman George "Whitey" Kurowski for twelve games. He then stepped in for shortstop Marion, who was continually nagged by back problems. Finally, he landed the starting second baseman's job when incumbent Emil Verban was traded to Philadelphia. Schoendienst responded well, leading the N.L. second sackers with a .984 fielding percentage. At the plate, he batted .281. Schoendienst and his teammates collected $3,742 each (before taxes) as winning shares in the Series. Life had quickly changed from the $75 a month minor leaguers in Union City received.

Another significant event shaped Schoendienst's career in 1946. "The luckiest break for me was when I became Stan Musial's roommate," he said during his Cooperstown induction speech. "We had great games and good times together. Stan and Lil [Stan's wife] are dear friends, and I'm glad once again we'll be roommates at the Hall of Fame." Musial returned the compliment, describing Red as having "the best pair of hands I've ever seen." But Schoendienst's admiration for his teammates doesn't stop with Musial, or with other Cardinal stars like Enos Slaughter, Terry Moore, or the Cooper brothers, Walker and Mort.

"One guy who comes to mind is George Kurowski,"

Schoendienst says of some of his unheralded co-workers. "I think he was one of the most underrated ballplayers I've played with. George was a good clutch hitter, a good third baseman and he could run faster than a lot of people thought. He knew how to cover the bases."

Schoendienst remembers two pitchers who saw promising careers extinguished by disabilities. "Joe Presko was a very good pitcher," he says of the small right-hander who worked in St. Louis from 1951 to 1954. "But then he hurt his arm." He offered additional praise for Dick Hughes, a hard throwing righty who helped launch the Cardinals to the 1967 World Championship when Schoendienst was manager. "He was one of the finest pitchers I ever saw that year. Hughes had great stuff and good control. He and Gibson were just terrific for me." After posting a 16-6 record in 1967 (which was the N.L.'s top winning percentage), an arm injury allowed Hughes to pitch just one more season in the majors.

During the 1940s, Schoendienst became a perennial All-Star. After missing a spot on the 1947 squad (when he hit a career-low .253, pacing the league with 659 at-bats), he was a fixture on the next eight straight N.L. squads. In the 1950 All-Star game at Chicago's Comiskey Park, Schoendienst slugged a game-winning home run off Detroit's Ted Gray. The 4-3 win was significant for the National Leaguers, who had been losers in the mid-season matchup since 1944.

The Cardinals valued Schoendienst's leadership and defense even more than his hitting. During his career, he set records by playing seventeen years at second base and by topping the N.L. in fielding percentage seven times. But the lean switch hitter was no slouch at the plate. In 1948, he tied a record with six doubles in a double-header. He made two-base hits an art form in 1950, when his 43 doubles were tops in the senior circuit. "I wasn't a home run hitter, I hit line drives," Schoendienst said. "I hit to all fields, wherever the ball was thrown. A lot of times I'd hit that screen in right field [in Sportsman's Park]. You'd have to run like heck to get a double there. If there had been an open fence, everyone would have hit more homers."

Schoendienst did have a surprising power spurt in 1953, when he clubbed 15 round trippers. How did he more than double his previous single season homer totals? With some much needed rest via a beaning at New York's Polo Grounds. "I got hit, and spent about three days in the hospital," he says, wincing as he recalls the memory. "I got hit above the eye. I didn't play for about a week. I just pinch hit. Right around the All-Star break, I'd always lose a lot of weight and I'd fade out. I'd hit .300 or better before, then I'd slump." Schoendienst says the recuperation gave him new strength when he resumed playing. "I think that was the big key," he adds. "I played almost every game and never got any rest at all. You couldn't afford to sit out. They had so many in the minor leagues who could take your place. So you played no matter what. If you had a broken foot, bad ankle or whatever, you didn't say anything." Homers weren't the only products of Schoendienst's season. His .342 average was just two points less than league leader Carl Furillo. For once, Musial (who hit an admirable .337) didn't lead the Cardinals in batting. Schoendienst also finished with career highs in runs scored (107), RBI (79; tied in 1954), walks and slugging percentage. In the field, Schoendienst was untouchable. He was first among N.L. second sackers in putouts, assists, double plays and fielding percentage.

The following year, Schoendienst reeled off a twenty-eight game hitting streak, just five games short of Rogers Hornsby's all-time Cardinals mark of thirty-three games. Red might have threatened Joe DiMaggio's major-league record of fifty-six games if not for Chicago Cubs pitcher Bob Rush.

"That was great," Schoendienst remembers of his month of glory. "I was really going. I really beared down once I got up to fifteen and twenty consecutive games. That's when I started thinking about it. But Bob Rush was the guy who stopped me. That night I hit three line drives to the fence, but they caught them. After that, I went for twenty to twenty-two more games before going to Chicago. And Rush stopped me again, although I think I hit the ball harder off him than I did anybody." With the aid of the hitting streak, Schoendienst's season average wound up at .315.

Although 1955 was another All-Star season for Schoendienst, it gave cause for the Cardinals to doubt the thirty-three-year-old's future. The veteran keystoner hit 11 homers with 51 RBI, but his average dropped to .268. In 1956, infielder Don Blasingame was promoted from Omaha. Although he began the season playing next to Schoendienst at shortstop, Blasingame would give the Cardinals cause to trade fan favorite Red. Despite hitting .314 in his first 40 games, Schoendienst was dispatched. On June 14, 1956, Cardinals general manager Frank Lane made a mammoth deal with the New York Giants. The man nicknamed "Trader Frank" exchanged Schoendienst, Jackie Brandt, Bobby Stephenson, Dick Littlefield and Bill Sarni for Alvin Dark, Ray Katt, Don Liddle and Whitey Lockman. Dark became the Cardinal shortstop to cover Blasingame's move to second.

St. Louis fans were irate over losing a long-time hero. Schoendienst, meanwhile, tried to take the transaction in stride. "In baseball, you feel sometime that you're going to get traded. But it was a shock to me," he says retrospectively. "That was the biggest disappointment I've ever had. I had come up through the organization years ago. I was established here in St. Louis. I wanted to finish my career here. But baseball is baseball. I hated to leave, but I had to."

In 1957, just one year and one day later, the Giants traded Schoendienst to the Milwaukee Braves in exchange for Ray Crone, Bobby Thomson and Danny O'Connell. During his split season, Schoendienst notched 200 hits, which was a personal high and a league best. Not since Charles "Piano Legs" Hickman, who had 194 hits in 1902, had anyone led the league in hits during the year in which he was traded. Awaiting in Milwaukee was the opportunity to play on two pennant winners, including the 1957 World Champions. Ironically, Schoendienst's respective World Series averages in 1957 and 1958 were .278 and .300. In the 1946 Series, Red's output was a mediocre .233.

When Schoendienst returned to the Redbirds in 1961, he was no longer a starter. Julian Javier occupied second base, and Alex Grammas played shortstop. Red was recruited strictly for bench strength. During his first year, he played just 32 of his 72 games at second base. The rest of the time was devoted to pinch hitting. Schoendienst was successful in 16 of 48 pinch-hitting appearances, good for a .333 average. His overall batting average was a cool .300. In 1962, he was tops in the league in pinch-hits (22) and pinch-hitting at-bats (72). Never before had a Cardinal switch hitter amassed so many pinch-hits in a single season. In his St.

Louis career, Schoendienst's 53 career pinch-hits rank second to Steve Braun's 60.

"You have to gear yourself to pinch hitting," Schoendienst says. "Manager Johnny Keane told me I was going to play part-time and pinch hit. That was my job." He says that he began to anticipate when Keane might call for pinch-hitters in a game. "I could tell when I was going to pinch hit. I'd loosen up on the bench, maybe run up and down the steps to get good and loose. You just don't sit there. I'd make sure I knew who was pitching and who was in the bullpen. I'd try to figure out what the current pitcher's best pitches were." Schoendienst refused to say that pinch hitting required a different attitude. "Playing everyday is a mental thing. You have to get yourself psyched up. Once you put your uniform on, you better start thinking about what you're going to do that particular day."

In 1962, the Cardinals made Schoendienst a player-coach. With several young players coming up in 1963, Schoendienst faced being released. But he was given a choice. "The team asked me if I wanted to go someplace else if other clubs were interested in me," he says. "Or, they said I could stay here and be Johnny Keane's coach." Schoendienst weighed his options quickly and objectively. "I told them I'd stay right here. I live here in St. Louis and my family is here. I knew I could have played two or three more years, but it would have been off and on. I was running out of time as a player."

As a player, Schoendienst rang up some impressive career statistics. In 2,216 games, he batted .289 with 2,449 hits. He collected 427 doubles, 78 triples, 84 homers, 773 RBI and 1,223 runs scored. Only Musial, Brock and Slaughter have more Redbirds seniority than Schoendienst's 1,795 games. He ranks among the top ten in seven all-time Cardinal offensive categories.

Schoendienst said he "didn't think that far ahead" about his eventual prospects as a manager. But his chance came early, when he replaced Keane as manager to start the 1965 season. By knowing and respecting his players, Schoendienst would win two pennants in his first four seasons at the helm. "You have to know what kind of players you have, and how to talk to them," Schoendienst says. "I got to know each individual. I tried to be fair and tried not to show the players up."

With the same grace he exhibited at second base, Schoendienst avoids saying which one of his managers influenced his own managerial style. "You don't want to be *like* anybody," he says. "You try to learn something from each manager." For instance, he says that he was inspired by Billy Southworth, "who started to bring in relievers quicker than anyone had before." About manager Haney in Milwaukee, Schoendienst says, "He was a real fair man. He treated his ballplayers great. He didn't try to over-manage."

From the examples of each of his previous managers, Schoendienst created his own brand of managing. "I had a lot of managers who wouldn't say anything when mistakes were made, but they called the players in to talk about it the next day. You get them in the office if they make a mistake." Furthermore, Schoendienst says he tried to keep from publicly criticizing one of his players through the media. "I might think something, but I never did say anything."

Schoendienst guided the Cardinals from 1965 through 1976, longer than anyone else has managed the club. Under Red, the Cards won 1,010 games and lost 925 (good for a .522 winning percentage). While everyone remembers that Schoendienst piloted the 1967 World Champions and the 1968 N.L. pennant winner, it's important to remember that he led his share of contenders. Schoendienst-managed teams took three seconds and a third from 1971 to 1975. The 1973 club, which finished at 81-81, ended the year just one and a half games behind the first place New York Mets. A duplicate ending occurred in 1974, with the Pittsburgh Pirates edging St. Louis for first by the same margin.

Schoendienst was dismissed following the 1976 season, and spent two years coaching in Oakland. He returned to St. Louis in 1979, and served as interim manager for the last thirty-seven games of the season in 1980 while Whitey Herzog took over the general manager's job temporarily.

When the Veteran's Committee named Schoendienst to the Hall of Fame in 1989, the sixty-six-year-old coach was marking his forty-fifth year in major league baseball. He graciously acknowledges every organization he's worked for, but he admits quickly that most of his greatest memories are from St. Louis. While in Cooperstown, he gleefully recounted how in St. Louis "Forty-two years ago, I met a dark haired, Irish girl, on a Grand Avenue streetcar. She asked me for my autograph. Well, two years later, I signed her up." Mary O'Reilly's autograph entitled her to a forty-two year marriage with the Cardinal stalwart.

Just as Joe DiMaggio and Lou Gehrig spoke with pride of their long-term association with the New York Yankees, Schoendienst has the same loyalty to the Cardinals and his adopted hometown of St. Louis. "First of all, I came up through the organization. I was here before Mr. Busch and Anheuser-Busch owned the club," Schoendienst says. "Sam Breadon and Branch Rickey had the team. They gave me the opportunity to play."

With a smile, he adds, "At least that's what Mr. Rickey told me. An opportunity to play. I told him that's all I needed. I'm just glad to be a part of it, and I hope I can stay a lot longer."

Red Schoendienst—Cardinal Stats

	G	AB	H	2B	3B	HR	R	RBI	BB	SO	SB	BA	SA
1945	137	565	157	22	6	1	89	47	21	17	26	.278	.343
1946	142	606	170	28	5	0	94	34	37	27	12	.281	.343
1947	151	659	167	25	9	3	91	48	48	27	6	.253	.332
1948	119	408	111	21	4	4	64	36	28	16	1	.272	.373
1949	151	640	190	25	2	3	102	54	51	18	8	.297	.356
1950	153	642	177	43	9	7	81	63	33	32	3	.276	.403
1951	135	553	160	32	7	6	88	54	35	23	0	.289	.405
1952	152	620	188	40	7	7	91	67	42	30	9	.303	.424
1953	146	564	193	35	5	15	107	79	60	23	3	.342	.502
1954	148	610	192	38	8	5	98	79	54	22	4	.315	.428
1955	145	553	148	21	3	11	68	51	54	28	7	.268	.376
1956	40	153	48	9	0	0	22	15	13	5	0	.314	.373
1961	72	120	36	9	0	1	9	12	12	6	1	.300	.400
1962	98	143	43	4	0	2	21	12	9	12	0	.301	.371
1963	6	5	0	0	0	0	0	0	0	1	0	.000	.000
World Series													
1946	7	30	7	1	0	0	3	1	0	2	1	.233	.267

MIKE SHANNON

Hometown Boy

Makes Good

It was a Sunday game in 1989, and the Cardinals were unable to do much against the visiting Reds' Danny Jackson. Sitting up in the radio booth with broadcasting partner Jack Buck, Mike Shannon attempted to turn things around by placing a "hex" on the Reds' pitching ace.

"Okay...here goes," he announced to millions of listeners. "Let's see if we can get to this guy. Z-z-z-z."

But the Cardinal batter failed to make contact.

"Let's try it again," Mike said, repeating the "hex sound."

Buck, not sure he was hearing his onetime protégé correctly, looked up from his scorecard and asked, "What in the *world* are you doing?"

"Z-z-z-z" came the reply, as the pitch was fouled off.

"Shannon, you're losing it. And what's worse, you're young enough that *you'll* have to pay for the treatment."

Both men laughed heartily, and those who heard the exchange laughed with them, even as Jackson retired the batter. Win or lose, Cardinal games are rarely dull with this broadcast team of nearly twenty years. Buck and Shannon provide their listeners with a clear understanding of the game and its nuances, but there is a shared sense of fun, too.

"My debut at the microphone was at a spring training game down in St. Petersburg, Florida, in 1972," Shannon recalls. "I got there early that day and was getting set, looking over the lineups and everything. They had a guy in the lineup—I don't even remember his name now—who had a very unusual spelling of his name, and this was before I learned that names were spelled phonetically in the *Green Book*.

"So, rather than try to pronounce the name myself, I waited for Jack to come in so I could ask him about it. I didn't want to mispronounce the guy's name on the air when he came to bat. So I asked Jack about the guy's name just as we were going on the air. And Jack said, 'Here's Mike for the starting lineups. By the way, his favorite player's here today...what's his name, Mike?' That was Jack's way of saying, well, big boy, now you're here. A baptism by fire. I started by doing just color, but after a while Jack worked me in for play-by-play."

When Shannon began his professional broadcasting career in 1972, he was only two spring trainings removed from a nine year hitch in the National League. He also, in his own words, "was happy that I was living."

Indeed, Shannon nearly died of nephritis, a rare kidney disease characterized by albumen in the urine and swelling of the tissue. Forced to retire a third of the way into the 1970 season, the St. Louis native began weighing his career options. In 1971 he joined the Cardinals' front office as assistant director of promotions and sales.

But the lure of being closer to the game he loved since childhood proved too much for the recently retired ballplayer, and Mike went behind the mike the following year.

"Our sponsors—the brewery people especially—had patience with me," Shannon said. "They stayed with me. So did Bob Hyland at KMOX and his people. Bing Devine with the Cardinals. So many people stuck with me. I got on-the-job training, man, just like catching in the big leagues, which I did for five games.

"I was very fortunate to have Jack there for me. He's been

such a great help to me over the years. He's another one who remained patient with me as I made the transition to the booth."

Considering Shannon's background, it's perhaps not that surprising that he made the grade as an announcer. In his youth he met challenges that would indicate his folks were raising an overachiever. At the very least, they were proud parents of a sports-crazy kid who was budding into a promising athlete.

"I was always playing some sport," Shannon said, "football in the fall, basketball in the winter and baseball in the spring and summer. When school wasn't in session, I left the house in the morning and didn't come home till it got dark.

"My mother would whistle—you could hear her for two blocks—and I'd come running. As a kid, we didn't have any organized thing as far as baseball goes until I was eleven, but there were always kids around, always pickup games goin' on somewhere. There were many times when I wound up playin' ball with kids older than me.

"The dad of a friend of mine managed a team of sixteen-year-olds, and we worked it out so that I played on that team. I'll never forget that first game I played in. It was at Roosevelt High School, and I played center field. I hit a home run over the right field fence there. After the game, the opposing coach wanted a forfeit because he said I wasn't old enough.

"It was pointed out to him that there wasn't any rule at the time that stated you couldn't be younger and play on a team with older kids, only a rule that you couldn't be *older* than sixteen. They let me play in that league for several more games. I think playing with older kids helped a lot in the development of my raw talent as a youngster.

"My dad would show me how to do certain things, how to improve certain aspects of my game," Shannon said. "He worked with me, and when I look back on that period in my life, it seems now that it wasn't always easy for him to find the time or energy. There were six kids in our family, plus, he was a policeman who was going to law school at the same time. He didn't have a lot of free time, which you can imagine, but he was there for us.

"When he was younger he played minor league ball, and later, for the police team. My dad never said anything about his own baseball career, but other people would bring it up. They'd tell me what a fine athlete he once was. Being a kid, it meant a lot to hear that, to discover that about my dad."

Something that Shannon discovered about himself was that his talents were more suited to football. He was a talented high school quarterback, leading Christian Brothers High School to an undefeated season his senior year, and seemed the perfect candidate for a collegiate gridiron career followed by one in professional football. But as Shannon points out, professional football didn't offer the same financial incentives back then that baseball did. He decided his future would be in baseball.

A number of major league teams scouted Shannon and tried to sign him right out of high school. At the time the majors' bonus rule was in effect, which stated that if a prospect was signed by a club for more than $10,000, the club was required to keep him on its major league roster the first two years rather than season him in the minors.

"I had a lot of ability, but I was really raw," Shannon said of his baseball prowess. "Nobody was going to sign me and keep me on the roster for two years. But I had appointments to go to both military academies...there was USC...I could have gone nearly anywhere in the country on a football scholarship.

"I played high school football with Stan Musial's son, Dick, so I knew Stan personally when I was a teenager. Stan had told me that the next year the baseball powers that be were going to get rid of that bonus rule. So, I thought, heck, I'll wait a year and go to college and then come back the next year and sign a baseball contract.

"The reason that I chose Missouri was Frank Broyles. He was a split-T coach and I was a split-T quarterback. He came in and recruited me. Recruited a great team, as a matter of fact. There was a national magazine at the time that said we were the best freshmen group of football players recruited at any time, any place. We had five high school All-Americans in the backfield and one on the line. Two of the five All-Americans in the backfield didn't even make the first string—that's how good the talent was when I played at Missouri."

As it turned out, Shannon attended the University of Missouri but one year, during which time he studied psychology. That one year of college lay the foundation for Shannon's continu-

ing interest in the role psychology plays in baseball, one subject
that still fascinates him.

Making his way through the Cardinals' farm system, Shannon for the most part played center field. But the parent club already had a steady, solid center fielder in Curt Flood, so it was
surprising to some—Mike included—that he debuted in center
when called up in September 1962.

It wasn't long before the Cardinal coaching staff saw what
Shannon's arm in right field could mean to the team's defense,
however, and he ended up patrolling there for most of his first five
years with St. Louis. At the end of the 1966 season he was approached about the possibility of being moved to third base.

"Their thinking was that the club needed a third baseman
who could drive in some runs," Shannon explained. "Charlie
Smith had driven in only about forty runs or so that year, and
what they were really looking for was a left-handed power hitter
in our lineup.

"There had been some talk of acquiring Eddie Mathews
from the Braves, but nothing ever materialized with that, so the
Cardinals went looking for a left-handed hitting outfielder who
could drive in some runs for us. That's how we acquired Roger
Maris from the Yankees—in a trade for Charlie Smith. But that ne-
cessitated my switching over to third base."

Shannon admits he wasn't initially thrilled with the prospect of leaving right field—a position he loved to play—for the hot
corner. Also, some of the media's negative coverage of Maris, plus
some of the rumors he'd heard, led Shannon to believe that his
new replacement might be a disruptive force on the Cardinal ballclub.

"It turned out great for us," Shannon said, "because we
won the pennant in '67 and '68, and Roger was a big part of that.
Just as important to me was the fact that Roger and I became best
friends—not just in baseball, but in life, as well.

"We had such a great time playin' together for the two years
he was with the Cardinals. After he retired in '68, he lived in Florida and ran the beer distributorship in Gainesville, but my family
and I would go down there and spend some time with Roger and
his family. Then, he'd come down and bring all his kids and stay
with us a week or so during spring training. His boys and my boys

and the two of us would go hunting in Kentucky every year. It's not often that you have a best friend and then your families become close, also, but that's what happened. We had some great times together."

So, when Maris finally succumbed to lymphoma, cancer of the lymph glands, in December of 1985, Mike Shannon was hurting from the loss of his buddy. It was a time for healing.

"When we went up to Roger's funeral in Fargo, we had to stop in Minnesota and change planes there," Shannon said, referring to a gathering of some of Roger's friends and former teammates.

"I'd come out of St. Louis, and Mantle had flown out from New York. Moose [Skowron] had come in from another city. Anyway, we met there at the airport in Minnesota and got to tellin' stories about Roger, and remembering what he meant to us as human beings. We were there for something like two hours, waitin' for the plane that would take us to Fargo for the services. We were sittin' in the bar, half in the tank, just talkin' about our friend. A toast, if you will.

"Roger was a winner. He did everything that was asked of him, regardless of what team he was on at the time. Everybody knows him for his 61 homers in 1961, but he was a good bunter, a good hit-and-run man, he could break up the double play at second base as well as anyone we saw, and his arm was strong and accurate out there. He was a complete ballplayer. A smart ballplayer.

"He was, as I said, my best friend in and out of baseball. But even if that wasn't the case, I'll say right now that Roger was one of the best all-round players of my era. He was steady; a dedicated family man who wasn't the surly, humorless guy he was portrayed to be, and why some of the writers and fans and Yankee brass treated him the way they did while he was in New York is beyond me.

"You know why he retired after the '68 season? It was because he wanted to spend more time with his family, plain and simple. I'll never forget the time in our clubhouse when he was summoned by Mr. Busch to his office. When Roger came back a while later, he said, 'Gussie wants me to play next year, but I told him I'd rather not, that I wanted to be with Pat and the kids more than another year in the game would allow.'

"So, I guess Mr. Busch told him that he wanted Roger to come back for one more year, but if that was the way Roger felt about it, he respected his feelings and said, 'You go ahead and be with your family, Roger.' Now, that's two men talkin' with each other, based on mutual respect."

When Maris joined the Cardinals for the 1967 campaign, he and his new teammates exchanged information about the opposing pitchers. Maris offered the lowdown on former American Leaguers who had come over to the National League, and Shannon and company gave Maris the scoop on N.L. hurlers he'd never faced.

Maris was particularly helpful at World Series time in 1967 and 1968, when the Cardinals battled the Red Sox and the Tigers, respectively, for the World Championship. But even the best scouting reports can't ensure a victory, as Shannon points out:

"I never will forget that in July of '68, when McLain was winnin' all those games over there for the Tigers and it looked as if we'd be playin' Detroit in the World Series...Roger came to me and said, 'Don't worry about McLain. The guy we have to worry about is [Mickey] Lolich. He's the one who's gonna give us trouble.' And dammit, he was *right*.''

Although Shannon played for all three Cardinal pennant winners of the 1960s, the 1967 and 1968 clubs remain his favorites. For starters, he says, he was more relaxed at the plate and had a better idea of what he was doing up there. He was also a regular on those teams, contributing at bat and in the field nearly every game.

"I was still a rookie in 1964," he said, "even though I'd played a little the two previous years. I came up at the All-Star break and from then until the end of the season I hit 9 home runs and nearly 45 RBIs. That's a hell of a second half, especially considering I was batting eighth.

"Then, in the World Series, in the first game, in my own hometown, I hit a home run off Whitey Ford. I thought, "Good Lord, a guy can't even dream this good.

"I will say that the '67 club didn't have as much talent as the '64 club, but both the '67 and the '68 clubs just never made many mistakes, the kind that can lose ballgames for you. Those two were well-balanced, well-oiled machines. When we walked onto the field, hell, we *knew* we were gonna win. That's the attitude any winning ballclub takes with them into each and every game, and that's the attitude those '67 and '68 clubs had.

"And after the game we'd go out to eat, and there'd be twelve, fifteen guys, sometimes, heading off to the same restaurant together. I mean, we'd break up into groups of three or four guys to sit down and eat. After all, it wasn't meant to be like a training table. And though we all had our own interests, and we didn't always hold the same philosophies about things, the guys would often share with each other, or take an interest in what the other guys were thinking or doing. All three of those teams—'64, '67 and '68—were filled with guys who respected one another and had fun to boot."

Shannon is a walking library of anecdotal material. Some of his stories involve him directly, some marginally. Either way, they prove that depending on the situation, a major league park can be one of amusement or bemusement.

One of Shannon's favorite stories spotlights friend and former teammate Julian Javier, whose graceful yet hard-nosed defensive style at second base was crucial to the Cardinals' success for more than a decade.

It seems "Hoolie" was standing on second base when Astro shortstop Julio Gotay quietly walked up behind him and said something that made Javier jump about a foot off the bag, at which point Gotay tagged him out. Once in the dugout, Shannon asked Javier what had happened out there.

Javier just shook his head and said, "No...no. No mas. No mas." But Shannon pressed him on the matter. Finally, Javier said, "Voodoo, voodoo," and walked away. "Evidently," Shannon said, "Gotay was into voodoo and Javier knew enough about it that whatever Gotay said scared the hell out of him."

An incident in Atlanta soon afterward was punctuated with a sense of déjà vu. This time, Shannon got into a little argument with the Braves Felix Millan at second base. Although the umpires stepped in to prevent a fight between those two, Braves left fielder Rico Carty joined the verbal fray when he barked at Shannon, "Pick on somebody your own size."

Just as Shannon snapped back with, "Well, come on, I'll fight you if that's what you want," Javier came running in and said to the angry Shannon, "No mas. No mas with him. He's voodoo, too." Mike shot Javier a withering glance and said, "I don't give a *damn* about any voodoo."

Players and umpires often find themselves forming an uneasy comedy team. Take, for example, this exchange between Shannon and umpire Billy Williams during a scoreless game in Atlanta in which the arbiter called a strike on the Cardinals third baseman:

"Hell, Billy, that was outside."

"Dammit, Shannon, I said that was a strike!"

"Who the hell are *you*? God?"

"Yeah, I'm God."

"In that case, make it rain, will ya? I'm 0-for-2."

It's unclear whether this next incident occurred during the same game, but it too, involved umpire Billy Williams in Atlanta. Former Cardinal Bob Uecker, then catching for the Braves, was behind the plate when Williams yelled "strike" on a pitch that was apparently wide of the mark. Uecker took off his mask and started arguing with Williams, who was puzzled by Ueck's outburst.

"Like hell that was a strike!"

"What the hell are you arguin' for? I called it in your favor."

"That doesn't matter. That pitch was a ball and you called it a strike. We're supposed to trust you guys!"

"Uecker," Shannon says, shaking his head and laughing, "was a real piece of work, let me tell you. We'd be on the bus and he'd have us laughin' so hard we'd have to get up and move away from him because our cheeks and ribs would start hurting. He was hilarious, even back then. He had a little problem with hitting, but let me tell you, he was a fine catcher. He really was."

Shannon too, caught in the big leagues, although he'd be the first to tell you that it was better to field than to receive.

"The first game I ever caught in my life was in the big leagues," Shannon said, "and wouldn't you know it, Billy Williams was the umpire in that situation, too.

"McCarver was out with a broken finger, so Uecker was catching this game. Rather than calling somebody up, the Cardinals decided I would be a backup to Uecker. This was 1965. On occasion I would go to the bullpen and warm the pitchers up. If anything happens, I was told, you'll be our catcher.

"We're playing the Giants at Sportsman's Park, and Dick Schofield is the hitter. First pitch, he swings and fouls it off Uecker's meat hand and splits—I don't know—a finger or his thumb. So, I gotta go in and catch the rest of the game. The home plate umpire, Billy Williams, looks at me and says, 'You ever catch before?' I told him, 'No,' and Billy was scared shitless right then.

"And later in the game, Red brought in Barney Schultz to pitch in relief, so I had to catch his knuckleball. I thought Williams was gonna faint. He had a tough afternoon. But he never got hurt, never got hit by a foul tip once that day."

Talk of Dick Schofield and the Giants segues into reminiscences about Candlestick Park and other points on the major league map. Echoing the sentiments of those who went before him and those who came later, Shannon talks of the "brutal wind" in San Francisco, the "rock-hard" infield at Dodger Stadium, fighting the sun in right at Wrigley Field, and learning to accept the reality of artificial turf inside the Houston Astrodome.

But, there were other "diamonds in the rough" as well.

"Naturally, I never paid much attention to the infields around the league until I moved to third base," Shannon said. "Crosley Field in Cincinnati was tough because they had a PA announcer who sat right down next to the dugout, and he had a plexiglass shield in front of him. The lights used to shine on that thing, and if you positioned yourself in just the right spot, you'd get a glare off it that kept you from seeing the ball in play.

"At Candlestick, you really had to know what you were doin' out there, regardless of where you were playing. Not just the wind, but all that garbage flyin' around out there...the hot dog wrappers and paper cups. With the high grass there you didn't have to play deep in the infield, but the Giants didn't have anybody who hit the ball on the ground, anyway. [Laughs] And if Mays *did* hit it on the ground he always hit to third, where I was playin.'

"Most of my career, I played on natural grass, with the exception of the Astrodome after their experiment with real grass failed. *That* was a learning experience down there. I didn't like the fake stuff at all. I didn't like playin' inside, either.

"The big problem there, for us outfielders, was that we couldn't see the ball in the air because the sun shone through the roof. Then, after they couldn't get the grass to grow, they installed the Astroturf and we all had to learn to play on this crazy new surface. When they first put it in, they kept the dirt part of the infield intact, which meant that there were pebbles and so forth that got on the carpet, making those true bounces not so true anymore.

"Wrigley Field could be tough. The sun in right field could make things interesting. There was a point in September, especially, when the ball was hit from say, the second baseman's normal position all the way over to the foul line. If you had to run in and get a ball hit in front of you, oh, man, was that scary, because the ball stayed in the sun almost the entire time the ball was in flight.

"As a hitter, though, I loved to play in Wrigley Field. See, I didn't figure it out until I was well into my career, but I could see the ball's spin better in the daytime. I could see it as soon as the pitcher let it go. In the five years that I was playing regular, I hit over .400 at Wrigley Field. And every time we went into Chicago for a series, for five straight years, I hit at least one home run."

An indication of how much Shannon liked to hit in Wrigley Field was given during the Cardinals' stretch drive in 1964. On September 13, he figured prominently in a 15-2 St. Louis victory over the Cubbies. Actually, *all* of the Cardinal starters figured prominently in the game's outcome.

The team scored at least one run in every inning. It remains only the second time since 1900 that the feat has been accomplished. Shannon hit a solo homer in the sixth to keep the scoring sequence intact, and brought in Ken Boyer from third with a sacrifice fly in the ninth for the Cardinals' final run. In all, Shannon went 2-for-5 with four RBI and a run scored.

"That whole game was like one long rally," Shannon quipped. "But I do remember another game at Cincinnati where we had nobody on base, two outs and the batter was in the hole, and we scored ten runs. Brock screwed it up because he hit a grand slam to kill the rally."

Despite his success at the plate that day, it wasn't until the 1966 season, Shannon relates, that he learned how to hit. He attributes his newfound success at the plate to manager Red

Schoendienst, who offered him tips on gripping the bat and beginning his stride toward the ball.

"I never put up big numbers," Shannon said, "but really, what I developed into was a clutch hitter more than anything. In '68, for example, I think I had something like twenty-six game-winning RBIs, or something like that. They didn't have that stat back then, but somebody in the Cardinals' front office who kept track of such things later told me that. But I never paid any attention to what my yearly stats were. I was only interested in winning.

"I usually hit fifth or sixth, depending on who was pitching against us that game. If it was a left-hander, I hit fifth and McCarver sixth; if it was a righty it was just the opposite. I used a 36-36 bat and choked up on it about an inch. I was an aggressive hitter up there, sometimes too aggressive, and I'd get out in front of the pitch. I had an open stance, and I was a hacker."

Shannon is, as he has always been, a student of baseball. He is interested in many aspects of the game: its history, the dramatic changes it has undergone—both on and off the field—in the past thirty years, the importance people place on it, the innovations.

"There's one thing that has always fascinated me about the game of baseball," he said. "You could apply this to other sports or even other professions, I suppose, but since baseball is my game I'll use it as an example.

"Right now there are twenty-four guys who are being reared by different families in all kinds of settings. They'll face both similar and dissimilar problems and challenges over the years. But somehow, some way, they're all going to come together—blacks, whites, Hispanics—with the right combination of talent and smarts and dedication and personality, and form a baseball team that can compete at the major league level. Never mind winning a pennant or World Series.

"Sometimes I think about that as it relates to the Cardinal teams I played for—the talent that was assembled on the field. We had a helluva team back then."

Mike Shannon—Cardinal Stats

	G	AB	H	2B	3B	HR	R	RBI	BB	SO	SB	BA	SA
1962	10	15	2	0	0	0	3	0	1	3	0	.133	.133
1963	32	26	8	0	0	1	3	2	0	6	0	.308	.423
1964	88	253	66	8	2	9	30	43	19	54	4	.261	.415
1965	124	244	54	17	3	3	32	25	28	46	2	.221	.352
1966	137	459	132	20	6	16	61	64	37	106	8	.288	.462
1967	130	482	118	18	3	12	53	77	37	89	2	.245	.369
1968	156	576	153	29	2	15	62	79	37	114	1	.266	.401
1969	150	551	140	15	5	12	51	55	49	87	1	.254	.365
1970	52	174	37	9	2	0	18	22	16	20	1	.213	.287

World Series

	G	AB	H	2B	3B	HR	R	RBI	BB	SO	SB	BA	SA
1964	7	28	6	0	0	1	6	2	0	9	1	.214	.321
1967	7	24	5	1	0	1	3	2	1	4	0	.208	.375
1968	7	29	8	1	0	1	3	4	1	5	0	.276	.414

ENOS SLAUGHTER

That Country Boy

Could Run...and

Hit...and Field

Sportswriters. Can't live with 'em, can't live without 'em.

Professional athletes frequently have mixed feelings about the men and women who cover their successes and failures in the sports world. Enos Slaughter is a case in point.

"You see, Fred Haney, a sportswriter for the *Durham Morning Herald* in North Carolina recommended me to the Cardinals," said the onetime St. Louis speedster who still lives near his native Roxboro home. "I guess they had asked him about any prospects he might have seen, and I'd been playin' with a local mill team. Back in those days every mill town had a baseball team.

"That's the way it was for me, and I went to this tryout camp in Greensboro in '34, right outta high school. The Cardinals signed me to a $75-a-month contract to play at Martinsville. Later I played at Columbus, Georgia, for a hundred dollars a month and then Columbus, Ohio, for $50 more. But, yeah, a sportswriter was the one who helped get things goin' for me."

Twelve years after Greensboro, sportswriters (and photographers and filmmakers) lionized Slaughter when his legendary "mad dash" from first to home scored the winning run in the Cardinals' 4-3, Game 7 win over the Red Sox in the 1946 World Series. Though proud of his 270-foot sprint into baseball's collective memory, Slaughter professes puzzlement—even irritation—that when his name is mentioned in baseball circles it is almost exclusively in connection with beating shortstop Johnny Pesky's relay to home.

"Well, I don't see nothin' unusual about that play," Slaughter said. "I think I just caught the whole Red Sox infield nappin' is all. If Bobby Doerr or Pinky Higgins would've hollered 'Home with it!' to Pesky, because he had his back to the infield, remember, when he took the throw from Leon Culberson, they probably would've thrown me out by ten feet.

"But you talk to these writers now and that's all they remember about me. To a lot of people that's all I ever did in my life is to score from first to win the World Series. Well, check out the record books. Look some stuff up about my nineteen years in the big leagues. I thought I had a great career."

Well, the man dubbed "Country" is right. Even a cursory glance at the numbers he put up between his inaugural year of 1938 and his swan song in 1959 will tell the reader that Slaughter hit for average (a .300 lifetime hitter); had pop in his bat (double figures in doubles for most of his career, twice the league leader in triples, and respectable home run totals with twice as many walks as strikeouts during his career) and both knocked in and scored runs with great regularity.

And, he was no slouch in the outfield, either, as one of his long-time running mates, Terry Moore, has maintained for years. Enos even stole a base or two, though only when necessary. ("I'd steal seven, eight, nine bases a year, or try to," he says, "but with the teams we had in St. Louis, I really didn't need to.")

A Hall of Fame career? A lot of people thought so once Slaughter retired after the 1959 season at the age of forty-three. But not a lot of the *right* people, apparently. The Baseball Writers' Association of America, whose members each year vote for those candidates they feel deserving of enshrinement in Cooperstown, passed on Slaughter—year after year after year—until he was no longer eligible for consideration by the BBWAA.

Sportswriters. Can't get in with 'em, can't get in without 'em.

But the Veterans' Committee *did* vote him in, eventually, and when Slaughter accepted baseball's highest honor during the 1985 induction ceremonies, there was something especially salient about that particular gathering. Sharing the podium with Enos was a St. Louis swifty from another era who that day also joined the game's elite: Lou Brock.

A few years after his big day in New York state, Slaughter touched upon some of his past glories and those of his Cardinal teammates. He chose not to cite a litany of his career accomplishments, preferring instead to cut loose in a sort of stream of consciousness:

"I grew up right on the farm where I'm livin' today. I got a farm joinin' my mother and dad's farm, and that's where I grew up. I'm still raisin' a little tobacco down there, even though I'm supposed to be retired. I'm playin' in a lot of celebrity golf tournaments, raisin' money for crippled kids—March of Dimes, Easter Seals, Multiple Sclerosis, things like that. I attend some of these card shows around the country, an' I'm booked to play in a number of these old-timers' games durin' the summer.

"One thing I'll say about growin' up in North Carolina... we had five boys and one girl in our family and everyone of us was sports-minded. My dad was an ol' ballplayer back in his days, an' one thing our folks did for us... we would work through the week and go to school, but when Saturday'd come we'd take off an' play baseball on Saturday afternoons. Every time we had a high school game they would knock off from work and take us there and see that we got back home. Yeah, still live seven miles outside of Roxboro.

"Straight through high school I was pitchin' and playin' second base an' the outfield. I was not real fast, not like later on. It's funny. When the Cardinals signed me and I was in Class D ball, I guess there was a question mark beside my name. They told me I was too damn slow, too clumsy, to make the big leagues, and the Cardinals wouldn't give me a second look if I didn't start doin' better. Billy Southworth, who'd been sent down there to take a look at us, told me to start runnin' on my toes more.

"So I practiced runnin' on my toes and increased my speed by four steps to first base and stayed in the game twenty-five years because I could run. Heck, when the Yankees bought me back from Kansas City in 1956, some guy had a stopwatch on me and I'm in the top twenty-five in baseball goin' to first base, an' I was forty years old by then."

Slaughter paused momentarily to consider the pitchers he faced in his lifetime. Two came readily to mind: Carl Erskine of the Dodgers and Walter "Jumbo" Brown of the Giants.

"I'm sure I got my hits off him, but Carl Erskine was one guy who caused me problems," Slaughter mused. "He caused me as much trouble as anybody in the National League. He had a good, live fastball, a good change and two different kinds of curves. He was tough.

"And Jumbo Brown...now there was a big, *big* man...300 pounds. He just threw fastballs, but he'd kinda short-arm his delivery, so when he released the ball it would come outta that big ol' body of his and I would lose the flight of the ball.

"Hubbell threw me curves, 'cause his screwball would come in to a left-handed hitter like me. He'd throw me curves and keep 'em up high in the strike zone so I couldn't pull 'em down the line. It was only 259 down the right field line at the Polo Grounds, but to center and the alleys it was considerably further. He knew what he was doin' out there. But I hit him pretty good.

"I changed the bat a little as I got older. I went to a lighter bat because I could handle it a little better. And after a while the people at Louisville Slugger got on me, sayin' everybody was goin' to a lighter bat because of me."

Slaughter was a Cardinal for thirteen years. It would have been sixteen but for three prime seasons he missed while serving in the U.S. Army Air Corps from 1943 to 1945. In April of 1954, when he was traded to the Yankees for Bill Virdon and two other would-have-been pinstripers, Slaughter wept publicly for all the world to see. But in a new uniform, playing in "the House that Ruth built" and other American League ballparks, the aging Enos continued to hit for average while socking just enough extra base hits to annoy the hell out of his adversaries on the mound.

He remained in the A.L. (ping-ponging between the Yanks and the Kansas City Athletics) for several years until the Milwaukee Braves claimed him on waivers in mid-September of 1959. Back in the league where it all began for him, Country's last contributions were for a Milwaukee club that lost a two-game playoff to the soon-to-be-crowned World Champion Los Angeles Dodgers.

In his first decade of retirement, Slaughter managed briefly at the minor league and collegiate levels. He says he also had skirmishes with baseball's powers-that-be over his retirement pension. And of course, there was always the matter of his absence from the National Baseball Hall of Fame for too many years.

But all that, as they say, is behind him now. So, when Enos Slaughter looks back on a baseball career that, counting his coaching activities in the 1960s, spanned four decades, there is little, if any, bitterness in his voice. And he's as good a storyteller as they come.

"Walker Cooper, when he was with the Cardinals, was always pullin' stuff, even on us," he began. "But one thing I remember him doin' to other ballplayers was this: At Sportsman's Park the visiting team would always have to walk through our dugout on the way to the ballfield.

"During battin' practice they would stop, you know, to have a last drag on their cigarettes. Well, Walker Cooper, he'd slide his *own* lit cigarette into the back pocket of one of 'em, and by the time that guy got up to the battin' cage you'd see him go 'O-o-h!' 'cause that thing'd burn a hole through his pants. An' you'd never dare go to sleep in the hotel lobby, 'cause Walker would give you the hotfoot.

"Another guy who would do that to you was Pepper Martin. He really was the 'Wild Horse of the Osage,' just like people said.

"We were playin' in St. Louis one day and George Magerkurth was umpirin' behind the plate. Pepper, he hit one off his fist and he drop-kicked the bat higher than the ball went and Magerkurth said, 'If it hits the ground it's gonna cost you fifty,' an' Pepper dove for the bat an' grabbed it before it hit the ground. You don't see things like that anymore."

Enos Slaughter—Cardinal Stats

	G	AB	H	2B	3B	HR	R	RBI	BB	SO	SB	BA	SA
1938	112	395	109	20	10	8	59	58	32	38	1	.276	.438
1939	149	604	193	52	5	12	95	86	44	53	2	.320	.482
1940	140	516	158	25	13	17	96	73	50	35	8	.306	.504
1941	113	425	132	22	9	13	71	76	53	28	4	.311	.496
1942	152	591	188	31	17	13	100	98	88	30	9	.318	.494
1946	156	609	183	30	8	18	100	130	69	41	9	.300	.465
1947	147	551	162	31	13	10	100	86	59	27	4	.294	.452
1948	146	549	176	27	11	11	91	90	81	29	4	.321	.470
1949	151	568	191	34	13	13	92	96	79	37	3	.336	.511
1950	148	556	161	26	7	10	82	101	66	33	3	.290	.415
1951	123	409	115	17	8	4	48	64	68	25	7	.281	.391
1952	140	510	153	17	12	11	73	101	70	25	6	.300	.445
1953	143	492	143	34	9	6	64	89	80	28	4	.291	.433

World Series

	G	AB	H	2B	3B	HR	R	RBI	BB	SO	SB	BA	SA
1942	5	19	5	1	0	1	3	2	3	2	0	.263	.474
1946	7	25	8	1	1	1	5	2	4	3	1	.320	.560

BILL VIRDON

"Billy, We Hardly
Knew Ya"

B ill Virdon could never have been clas-sified as a high school "phenom" by baseball scouts.

Oh, it wasn't because he lacked talent. Or desire. It's just that scouts had no reason to visit the boy's school in southern Missouri near the Arkansas border: it didn't have a baseball program.

"I played *one* high school baseball game back in West Plains," Virdon recalled. "School officials at the time were considering putting something together, and during the course of my senior year we played one game with one of the other towns in the area. I don't remember the score, but I know we got beat. I played shortstop and pitched a little bit."

Despite the dearth of organized youth baseball young Bill Virdon encountered, he was one of these kids who seem to have their eyes focused on becoming major leaguers the moment they're drawn to the National Pastime. Virdon says it was one of his "priorities" to play baseball—perhaps the one thing he always wanted to do with his life.

Born in Hazel Park, Michigan, where his family lived until he was about thirteen years old, Virdon followed the Detroit Tigers. He listened to radio broadcasts of the Tigers' games, and joined the ranks of those who adored Hank Greenberg.

"I guess that's often the case with young boys," Virdon said, "they root for the big home run hitters. But he was more than just a slugger and big run producer. He was a fine all-round ballplayer, a real hero. And like him, I wanted to be an everyday player. I wasn't interested in pitching."

Up until the time when the Virdon family left Michigan and moved to South Fork, Missouri, Bill's baseball world pretty much revolved around two places: the grade school playground and home, during moments shared with his father.

"He played baseball himself, somewhat, when he was younger," Virdon said. "He worked a lot, and wasn't home much because of it, but he played catch with me when it was possible. I know he always enjoyed participating with me. I'm sure he helped in my early development."

In South Fork, which is about ten miles outside West Plains, Virdon's parents owned and operated a combination gas station/country store. Bill worked there on and off during the two years the family lived in South Fork. Then it was on to West Plains.

And still no organized baseball.

"I went looking for a place to play," Virdon said of his frustration in not finding a baseball program to suit his needs. "A friend of mine had been to a tryout camp in Kansas, and they asked him to come out and play amateur baseball there for the summer. It was similar to Ban Johnson Baseball. It was called ABLA—the Amateur Baseball League of America.

"I think the major leagues would kind of organize it, and maybe subsidize it a little bit, too, for their players they didn't feel were quite ready to play pro ball, or college players who wanted to take part in an organized program.

"Anyway, I went with my friend down to Kansas to try out. We tried out over a week's time, I think. I made the club, he didn't. And he went back to West Plains while I stayed in Kansas for the summer. This was 1948—between my junior and senior years in high school. I went back the next summer, too, after my senior year, and played. That's where I was scouted. So, even though I played only one game of high school ball, I was finally in an organized program during that period."

The ABLA team for which Virdon played already had a potential major leaguer at shortstop—Virdon's position—so the West Plains teenager was moved to left field that first summer and center field the next. From then, until he retired from baseball as an active player in 1968, Virdon started at center field most of his career.

"Once I learned how to play the position, I came to enjoy it," Virdon said. "Of course, I was happy just to play. I wasn't concerned where I played...that didn't bother me in the least."

While roaming the outfield under that hot Kansas sun, Virdon caught the eye of several major league scouts. He even got as far as talking with the Chicago Cubs' representative. But it was with the Yankees that he signed.

"Actually, New York signed me out of one of the Yankee tryout camps, held in Branson, Missouri," Virdon said. "I had finished playing at Clay Center, Kansas, that summer of '49, and went to the tryout camp at Branson for a week or ten days.

"Tom Greenwade, who lived in Willard, which is close to Springfield, came to our home in West Plains and signed me about a month after that tryout camp. The club signed me for the 1950 season, and I started my minor league career at Independence, Kansas, which at the time has D ball, the lowest level there was in baseball back then.

"I played there a year, and that was the year right after Mickey Mantle played there. Another 'Mick,' Bunny Mick, was the manager at Independence when I was there. Some of today's Cardinal fans might recognize that name because Bunny Mick has worked with Vince Coleman, among others.

"Bunny had been with the Yankee organization for a couple of years by then, and he was a good teacher to me. Probably as much as anyone, he helped me early in my professional career. Later, he and I worked together when I was managing the Astros. He was a bunting coach."

In 1951, Virdon played for Mayo Smith at Norfolk, Virginia, in the Piedmont League. As he moved through the Yankee farm system, Virdon also played for Harry Craft and Jim Gleeson, who, like Smith and Mick before them, were outfielders in their day.

Virdon says he was "fortunate to have played" under the tutelage of former outfielders, all of whom offered the youngster their expertise at each step of the way.

Virdon went to spring training with the Yankees in 1954. It was his first exposure to a major league camp, and his only one with the Yankee organization. On April 11, he was one of several pinstripers who went to the Cardinals in exchange for Enos Slaughter. Virdon was then assigned to Rochester.

"The trade didn't bother me," Virdon said. "In fact, it was probably the biggest break that I had gotten up to that point, for the simple reason that the Yankees were loaded with outfielders at the time, and the Cardinals were searching for some young outfield talent. So, that move gave me a chance to play every day when I did finally make the parent club."

Almost exactly a year to the day after the trade, Virdon debuted in a Cardinal uniform.

"I played winter ball that winter of '54-'55, and went almost right from Cuba to spring training with the Cardinals," Virdon said, "so there really wasn't a lot of time to dwell on what was going to happen to me as a member of the Cardinals organization.

"But it was not a fun spring for me. I didn't hit well. I played all the time, and I knew I was going to get a shot at playing in the big leagues, but there was some concern about my lack of hitting. Eddie Stanky was managing the Cardinals at that time, and three or four days before the '55 season opened he told me I was gonna start for him in center field. I was relieved to hear that.

"The first game we played was in Chicago against Paul Minner, a pretty good lefty. I got a base hit up the middle; the fielder got to the ball but I beat the throw.

"Then, in the seventh or eighth inning I got a double that hit off the left field wall, which was nice. A good, solid hit. Things started out right for me, and I hit pretty well from that day on, although I hit better earlier in the season than I did later on."

Virdon's numbers in 1955 were good enough to garner National League Rookie of the Year honors. He hit .281 with 68 runs batted in and 58 runs scored. He cracked 18 doubles, 6 triples and 17 home runs.

"My batting style changed as I went to different ballparks," Virdon said. "At Sportsman's in St. Louis, for example, there was the short right field fence. Being as I was a left-handed batter, I tried to pull the ball more in St. Louis and hit it out of the park. It was only about 300 feet or so down the line and about 350 to right-center. I always seemed to hit better at Sportsman's than I did at the other parks.

"When we went into other cities, other ballparks, I changed my style of hitting to accommodate the situation. Forbes Field in Pittsburgh, for example, was a large ballpark. Right field wasn't that close except for right down the line, and right-center was more than 400 feet away, so I was wastin' my time trying to hit the ball out of the park there. That was one of the places where I made an extra effort to hit the ball to all fields, and get away from thinking long ball."

Former Cardinal great Terry Moore, who starred in center field for eleven years, worked with Virdon on learning to play the position at Sportsman's Park. Virdon calls him "one of the best there was." And in keeping with the outfielder connection that Virdon enjoyed throughout much of his professional career, he also played for Harry Walker when "The Hat" replaced Stanky as manager about six weeks into the 1955 season.

"At Sportsman's, the fences were a little closer than they were at some ballparks, so you had to be a bit more cautious out there as far as playing the ball on the bounce.

"But Sportsman's was pretty good to roam around in, too, and that's what I loved about playing center field during my career. I loved that feeling of tearing after the ball and catching it. There were some ballparks that were so spacious I didn't have to worry about the walls or the fences—I could just go get 'em without any fear."

Virdon played nearly all of his games in center field during his rookie season with St. Louis. His usual partners in the pasture were right fielder Wally Moon, the league's Rookie of the Year the previous season, and left fielder Rip Repulski.

Because Virdon came up through the Yankee organization, he gave little thought to facing National League pitching. But once he came over to the senior circuit for the 1955 campaign, Virdon learned quickly that it, too, was brimming with tough hurlers.

"It really wasn't a whole lot of fun facing any of them," Virdon said. "The Dodgers, for instance, who wound up World

Champions my first year, had a bunch of people who were very good: Don Newcombe, Johnny Podres, Carl Erskine, Clem Labine, Billy Loes. Later on they added [Don] Drysdale and [Sandy] Koufax and [Ron] Perranoski. Koufax, I think, was the best pitcher I ever faced. A lot of former hitters will probably tell you that.

"Then of course, you had the Braves, with [Warren] Spahn and [Lew] Burdette and [Bob] Buhl. After I left the Cardinals in '56, I found out just how tough Harvey Haddix could be. And Brooks Lawrence, who was with the Cardinals when I joined the club in '55, later had some good years with Cincinnati. He was tough.

"Let's see . . . other guys I remember *trying* to hit were Lindy McDaniel in relief—he had a mean forkball, and was one of the toughest right-handers I had to face—and Jim Maloney of the Reds. The right-hander I had as much trouble with as anybody in my career—but this was after he came up with that screwball—was Juan Marichal of the Giants."

The Cardinals finished in seventh place in 1955, more than thirty games behind Brooklyn. In that dismal year Virdon was one of the squad's bright spots. He had put up some solid numbers on his way to winning Rookie of the Year honors over pitchers Jack Meyer (Phillies) and Don Bessent (Dodgers), and was looking forward to his second season in a Cardinal uniform.

The honeymoon, as they say, lasted all of 24 games. Virdon got off to a slow start, hitting .211, and on May 17 was traded to Pittsburgh for pitcher Dick Littlefield and outfielder Bobby Del Greco. It turned out to be a great trade—for the Pirates, that is—as Virdon established himself as a decent hitter (.267 lifetime batting average) and a fine center fielder for the Buccos for many years.

He was part of the Pittsburgh team that, in storybook fashion, beat the Yankees in Game 7 of the 1960 World Series on Bill Mazeroski's bottom-of-the-ninth-inning shot over the left field wall at Forbes Field. (In the eighth inning, Virdon's bad hop single that struck Yankee shortstop Tony Kubek in the throat was a key play in the Pirates' five-run outburst that briefly gave them the lead.)

Slightly more than one full season. That's all the time that Cardinal fans had to enjoy the all-round play of Bill Virdon before general manager Frank Lane traded the promising youngster to the Pirates.

"I had a good career at Pittsburgh, and I enjoyed it very much, but I was surprised when the Cardinals traded me," Virdon said. "They're part of the game—trades that is—but I didn't figure on leaving St. Louis so soon, especially after my rookie season. I thought I was going to be there for a while. But the fans were good to me there. It's a good baseball town."

Bill Virdon—Cardinal Stats

	G	AB	H	2B	3B	HR	R	RBI	BB	SO	SB	BA	SA
1955	144	534	150	18	6	17	58	68	36	64	2	.281	.433
1956	24	71	15	2	0	2	10	9	5	8	0	.211	.324

HARRY WALKER

Have Bat,

Will Travel

A dazzling moment in Cardinals history, and an image that is indelibly etched in baseball's memory, is Enos Slaughter's "mad dash" from first to score the winning run in Game 7 of the 1946 World Series. The man whose two-out hit propelled "Country" around the bases and across the plate was Harry "The Hat" Walker—so named because of his constant fidgeting with his baseball cap while standing in the batter's box.

Standing out there on second base with the Cardinals' fourth two-bagger of the game, Walker watched his animated teammates welcome Slaughter back to the bench as thousands of delirious fans rocked Sportsman's Park. It was Walker's sweetest day as a Cardinal.

But as it turned out, his days as a Cardinal were numbered. After appearing in ten games for St. Louis the following season, Walker was traded to the Phillies.

The change of scenery did him good. He led the majors with a .363 batting average and 16 triples. And as he played out the string with the Phillies,

the Cubs, the Reds and the Cardinals (again), Walker saw limited action but still managed to hit well. For his eleven major league seasons (in which he averaged only 241 official at-bats per year) Walker fashioned a .296 average and walked a total of 70 times more than he struck out.

Walker served as player-manager for the Cardinals in 1955, the latter role becoming a full-time occupation for him with the Pirates and Astros from 1965 through 1972.

Walker authored a baseball book some thirty years ago. He has been a major contributor—financially and otherwise—to the University of Alabama's (Birmingham) baseball program. And, he demonstrates what he calls "the right and wrong things in hitting" in a popular mail-order video that he and a friend updated in 1986. ("It was hotter than Hades that day," Walker says, "so we started taping it and never stopped...left all the mistakes in, no cuts. I helped build that beautiful ballpark you see in the video. Put $50,000 into it.")

The native of Pascagoula, Mississippi, also continues to travel the country, working with struggling major leaguers to rid them of bad habits at the plate and fine-tune their hitting. Walker is baseball's version of TV's "Paladin"—only Harry's business card might read, "Have Bat, Will Travel."

"It's not that I can wave a magic wand that can turn 'em into great hitters," Walker cautioned, "but I do know how to work with these fellas, know how to respond to 'em and teach 'em. You know, it's funny. No one ever talked to me about hitting all that much when I was a player. Sometimes my brother, Dixie, would say somethin' to me once in a while, but mostly I worked out my problems on my own."

Dixie undoubtedly gave sound advice. "The People's Cherce"—as he was dubbed—was a career .306 hitter who played eighteen years in the major leagues, many of them with the Brooklyn Dodgers in the 1940s. The Walker family also included dad Dixie, Sr., who roomed with Walter Johnson when the two men both pitched for the Senators from 1909 to 1912. And Dixie, Sr.'s, brother, Ernie, was an outfielder for the Branch Rickey-managed Browns from 1913 to 1915. With a family history like that one, could little Harry's future ever be in doubt?

"When I was in school, one of the first things the teacher

asked us was what did we want to be when we grew up," Harry recalled. "Kids in those days talked about bein' a policeman, a fireman, somethin' like that. I piped up that I wanted to be a baseball player. I'm not sure if the teacher approved. In fact, they probably thought I was being cute.

"But all through my young life, it seemed, I did nothin' but carry around a bat and ball with me. I played whenever and wherever I could. As a kid I was thin, rundown from not eatin' my meals. Some mornings I'd leave a full breakfast behind on the table to go out and play baseball with my friends.

"We lived in a residential area, and there were a lot of kids there. There was only one decent diamond, really, and a lot of times we couldn't get on the field because the older boys would have it. So we played in backyards, mostly. We'd have to hit opposite from our normal stances so as not to break nearby windows or lose the ball after a long hit. But I never followed up on it—switch hittin' I mean."

Another pursuit that Walker left behind was football, and with good reason. Brother Dixie once suffered a broken collarbone playing it, and in the seventh grade Harry's leg was broken when he wound up on the bottom of a gang tackle.

His infatuation with the gridiron behind him, Harry concentrated on baseball. After his high school career was over, Walker played semi-pro baseball in several coal mining towns in Kentucky. He would make as much as a hundred dollars a month. Coming as it did during the Great Depression, that was good money.

"Whether it was a coal mining town, or a cotton mill town or lumber, those places had no entertainment for the people there," Walker said. "People were workin' hard for their livin' and they had no movies, no theaters, no TV, and radio was just comin' into some of those areas, so baseball became a big part of their lives.

"Here I was, about seventeen or eighteen at the time, playin' ball with grown men who played hard to win. The equipment we used wasn't too bad, actually. Pretty modern for that time and place. As you know, even the outfielders' gloves were small back then, but after I got to the Cardinals and played outfield for 'em I kept usin' a small glove, more like what a second baseman might use, like Lonny Frey. He was an infielder with the Dodgers and Reds years ago. I wanted to get the ball out of my glove in a hurry if I had to."

Walker credits Terry Moore, more than anyone else, with helping him learn the nuances of playing the outfield at Sportsman's Park once Walker reached the majors:

"I played with some fine ballplayers over the years, and I saw a lot of good ones on other teams, but Terry was the best in center field I ever saw. Not only that, he was the team leader of the Cardinals when I was there. Everybody respected him. I named my son after Terry."

Although he can recite numerous individual and team highlights from his pre-big league days, Walker's minor league career was marred by an occasional unsympathetic coach, injuries, contract disputes and haggling over money. And that was *before* the Cardinals caught sight of the rangy hitter. The Yankees and the Tigers previously had their chances to sign him, but failed.

"There's a team picture from spring training in '36 with the Yankees," Walker said, "with [Joe] DiMaggio and the rest, and I'm in there. [Jacob] Ruppert, the owner, was there, and [Joe] McCarthy, their manager. We couldn't agree on the money, though.

"And DEE-troit, I worked out with them in '37, but they released me 'cause they felt my throwing arm was suspect. But I just didn't want to let go with every single throw during practice and hurt my arm. I wanted to save my arm for game situations that meant something."

And Walker did. Beginning in the minors.

In a game played in Tyler, Texas, Walker threw two men out, a first for him.

"That got the fans all excited and everything, and they began hollerin' 'Shotgun arm!' at me when I resumed my position in the outfield," Walker said. "So I started to work on that aspect of my game as the season went on by getting about a dozen balls and throwing 'em into a box I'd set up in the infield. In the short time I was there I threw out nine or ten men from the outfield. That really turned me around as far as my defense was concerned."

Finally, Walker says, he was summoned by the Cardinals' front office to come to St. Louis and meet with general manager

Branch Rickey. They talked about family, character, the great game of baseball. . .and a contract.

"When I told him I'd play for $5,000, why he'd like to swallow his CEE-gar," Walker recalled. "He told me, 'Judas Priest, boy, we don't have that kind of money! We're not the Reds or some other club that can afford huge salaries.' "

But Rickey looked over at another Cardinal official who was present at the meeting and asked, "Has anybody else shown interest in this boy?"

"Yessir," came the reply, "the Dodgers, for one."

Rickey paused, blew some cigar smoke, looked at Harry and said, "Let me think this over, and I'll get back to you."

A few days later, Rickey offered Walker a thousand dollars. Walker countered with, "No, I'll take $2,500 or I'm goin' home." Rickey, no doubt biting his omnipresent cigar in half, said, "OK."

Stints at two of the Cardinals' farm clubs, Rochester and Columbus, followed. It was at Columbus in 1940 where Walker briefly—and bravely—tried his hand, and backhand, at shortstop for about twenty games before going back to the outfield. The Cardinals brought him up in September of that year.

"I guess I didn't impress 'em too much," Walker said of his seven-game "cup of coffee" in 1940. "I barely hit above my weight. But I did knock in six runs while I was there."

In 1941 Walker went to spring training with the Cardinals but was sent back to the minors for more seasoning. He says he didn't have as much success at the Triple A level as he did the previous season, but in the Little World Series he clubbed three home runs in three days. It was around that time when the famous "Walker finish" bat came to be.

"I was in Louisville for the playoffs, and I didn't have my model of bat, so I asked Mr. Hillerich, of Hillerich and Bradsby, the bat manufacturers, about getting one," Walker said. "He told me that he was sorry but the plant was closed. He said they'd be open Monday and he could get me one of my model bats by Wednesday.

"I told him we might be out of the playoffs by then. I needed a bat right now when it could do me some good. And so I started to leave. As I was goin' he said, 'Wait a minute, Harry. I just happened to think, I was experimentin' with some stain, using your bat to stir the mixture. It's kind of brown at one end where it was in the stain... '

"I said, 'Nahhh, that don't bother me.' So the first time I used the thing I hit a home run in the playoffs. I still have that bat, that two-tone bat they later called 'the Walker finish.' "

But even an unusual bat and the ability to hit to all fields couldn't keep Walker in the starting lineup on a regular basis once he made the Cardinals for keeps. It was only when Stan Musial was moved to first base that Walker saw much playing time in the outfield. Harry also filled in at first and second during his initial go-round with St. Louis.

Using a fairly closed stance, with a crouch not quite as pronounced as Musial's, Walker took a fairly normal stride as he brought his bat through the strike zone. A dead pull hitter while at Columbus, he soon learned that the fences in major league ballparks weren't nearly so inviting. So he began using the whole field.

Numbers-wise, Walker's best totals with the Cardinals came in the championship years of 1942, when he hit .314 in limited action, and 1943, when he hit .294 with 53 runs batted in over the course of a full season.

"I couldn't get that great bat speed that fellas like Musial and Johnny Mize could get," Walker said, "but I did have good bat control. And with that big barrel, all I had to do was make contact and that bat would send line drives out there.

"Once I accepted the fact that I wasn't gonna slug a bunch of home runs in the big leagues, I just never looked anywhere except the middle of the diamond. Never looked at right field. Once I hit 16 triples in a season in the big leagues, and when I got a chance to play more often I was usually around 30 doubles a year."

Individually, Walker's greatest single season was 1947—*after* he had donned a Phillies uniform. But in listening to him retrace his professional baseball career, it's apparent that he feels himself a part of the Cardinals' extended family.

"The best club I ever played for? The 1942 Cardinals. They were super. Oh, the pitching we had, and the hitting and fielding, too. All through the 1940s we had great teams, but that '42 club was something special. The '46 club was another good one, especially the way we won the pennant that year [by defeating the Dodgers in a best-of-three playoff series, two games to none].

"We had great pitching throughout the '40s. Howie Pollet, Harry Brecheen, Johnny Beazley, Max Lanier, Murry Dickson...I can't even remember 'em all. Mort Cooper was one of the finest pitchers I ever saw, even though I played only a few years with Mort. Mort would pitch a game where he'd throw ninety, a hundred pitches, and the game's over. With him, you were always alert, always focused on your job.

"Murry, on the other hand, would say to us, 'You don't make plays like that for me when I'm out there.' Well, Murry was a fine pitcher, but when he'd pitch he'd get two strikes on a guy and then ball one, ball two, ball three. He'd be out there pitchin' too fine, or experimentin' with his knuckler or something. Drove us nuts. By the sixth inning we were wore out, back on our heels, not as alert as we should be, so we were more prone to errors. But Murry was a good one, especially in '46.

"And you know, those fellas we had back then...all those pitches you hear about today, like the split-fingered fastball and all? They threw 'em back then. Guys today just give 'em new names."

In his free time Walker was an avid moviegoer. In fact, if the team had an off-day, he would catch a matinee somewhere and then head off to another theater at night to watch a twin bill. Although he stayed away from booze and smokes throughout his life, Walker was often the life of the party. Or, at least, its host.

"In 1942, I think it was, I was livin' out west of town. At some point in the season I told the guys that if we tied for first place I'd hold a barbecue at my place. And we did, so I did. There was a pretty good-sized garden out where I lived. Dizzy Dean asked if he could bring some of his friends to the barbecue, and I said 'sure.' So Diz brought his friends, includin' a country band and singers, complete with a sound system and these big ol' speakers.

"All the ballplayers and their wives were there, and we barbecued chicken and ribs and had a great time. But the band was loud, and this being a residential neighborhood I was sure the neighbors would run us off, even though we did have a policeman on guard at the entrance.

"It wasn't long before some of the neighbors started comin' through our place, but when they saw what was goin' on and saw all the Cardinal ballplayers, their eyes lit up and they asked if they could join us. We wound up with all kinds of people comin' in. In fact, we ran outta food at one point. But one of the neighbors livin' across the road from me had a meat market, so he went down and brought back a bunch of weinies and hamburger so we could feed all those extra people."

Walker's sociable inclinations resumed years later when he coached for the Cardinals. He'd host barbecues for the players and their families, as well as some of the Cardinals' front office people and their families.

"We'd go out to Creve Coeur Lake and I'd have a bunch of pits goin' all at once," Walker said. "I'd make the sauce the night before and get everything organized. We'd cook up 75 pounds or more of ribs and 125 pounds of chicken. We'd do that every year."

Walker now resides in Leeds, Alabama, about fifteen miles east of Birmingham, on a fifty-acre spread. He once raised cattle, but now just "monkeys around with" several crops, including corn, beans, cantaloupe and tomatoes. There's a little river that runs by his place, and he has a small pond that's home to dozens of catfish.

Occasionally a former ballplayer will visit the Walker place, but Harry usually sees his former teammates, men he coached or managed, and other baseball friends at card shows, fantasy camps, old-timers games or celebrity golf tournaments. For years, in fact, Birmingham has served as the site of the Harry Walker Invitational.

"I enjoy seein' some of the other guys," Walker said. "We visit and find out how things are goin'. I don't write or call much, if at all. But it's sure nice to see 'em when I get the chance. I just got done visitin' with Bill White, a former Cardinal, up at his place in Pennsylvania.

"I'm real excited about Bill being named National League president. He'll do an outstanding job. He's a first-class man."

Then, switching gears, "The Hat" again starts talking about hitting, his favorite subject.

"Say, have I told you who I think the best hitters in baseball have been over the years? Let's start with Musial . . ."

Rising from his chair, Harry assumes a batting stance familiar to most Cardinal fans and swings an imaginary bat into an
equally imaginary slider. Looks like a hit to left-center, Harry.

Harry Walker—Cardinal Stats

	G	AB	H	2B	3B	HR	R	RBI	BB	SO	SB	BA	SA
1940	7	27	5	2	0	0	2	6	0	2	0	.185	.259
1941	7	15	4	1	0	0	3	1	2	1	0	.267	.333
1942	74	191	60	12	2	0	38	16	11	14	2	.314	.398
1943	148	564	166	28	6	2	76	53	40	24	5	.294	.376
1946	112	346	82	14	6	3	53	27	30	29	12	.237	.338
1947	10	25	5	1	0	0	2	0	4	2	0	.200	.240
1950	60	150	31	5	0	0	17	7	18	12	0	.207	.240
1951	8	26	8	1	0	0	6	2	2	1	0	.308	.346
1955	11	14	5	2	0	0	2	1	1	0	0	.357	.500
World Series													
1942	1	1	0	0	0	0	0	0	0	1	0	.000	.000
1943	5	18	3	1	0	0	0	0	0	2	0	.167	.222
1946	7	17	7	2	0	0	3	6	4	2	0	.412	.529

RAY WASHBURN

A Moment of

Glory

"Ray Washburn is one of the most promising young pitchers to come up from the minors in years."

—1962 Cardinals Yearbook

"It's been a long, hard battle for Ray Washburn..."

—1969 Cardinals Yearbook

When pitcher Ray Washburn began his professional baseball career in 1960, the St. Louis Cardinals projected greatness for the young right-hander. After discovering Washburn playing for Whitworth College in the NAIA World Series, the Cardinals signed him for a reported bonus of $50,000. After just two minor league seasons, the twenty-four-year-old hurler was in the starting rotation for the Redbirds.

In 1962, Washburn was 12-9 with St. Louis. The following year he was 5-3 with two shutouts and a 3.09 ERA, but a shoulder injury blighted his season. Suddenly, Washburn's biggest goal was survival. He had to pass minor league

rehabilitation assignments in 1963 and 1964 to regain his spot with the Cardinals.

"He could have been as good as anybody," longtime manager Red Schoendienst remembers about Washburn. "He would have been a consistent 15 to 20-game winner if he hadn't hurt his arm. He had a real good hard breaking ball and a tough sinker. He had good control, he could run the ball in on you and he picked his spots well when he threw. It's just too bad he got hurt in 1963. He was an outstanding pitcher."

But Washburn did more than exist. He aided the Cardinals for nine seasons, posting a 68-60 record from 1961 to 1969. Although Washburn was "damaged goods" for the remainder of his career, he posted winning marks with six of his nine Cardinal teams.

Fate did smile kindly upon Washburn in the twilight of his career. With the 1968 pennant winning Cards, the man nicknamed "Washie" won a career-high 14 games. He notched career highs in starts (30), complete games (8), strikeouts (124) and ERA (2.26). He beat every team but Chicago that year, and notched three victories apiece against Los Angeles and Atlanta. Most importantly, Washburn gained a lasting place in baseball history on Sept. 18, 1968.

The Cardinals had clinched their pennant almost two weeks early while in Houston. The next stop of the road trip was San Francisco. Gaylord Perry greeted the Cardinals on September 17 with a 1-0 no-hitter. Ironically, Washburn wasn't even present for Perry's gem. "Before starting the series in San Francisco, we had an off-day after coming from Houston," Washburn recalls. "I had permission to fly back home to Washington." Because he wasn't pitching until the next day, Washburn didn't see Perry spin his masterpiece. "I had gone back to the hotel. I didn't even know about it until the next morning." He says that his teammates, considering their clinched pennant, didn't seem especially distressed about Perry's no-hitter. "They didn't like it, of course," he adds. "The San Francisco press wasn't too kind about it."

Evidently, the quick trip home did wonders for Washburn's morale. The next day, he avenged his teammates with a 2-0 no-hitter against the Giants. The baseball world was buzzing over the news of back-to-back no-hitters. Washburn's hitless victory was smooth sailing for the unflappable veteran. Giant batters hit only two balls to the outfield during the entire game.

Yes, Washburn says that he was keenly aware of his no-hit bid. "It's a goal that every pitcher has," he admits. "You think about it every time you go out there." True to the baseball tradition of not ruining a pitcher's luck, Washburn's no-hit quest remained a solitary journey. "No, nobody really said anything during the game in the dugout," he says. "That's pretty well established." He says that his biggest concern came "when I wanted the final three outs. For two of those outs, I had to face Mays and McCovey."

But after a successful showdown with the final two San Francisco sluggers, Washburn grabbed a special spot in the Cardinals' record book. The last Redbird to throw a no-hitter was Lon Warneke, who stymied the Cincinnati Reds on Aug. 30, 1941. More than a quarter of a century passed before another no-hit gem was uncovered. Washburn became just the fifth Cardinals pitcher (the fourth in the twentieth century) to earn the honor.

For an encore, Washburn won the third game of the World Series against the Detroit Tigers. After a two-inning relief stint in the 1967 Series versus the Red Sox, the Cardinals gave Washburn starting assignments in games three and six versus the Bengals.

Washburn's unqualified success came years after he was a highly-touted prospect. He credited Cardinals pitching coach Billy Muffett for helping him compensate for arm problems. "My best years were when Billy was there," Washburn says. "He encouraged me to throw more off-speed pitches to keep hitters off balance." This older, wiser Washburn must have been a far cry from the hard throwing rookie who led the International League with a 16-9 mark and a 2.34 ERA in 1961. "Basically, I was a two-pitch pitcher," he says, assessing his early days in baseball. "I had command of my pitches, and I threw pretty hard. I threw in the nineties with good movement on the ball."

While Washburn struggled with arm problems, he kept winning for St. Louis. He won nine games in 1965, eleven in 1966 and ten in 1967. Due to stints on the disabled list in 1964, Washburn was left off the World Series roster that season. He remembers being relegated to the bench during the Series, one of his most frustrating experiences. However, that year Washburn was 3-4 in 15 appearances (10 as a starter). Considering that the

Cardinals took the pennant from Cincinnati and Philadelphia by just one game, Washburn's contributions are even more immense.

Following the 1969 season, the Cardinals traded Washburn, just as they did many other regulars from the two previous World Series teams. He was swapped to the Cincinnati Reds for pitcher George Culver on Nov. 5, 1969. Coincidentally, Culver joined Perry and Washburn as the only National Leaguers to hurl no-hitters in 1968. In his final season, Washburn got to ride on Cincinnati's "Big Red Machine." He made his third World Series appearance, hurling one and a third innings of relief in the fifth game versus Baltimore.

Washburn earned a Bachelor of Arts degree in history and physical science at Whitworth College before starting his pro career. So, after his retirement from baseball, Ray became a teacher and athletic director at Bellevue Community College near Seattle, Washington. In his corner office of the school's physical education building, few indications of his baseball career can be found. But he still wears his Cardinals World Series ring, and he displays one modest 8-by-10" action pose of himself on a bookshelf.

With the exception of a little more gray in his hair, the 6-foot-2, 190-pounder is still the spitting image of his baseball cards. He will talk admiringly and reverently about teammates like Lou Brock, Orlando Cepeda and Bob Gibson. He seems to almost blush when told of the greatness of his no-hitter. However, he sees a simple explanation in the greatness of those 1960s Cardinals teams.

"We were close, and we knew what it took to win," he says. "Sometimes I think we would have played the same with or without a manager. You felt like you belonged in St. Louis. You felt like the Cardinals were your home."

Ray Washburn—Cardinal Stats

	W	L	PCT	ERA	G	GS	CG	IP	H	BB	SO	SHO	SV
1961	1	1	.500	1.77	3	2	1	20.1	10	7	12	0	0
1962	12	9	.571	4.10	34	25	2	175.2	187	58	109	1	0
1963	5	3	.625	3.08	11	11	4	64.1	50	14	47	2	0
1964	3	4	.429	4.05	15	10	0	60	60	17	28	0	2
1965	9	11	.450	3.62	28	16	1	119.1	114	28	67	1	2
1966	11	9	.550	3.76	27	26	4	170	183	44	98	1	0
1967	10	7	.588	3.53	27	27	3	186.1	190	42	98	1	0
1968	14	8	.636	2.26	31	30	8	215.1	191	47	124	4	0
1969	3	8	.273	3.07	28	16	2	132	133	49	80	0	1
World Series													
1967	0	0	—	0.00	2	0	0	2.1	1	1	2	0	0
1968	1	1	.500	9.82	2	2	0	7.1	7	7	6	0	0